Word Identification Strategies

Phonics from a New Perspective

Second Edition

Barbara J. Fox
North Carolina State University

Merrill
an imprint of Prentice Hall
Upper Saddle River, New Jersey   *Columbus, Ohio*

Library of Congress Cataloging-in-Publication Data

Fox, Barbara J.
  Word identification strategies: phonics from a new perspective /
Barbara J. Fox.   — 2nd ed.
      p.   cm.
    Rev. ed. of: Strategies for word identification, c1996.
    Includes bibliographical references and index.
    ISBN 0-13-020342-4
    1. Reading—Phonetic method—Study and teaching (Higher)   I. Fox,
Barbara J.   Strategies for word identification.   II. Title.
  LB1050.34.F69   2000   99-20620
  372.4′ 145—dc21   CIP

Cover photo: Index Stock
Editor: Bradley J. Potthoff
Production Editor: Mary M. Irvin
Design Coordinator: Diane C. Lorenzo
Text Designer: Carlisle Publishers Services
Cover Design: Rod Harris
Production Manager: Pamela D. Bennett
Director of Marketing: Kevin Flanagan
Marketing Manager: Megan McCauley
Marketing Coordinator: Krista Groshong
Production Management and Editorial Supervision: Carlisle Publishers Services

This book was set in 10/12 Palatino by Carlisle Communications, Ltd. and was printed and bound by R.R. Donnelley & Sons Company. The cover was printed by Phoenix Color Corp.

© 2000 by Prentice-Hall, Inc.
Pearson Education
Upper Saddle River, New Jersey 07458

Printed in the United States of America

10 9 8 7 6 5 4 3 2 1

ISBN: 0-13-020342-4

Prentice-Hall International (UK) Limited, *London*
Prentice-Hall of Australia Pty. Limited, *Sydney*
Prentice-Hall of Canada, Inc., *Toronto*
Prentice-Hall Hispanoamericana, S. A., *Mexico*
Prentice-Hall of India Private Limited, *New Delhi*
Prentice-Hall of Japan, Inc., *Tokyo*
Prentice-Hall (Singapore) Pte. Ltd., *Singapore*
Editora Prentice-Hall do Brasil, Ltda., *Rio de Janeiro*

Preface

This book about phonics and word identification has 19 three-part lessons and 73 learning activities for you to use when teaching word identification. You will find a concise explanation of the letter-sound relationships of phonics, a phonics teaching and learning sequence, and guidelines for effective phonics lessons. For many years, we have been caught up in a debate between those who champion spending a lot of time on letter-sound instruction and those who do not. That is why Chapter 1 begins with an explanation of the place of word identification in today's balanced reading programs. Chapter 2 focuses on phonemic awareness, which is the necessary awareness and conscious manipulation of the words, rhymes, and sounds in spoken language. You will find in this chapter effective classroom activities for teaching children how to identify the rhyme and sounds in language, and how to blend sounds together into spoken words.

In Chapters 3 through 6, you will learn about seven word identification strategies children develop on the way to becoming accomplished readers, and how different strategies correspond to different phases of movement toward fluent word recognition and conventional spelling. Chapter 3 explains the word identification strategies children use as they begin their journey toward literacy. Chapters 4, 5, and 6 describe the three mainstays of word identification—the analogy strategy with onsets and rimes, the letter-sound strategy, and the multiletter chunk strategy, respectively.

Chapter 4 includes 20 lessons and activities for teaching the use of analogous letter patterns in known words to unlock the pronunciation of unknown words. Chapter 5 has 22 lessons and activities for teaching children to sound out words with phonics. Chapter 6 explains the multiletter chunks readers use to identify long words, including prefixes, suffixes, compound words, contractions, the Greek and Latin roots in our language, and syllables. There are guidelines for dividing words into syllables, and 21 lessons and activities for teaching children to use multiletter chunks.

Chapter 7 focuses on children who need extra help. Profiles of struggling readers are explained, examples of children's work are examined, and specific teaching suggestions, drawn from earlier chapters, are made for each child.

When you finish reading this book, you will know how to teach the children in your classroom who are making normal progress and those who are struggling. You will know the word identification strategies children develop as they learn to read, the phases of word identification and spelling that correspond to the use of different strategies, and many appropriate, effective teaching techniques. You will know how to match what you teach to what children need to learn. And, what's more, you will have the knowledge you need to make word identification an integral part of the ongoing learning in your classroom and to assure that the children whom you teach successfully progress toward becoming accomplished readers who instantly recognize all the words they read.

ACKNOWLEDGMENTS

I am indebted to the many teachers who welcomed me into their classrooms, to the children who were willing readers and eager participants in the activities their teachers shared, and to the principals who encouraged and supported their teachers. Without them this book could not have been written. Of the teachers I visited and who shared their classrooms with me, I would like to especially thank: Elo Goodman of Cary Elementary School; Judy Goodnight, Supervisor, and Tamara Jones and Traci Ashbaugh of the Kannapolis City Schools; Cristine Greene of Holly Springs Elementary School; Judy Skroch of Effie Green; Joan Perry of Emma Conn; Sarah Rodgers of Fox Road School; Denise Rhodes, principal, and David Wall of Franklinton Elementary; William Abel, principal, and Amy Stone of Immaculata Catholic School; Donna Dysert, Donna Kocur, and Karen Royall of Lacy Elementary; Helen Collier, principal, Gail Ace, and Marilyn Gray of Penny Road School; Moria O'Connor, principal, Carolyn Banks, Diana Callaghan, Debbie Faulkner, Pat Lemmons, and Gail Walker of Poe International Magnet School; Pam Bridges, principal, Judy Honeycutt and Patricia Gonzales of Willow Springs; JoAnn Everson; and Ronald Honeycutt. A special thanks to Catherine Clements for her good advice, to Celia Jolley for her helpful words, and to Elizabeth Beecher for her wise counsel. Thanks also goes to the reviewers of this text: Beth C. Anderson, Moorhead State University; Diane E. Bushner, Salem State College; Patricia P. Kelly, Virginia Tech University; and Thomas Gunning, Central Connecticut State University. Finally, thanks to Brad Potthoff, my editor at Merrill, for his guidance and vision.

DISCOVER THE COMPANION WEBSITE ACCOMPANYING THIS BOOK

The Prentice Hall Companion Website: A Virtual Learning Environment

Technology is a constantly growing and changing aspect of our field that is creating a need for content and resources. To address this emerging need, Prentice Hall has developed an online learning environment for students and professors alike—Companion Websites—to support our textbooks.

In creating a Companion Website, our goal is to build on and enhance what the textbook already offers. For this reason, the content for each user-friendly website is organized by chapter and provides the professor and student with a variety of meaningful resources. Common features of a Companion Website include:

For the Professor

Every Companion Website integrates **Syllabus Manager**™, an online syllabus creation and management utility.

- **Syllabus Manager**™ provides you, the instructor, with an easy, step-by-step process to create and revise syllabi, with direct links into Companion Website and other online content without having to learn HTML.
- Students may logon to your syllabus during any study session. All they need to know is the web address for the Companion Website and the password you've assigned to your syllabus.
- After you have created a syllabus using **Syllabus Manager**™, students may enter the syllabus for their course section from any point in the Companion Website.
- Class dates are highlighted in white and assignment due dates appear in blue. Clicking on a date, the student is shown the list of activities for the assignment. The activities for each assignment are linked directly to actual content, saving time for students.
- Adding assignments consists of clicking on the desired due date, then filling in the details of the assignment—name of the assignment, instructions, and whether or not it is a one-time or repeating assignment.
- In addition, links to other activities can be created easily. If the activity is online, a URL can be entered in the space provided, and it will be linked automatically in the final syllabus.
- Your completed syllabus is hosted on our servers, allowing convenient updates from any computer on the Internet. Changes you make to your syllabus are immediately available to your students at their next logon.

For the Student

- **Chapter Objectives**—outline key concepts from the text
- **Interactive self-quizzes**—complete with hints and automatic grading that provide immediate feedback for students

  After students submit their answers for the interactive self-quizzes, the Companion Website **Results Reporter** computes a percentage grade, provides a graphic representation of how many questions were answered correctly and incorrectly, and gives a question by question analysis of the quiz. Students are given the option to send their quiz to up to four email addresses (professor, teaching assistant, study partner, etc.).

- **Message Board**—serves as a virtual bulletin board to post—or respond to—questions or comments to/from a national audience
- **Net Searches**—offer links by key terms from each chapter to related Internet content
- **Web Destinations**—links to www sites that relate to chapter content

To take advantage of these and other resources, please visit the *Word Identification Strategies: Phonics from a New Perspective* Companion Website at www.prenhall.com/fox

Contents

CHAPTER 3

Early Strategies: Using Logos, Pictures, Smudges, and Rudimentary Letter-Sound Associations to Identify Words   53

CHAPTER 4

The Analogy Strategy with Onsets and Rimes: Using Familiar Words to Identify Unfamiliar Words   69

CHAPTER 5

The Letter-Sound Strategy: Identifying Words by Their Letters and Sounds   101

CHAPTER 6

The Multiletter Chunk Strategy: Using Groups of Letters to Identify Words   139

CHAPTER 7

Children Who Need Extra Help   177

APPENDIX A

APPENDIX B

APPENDIX C

APPENDIX D

APPENDIX E

APPENDIX F

1

Word Identification in a Balanced Reading Program

This chapter explains the proper place of word identification in a balanced classroom reading program and how you, the teacher, can determine the most appropriate balance for the children whom you teach. You will also learn how readers use letter-sound and context cues to identify unfamiliar words, and how to plan instruction so as to help children apply word identification strategies when reading.

KEY IDEAS

➤ In balanced reading programs, the emphasis on word identification is in proportion to children's individual needs.

➤ We teach the letter and sound relationships of phonics because it is a shortcut for learning words, it helps children develop fluent, automatic word recognition, and it helps children become independent readers.

➤ Readers use alphabetic cues from our writing system, syntactic cues, and semantic cues to identify unfamiliar words when reading.

➤ Word identification strategies develop when children have opportunities to learn how our English alphabetic writing system represents speech, and when children use this information while reading and writing.

You automatically recognize all the words you commonly encounter when reading. Instead of figuring out words, you focus on comprehension. This is exactly as it should be. But consider what it is like for young readers who come across many unfamiliar words in books and everyday surroundings. Meeting a large number of new words is a major impediment to comprehension, and so it is not surprising that these children concentrate on developing their reading vocabularies. One way to do this is to use the cues in the reading context, including cues from our alphabetic writing system, to figure out the identity of words that have never been seen before.

Consider the note Maria wrote (see Figure 1–1). If you speak and read Spanish, Maria's message is crystal clear. The words are easy to recognize, the sentences are well formed, and you know why the picture and the message are a perfect match. Suppose instead that you speak Spanish but cannot read it. Now the format of the note and Maria's drawing are the only reliable clues to meaning. You might make an educated guess based on information gleaned from the picture and your own background knowledge. From the heart-shaped drawing, you might logically infer that this is either a Valentine or a love letter. But unless you recognize the words Maria wrote, your grasp of meaning is limited, and your comprehension is only a gross approximation of Maria's message.

To go beyond supposition, you must learn the same things beginning readers learn: You must learn how to strategically use the letter and sound relationships of our alphabet to identify unfamiliar words in the reading contexts in which they appear. You must develop, through reading, writing, and using symbol-sound relationships, a vast reservoir of fluently recognized words. Just recognizing words is not enough, however. You must also know the meaning of the words Maria wrote, understand the sentence structure, have a specific purpose for reading, and appreciate the social context in which notes such as this are written and read. (See the translation of Maria's note at the end of this chapter.)

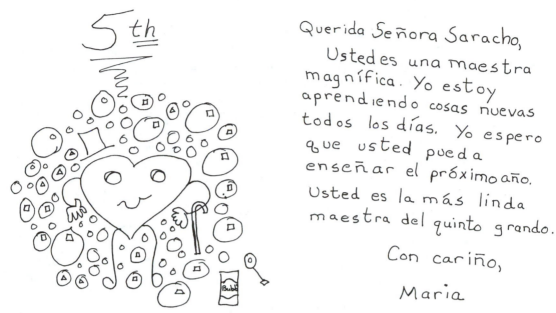

Figure 1–1 Maria's note: Can you get the message?

WHAT IS PHONICS, WHO TEACHES IT AND WHY?

Phonics is the relationship between the letters in written words and the sounds in spoken words. The letter-sound relationships of phonics are a set of visual directions—a map, if you will—telling readers how to pronounce words they have never seen before. Many languages use an alphabet to represent speech, among them English, Spanish, Arabic, Russian, French, and Icelandic. Each of these languages is based on the alphabetic principle—the principle that letters represent sounds. When you teach phonics, you help the children in your classroom learn how the alphabetic principle is applied by our own English writing system. Though figuring out pronunciation letter-sound by letter-sound is the common perception of how readers use phonics, this is only one of several word identification strategies you will learn about in this book.

You teach phonics whenever you help children understand our alphabetic writing system: When you demonstrate that **b** represents the sound heard at the beginning of **banana, boat,** and **bubble,** you are teaching phonics. When you help children compare and contrast the sounds represented by the vowels in words such as **hid, pin,** and **mad,** and **hide, pine,** and **made,** you are a phonics teacher. When you challenge readers to think about a word that begins with **c,** ends with **t,** and makes sense in the sentence, **Mark's _____ eats tuna fish,** you are teaching phonics. When you encourage writers to spell a word "the way it sounds," you help writers think about and analyze our alphabetic writing system, which is what you do when you teach phonics.

Every teacher, whether an advocate of whole language, literature-based, basal, or skills instruction, includes word identification in a balanced classroom reading program. There are three reasons teachers do this.

First, phonics is a short cut to word learning. With a relatively small amount of information readers can identify a large number of words. For instance, the children in your class who know the sounds that **t** and **ur** represent can figure out the pronunciation of words that share these letters, such as **turn, turkey, turban, turmoil, turnip,** and **turtle.** Should children ignore letter-sound combinations, they are faced with the daunting task of remembering every single word by sight alone. By and large, this is how words are learned in languages like Chinese that do not use the alphabetic principle. Remembering English words by sight alone takes a very long time and a tremendous effort because our alphabet uses only twenty-six letters to spell literally thousands upon thousands of words. As a result, many words look a lot alike, **park, perk,** and **pork,** for example. Paying attention to, and ultimately remembering, the connections among the letters in written words and the sounds in spoken words helps cement words in memory, even when words are visually similar (Adams, 1990). The combination of letters and ear sounds is suited to learning words written in an alphabet because, after all, this is the premise upon which alphabetic writing is based.

Second, knowing phonics helps children develop a large vocabulary of words that are recognized accurately, effortlessly, and instantly—within a second of seeing them (Ehri, 1997). These words are "on the tip of the tongue," always ready and instantly available anytime children see them. A large vocabulary of automatically recognized words is critical, for this permits readers to concentrate on comprehension rather than on word identification. The relationship works like this: When word identification is automatic, comprehension takes precedence. Children who recognize words automatically pay utmost attention to meaning because they are not distracted by unfamiliar words. On the other hand, when readers stumble over many unfamiliar words, comprehension suffers because readers have to allocate to word identification attention that should be going to comprehension.

Reading is a highly complex process made up of many different subprocesses, such as recognizing words, comprehending, relating background knowledge to information from the text, adjusting reading rate, and so on. While these subprocesses, and many others not mentioned, occur simultaneously while reading, readers cannot pay conscious attention to all of them at once. Some have to be carried out automatically, that is, without conscious attention. Word recognition is one of the automatic subprocesses. Some attention is needed, of course, but the level is minimal in comparison with the mental resources readers have available to them. Word recognition can be an automatic subprocess because there is a lot of uniformity, or sameness, to word identification—the same words are spelled the same way every time readers see them. Unlike word recognition which has a large measure of stability, comprehension is continuously changing and, therefore, all readers must put some attention and effort into it (Samuels & Flor, 1997). The advantage of word recognition fluency is that it frees readers—mature readers like you and me, as well as readers in grades 1 through 8—to concentrate on comprehension rather than word identification.

Third and last, phonics helps children become independent readers. Children who are good at word identification are also good readers, and this is true up through the elementary school (Carver, 1998). Children who know now to use phonics can identify many different words in text. Consequently, they can read any book at any time in any place. They do not have to rely on their teachers to tell them words; they read independently. Of course, phonics alone is not enough. Children must understand what they read, and they must spend time reading in and out of school. Exposure to print, the opportunities children take to read and enjoy all sorts of literature in elementary, middle, and high school, is related to reading comprehension in the eleventh grade (Cunningham & Stanovich, 1997). Eleventh graders' exposure to print is, in turn, predicted by how readily they learned to read in first grade. And, not surprisingly, knowing how to use the alphabetic principle helps beginning readers get off to a good start. What may be at work here, say Cunningham and Stanovich, is a reciprocal relationship where children who learn to read easily as first graders are likely to find reading enjoyable and hence to spend more time reading outside school.

PHONICS IN A BALANCED READING PROGRAM

When something is balanced it is in proportion. Your checking account is balanced when your end-of-month total equals the one on your bank statement; the United States will achieve a balance of trade when our nation's exports are in proportion to our imports. Your classroom reading program is in balance when all components are in proportion to children's needs at a given time in their reading development. The things children need to know to improve their reading achievement change as their reading ability develops. As a consequence, the role of phonics in a balanced reading program in a first-grade classroom is quite different from its proper place in a fourth-grade classroom. Yet the goal of phonics—to give children the tools they need to develop automatic word recognition—remains the same across grades. To this end, teaching is systematic and planful, and includes the use of many different materials. Teachers explain, model, and demonstrate phonics knowledge and how to use it when reading and spelling (Warton-McDonald et al., 1997). Children learn to identify words by letter-sound associations, which is the traditional grist of phonics (Chapter 5). However, in this book we will also include in a balanced classroom reading program the teaching of analogous groups of shared letters (Chapter 4), such as the **at** in **hat** and **fat,** and large multiletter structural features of words (Chapter 6), such as prefixes and suffixes. And, of course, balanced programs ensure that children have frequent, meaningful opportunities to use their knowledge of phonics, analogous letter groups, and multiletter structural features when they read and spell.

The International Reading Association's (1997) position is that teachers should ask *when, how, how much,* and *under what circumstances* to teach phonics. The answer to *when* depends on the level of children's development as readers. For children to develop word fluency (automatic, rapid word identification) and reading independence by third grade (certainly no later than the beginning of fourth grade), a balanced reading program must dedicate a significant amount of time to phonics in the early grades. This is what happens in practice, for over half the first-grade teachers in a nationwide survey said they spend significant time teaching phonics, while only a handful of fourth- and fifth-grade teachers report doing so (Bauman, Hoffman, Moon, & Duffy-Hester, 1998). Because children in grade four and above know how to use letter-sound associations, a balanced program for these children focuses on the multiletter structural features of words (prefixes, suffixes, contractions, syllables, and roots words, including Greek and Latin roots), advanced comprehension strategies and study skills. Thus, the answer to the question of *when* to teach phonics is that it should be taught early, which brings us to the next point—*how* to teach phonics (Snow, Burns, & Griffin, 1998).

Though there is a plethora of phonics teaching materials published today, phonics instruction can be distilled into a choice between synthetic (sometimes called direct instruction) and analytic (sometimes called indirect instruction). Synthetic phonics is part-to-whole instruction. This approach begins with the parts of words—letter-sound relationships—and progresses to the whole—complete words and the text in stories and poems. Analytic phonics is whole-to-part-to-whole instruction. This approach begins with the whole words in stories and poems, moves to the letter-sound parts in these words, and then back again to the whole words. Figure 1–2 illustrates how part-to-whole and whole-to-part-to-whole lessons might be sequenced. You should expect to see the most obvious differences between synthetic and analytic phonics in the early grades when children are learning to read.

In addition to traditional synthetic and analytic instruction, contemporary approaches include (1) spelling-based programs where children learn phonics through spelling, (2) analogy-based instruction where children learn to use known word parts to identify unknown words, and (3) embedded phonics where phonics instruction is part of authentic reading and writing activities (Stahl, Duffy-Hester, & Stahl, 1998). Each approach is effective for some of the teachers and children who use it. However, generally speaking, synthetic phonics—direct instruction in print and speech relationships—appears to be more effective than analytic, particularly for children at-risk (Chall, Jacobs, & Baldwin, 1990; Foorman, Francis, Beeler, Winikates, & Fletcher, 1997; Foorman, Francis, Fletcher, Schatschneider, & Mehta, 1998).

When you teach phonics in your own balanced classroom reading program, make lessons interesting and include (1) some direct, teacher-led lessons; (2) instruction in awareness of the sounds in spoken words (called phonemic awareness and explained in Chapter 2); (3) instruction in knowledge of letters and letter-sounds; and (4) lots of practice reading words in many contexts (Stahl et al., 1998).

The abbreviated lessons focus on the **VCe** pattern in which the final, silent **e** usually indicates that the first vowel represents a long sound, as in **mine** and **tile.**

Part-to-Whole	Whole-to-Part-to-Whole
Introduce the Letter-Sound Correspondence The teacher (1) explains that the final **e** in the **VCe** pattern helps the **i** say its name thus indicating a long vowel sound; (2) demonstrates how a consonant in the blank **i____e** completes the **VCe** pattern as in the words **like, time, hide,** and **drive;** and (3) may contrast the long **i** (**hide**) with the short **i** (**hid**) and review other long **i** spellings.	**Reading Connected Text** The teacher supports children as they read stories and poetry where the primary focus is on meaning and the secondary focus is on developing word identification strategies.
Blending Children blend words sound by sound (l+i+ke). Children may also segment words into sounds, which may include identifying the beginning, middle, and ending sounds; deleting sounds; and substituting sounds.	**Introduce the Letter-Sound Correspondence** The teacher (or children) reread part of the story. The teacher points out a word with the long **i** sound. Children repeat the word, listening for the long **i.** The teacher finds a long **i** word in the story and helps children conclude that the **i** represents a long vowel sound. The teacher writes **like** on the chalkboard and calls attention to the **VCe** pattern.
Practice Children find long **i** words in sentences and participate in other activities in which they pay attention to the **VCe** pattern and to other spellings of long **i** (as in **night**).	**Practice** The teacher writes **like** on a chart. Children read **like** and tell the vowel sound. The teacher writes another **ike** word, **bike,** and children read it. Children, perhaps with the teacher's help, add more **ike** words.
Application *Reading:* Children read a story and apply the **VCe** pattern to identify unfamiliar words. *Dictation:* Children write, from dictation, words and sentences with long **i** words.	**Application** Children read and write using their knowledge of the long **i** sound in words such as **like** and **bike.**

*For brevity, **C** stands for consonant; **V** for vowel.
 Examples of the **VCe** pattern are: **ice, fame, vote,** and **huge.**

Figure 1–2   A Comparison of Part-to-Whole and Whole-to-Part-to-Whole Phonics Lessons

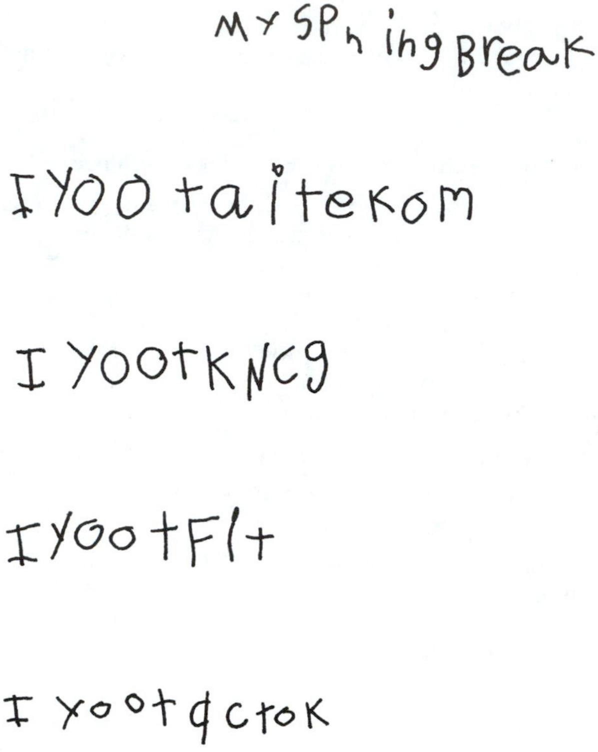

Figure 1–3 At the end of the first grade, Greg knows only a handful of words. He will benefit from explicit instruction in all aspects of reading, including phonics, and from opportunities to use letter and sound relationships when reading and spelling.

M Y SP h ing Break

I YOO t a i te K o m

I YOOtK NC g

I YGo t F l t

I X o o t q c t o K

In the chapters that follow, you will find many flexible lessons and activities that make phonics learning interesting without resorting to the kind of mindless drill that is divorced from using phonics while reading and writing.

How much time and energy teachers spend on phonics instruction depends on children's knowledge of the alphabetic principle, and their ability to use this knowledge when reading and writing. To strike the right balance in your own classroom, consider children's needs and then select the intensity (how much) that is the best match for the individuals and groups you teach (Strickland, 1998). Greg and Sharon (Figures 1–3 and 1–4, respectively) show how beginning readers from the same first-grade class have different levels of phonics knowledge. Greg and Sharon wrote the descriptions of what they did on their spring break in late March. Greg (Figure 1–3) fluently recognizes only a few words, depends almost entirely on pictures to guess at meaning, inconsistently uses beginning and ending letter-sounds to identify words, and forgets words from one day to the next. He does not consistently separate words with white spaces when he writes, and does not consistently use letters to represent sounds.

Sharon (Figure 1–4) understands what she reads, uses phonics and context cues to identify new words, and applies sound-letter relationships when spelling. Her fluent reading vocabulary is growing rapidly and she is gaining reading independence.

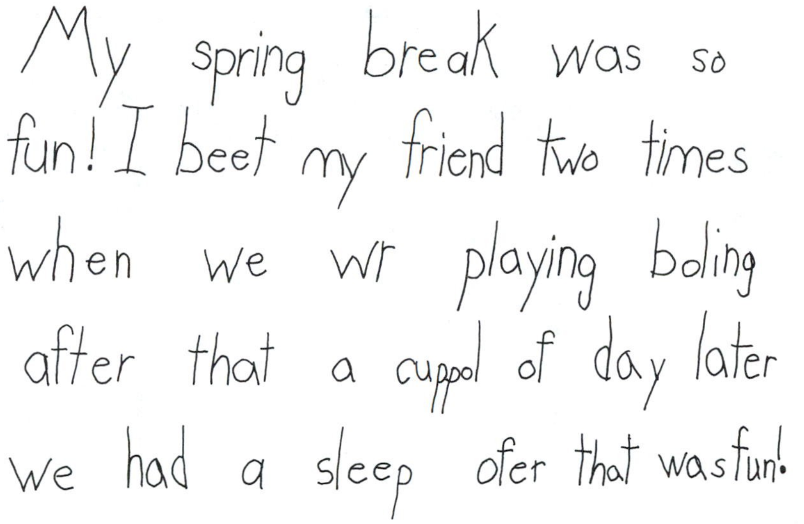

Figure 1–4 While Sharon, Greg's first-grade classmate, will benefit from learning more about alphabetic cues, she knows and uses many more letter-sound associations when she reads and writes than Greg. An appropriate classroom balance would include less concentration on phonics for Sharon than it would for Greg.

My spring break was so fun! I beet my friend two times when we wr playing boling after that a cuppol of day later we had a sleep ofer that was fun!

We can see from her writing that Sharon correctly spells many words in her fluent reading vocabulary, understands the sounds most consonants represent, and is developing knowledge of how vowels represent sounds. While both Greg and Sharon will benefit from more phonics knowledge, Greg has far more to learn than Sharon. For this reason, an appropriate classroom balance would include more phonics instruction for Greg than it would for Sharon. So, we see that the answer to *how much* phonics to teach depends on children's knowledge of the alphabetic principle and on their ability to use phonics in everyday reading and writing.

The answer to *under what circumstances* depends on how teachers differentiate instruction. In balanced classrooms, children learn in large groups, small groups, flexible skill groups, and individually. Large groups typically include everyone, or nearly everyone, in the class. Learning focuses on information and strategies that everyone needs to learn. Unlike large group instruction where the whole class learns and does the same thing, small groups focus on just a few children. While there are many ways to form small groups, ability groups and literature study groups are the most prominent. Small ability groups consist of children who read books written on their instructional level—not so easy that children have nothing new to learn and not so hard that reading is frustrating. The emphasis is on teaching the particular knowledge and strategies children need to develop. Reading ability is not so tightly controlled in literature study groups where children read, discuss and react to self-selected books. Flexible skill groups may consist of children reading at vastly different levels; they target specific aspects of our alphabetic writing system children need to know more about. These groups are disbanded once children know and apply information and strategies when reading (Au, Carroll, & Scheu, 1997).

You will find that different teachers in your school conceptualize balance differently. Naturally, when teachers' views differ, so too does the emphasis they place on phonics (Freppon & Dahl, 1998). There are many factors that go into finding the right balance among phonics and other components of the classroom reading program—the grade taught, children's ability to use letter-sound relationships, multiletter structural features and analogous letter groups when reading and writing, and the size and growth of children's fluent reading vocabulary, to name a few. A well-balanced program for a child like Greg, who brings less phonics knowledge to reading and writing, may look quite different from a well-balanced program for a child like Sharon, who has more phonics knowledge. Even though the individual teachers in your school may not all agree on the answers to when, how, how much, and under what circumstances to teach phonics in a balanced program, they will all teach children how to use letter-sound cues and context cues to identify unfamiliar words in text, which is the topic of the next section.

CUES FOR IDENTIFYING WORDS

Readers interpret storybooks, novels, textbooks, magazine articles, newspaper editorials—virtually all written material—within their unique framework of personal knowledge and experience. For instance, the tongue-in-cheek humor of Scieszka's (1989) book, *The True Story of the Three Little Pigs!*, is fully appreciated only when readers know the original version of the story. In addition, readers must bring to this storybook social-cultural knowledge and an understanding of point of view and current practices of reporting the news. The author counts on his readers knowing all these things when he writes about the first little pig thinking, "It seemed like a shame to leave a perfectly good ham dinner lying there in the straw" and when he compares the first little pig to "a big cheeseburger" (p. 15).

Along with social-cultural background knowledge, readers use the cues in spoken and written language. Readers bring to print a deep understanding of the word order, meaning, and sounds of the spoken language. Knowing a great deal about spoken language is a tremendous asset, for the predictable patterns of speech are also present in written language. Information about grammar, meaning, and our alphabetic writing system represent three types of information, or cueing systems, that support readers as they make sense of authors' messages.

Syntax is the grammatical arrangement of words in phrases, sentences, and paragraphs. **Syntactic cues** are the basis on which readers decide whether an author's word order is consistent with English grammar. Syntactic cues help readers predict words in phrases and sentences. For instance, in **The little _____ chewed on a bone,** readers know that the word following **little** is a person or an animal (a noun). Likewise, readers know that the word following **dog** in **The little dog _____ on a bone.** is an action word (a verb). Syntactic cues also give readers insight into the meaning of sentences. Readers who use these cues know that the meaning of phrases, sentences, and paragraphs may change when words are sequenced in different ways, for example, **The little dog chewed on a bone.** versus **The dog chewed on a little bone.** Though the first sentence refers to a small dog and the other to a small bone, both conform to the structure of English. But the sentence **The chewed on a dog bone little.** makes no sense at all. Word order is not consistent with English structure, and so the sentence is not meaningful language. Hence, when readers use syntactic cues, they ask themselves, "Does this seem like language?"

Semantic cues, a second source of information, are the meaningful relationships among words in phrases, sentences, and paragraphs. This is the basis on which readers decide if an author's message is logical and represents real-world events, relationships, and phenomena. Readers draw on their knowledge of the meaningful relationships among words and on their prior knowledge of the topic they are reading about. In so doing, readers look for meaning that is consistent with both the text and their experiences. For example, readers use semantic cues to determine that the relationship among words in **The little dog chewed on the bone.** is meaningful and that the relationship among the words in **The little bone chewed on the dog.** is not. Hence, when readers use semantic context cues, they ask themselves, "Does this make sense?"

From a broader perspective, the reading context also includes the overall conditions under which materials are read and readers' reasons for reading. As a consequence, when readers consider both syntactic and semantic cues, they do so in light of the reading environment (such as noisy or quiet, shared reading or reading independently, with time limits or without time limits) and reasons for reading (such as for pleasure or for study, to get the gist or to locate facts).

Syntactic and semantic cues, together with the overall conditions under which materials are read, create a rich base on which word identification and reading comprehension rest. When readers use the reading context, they draw upon all the cues available to them, selecting and combining information to construct authors' messages. Brian's note (Figure 1–5) illustrates how syntactic and semantic context cues work together. You, the reader, automatically recognize all the words as belonging to your fluent reading vocabulary except one: **spreencler.** If you were to try to decode this word without thinking about context, it would be difficult to figure out just what Brian meant to say. However, **spreencler** is surrounded by other words that contribute valuable clues to its identity.

From syntactic cues, you infer that **spreencler** is a noun, not a verb, adverb, or adjective. From semantic cues, you surmise that this unknown object is something children play with, which rules out such things as spoons or spigots. If you know the types of activities Brian and Mike enjoy, and if you also know the types of things Mike has to play with, you can use this background knowledge to narrow your choices even further. For many readers, this information is enough to deduce the identity of **spreencler.**

Though the syntactic cues and semantic cues are rich, if you want to be absolutely certain about the word, you will turn your attention to cues that are a combination of how words look and sound. Goodman (1996) coined the term **graphophonic** for these cues and other visual cues indicated by punctuation. In this book we will use the term **letter and sound cues** to describe a specific focus on the associations

Figure 1–5 Brian's
note: How do you
figure out the meaning?

among letters and sounds that are the backbone of our writing system. Letter and
sound cues help you further narrow the field of possible words. When readers use alphabetic cues, they ask themselves, "Does this word sound and look right?"

When using syntactic, semantic, and letter and sound cues to identify words,
readers keep the focus on meaning since they need to think about words that make
sense in passages. Given the unconventional way Brian spelled **spreencler,** letter
and sound cues might help you approximate pronunciation. The easiest way to
combine letter and sound cues with syntactic and semantic context cues is to ask
yourself, "What word begins with **spr,** ends with **er,** and makes sense in Brian's
message?" With this combination of cues, your chance of making a good educated
guess increases substantially because letter and sound cues help you narrow the
field of possible words. If the guess you make is sensible, you discontinue decoding, confident that you understand Brian's message.

If the beginning and ending letter and sound cues in **spreencler,** as well as the
syntactic cues and semantic cues are not enough to figure out this word's identity,
then you consider all the letters in spelling. Should you choose to do this, you
would probably sound out **spreencler** letter-sound by letter-sound. But, having
sounded out **spreencler,** you still have not pronounced a recognizable word.
Brian's spelling is unconventional, and so the outcome of sounding out is a non-

sense word. Yet this nonsense word is quite similar in sound to a meaningful word in your speaking vocabulary that fits nicely into the overall reading context.

There is a curious and very interesting phenomenon at work here: In using letter and sound cues, readers do not always have to perfectly pronounce the words they are figuring out. Pronunciation need only sound enough like a real word to trigger recognition. By combining information from different cues, you know without a shadow of a doubt that Brian intended to write that he is playing in Mike's **sprinkler.**

While use of all types of cues contributes to understanding messages like the one Brian wrote, this does not imply that every cue is equally helpful in every reading situation. Children's reasons for reading affect the importance they assign to accurate word identification. For example, a fifth grader who reads her science textbook for information needs to pay close attention to the words the author wrote. A second grader who is reading an article in the children's magazine *Ranger Rick* is more likely to be concerned with the overall ideas in the article, not with detailed information. Correct identification of nearly all words is far more important for understanding the information in science textbooks than it is for enjoying articles in *Ranger Rick.*

Insofar as Brian's note is concerned, if your reason for reading is to find out who Brian is playing with, you might make an educated guess for **spreencler,** having found out that Brian is in Mike's company. Conversely, if you are concerned with knowing precisely what Brian is doing, you will analyze **spreencler** to determine exactly what type of play Brian is engaged in. All in all, the amount of mental attention you allot to word identification depends on how concerned you are about absolute understanding. Your concern for understanding is, in turn, determined in part by the reason you are reading Brian's note in the first place.

Overrelying on any one cue is inefficient, time-consuming, and likely to result in poor comprehension. Good readers know this and hence balance syntactic, semantic, and letter and sound cues with the type of text they are reading, the reading environment, their own reasons for reading, and their own background knowledge. Though it is not necessary to distribute attention equally to all cues, it is necessary to be able to take maximum advantage of the information cues provide, should reading situations call for it. When all is said and done, the strategic use of the reading context hinges on taking advantage of syntactic, semantic, and letter and sound cues. And, of course, the reasons for reading and the background knowledge readers bring to text help determine how much attention readers choose to pay to the cues available to them.

TEACHING CHILDREN TO IDENTIFY WORDS STRATEGICALLY

Unlike the Greek goddess Athena who sprang fully grown from Zeus's head, word identification strategies do not emerge fully formed from a few incidental experiences with print. Strategies are systematic, organized procedures for identifying words and as such require careful nurturing and a supportive environment in which to develop. This does not mean a drill-and-kill approach to learning where readers memorize isolated letter-sound combinations. Rather, it means giving readers many opportunities to understand how our alphabetic writing system works and many chances to strategically use this information as they read and write every day. Your role as the teacher is to explain how our alphabetic writing system represents speech, to guide children, to model and demonstrate strategies, and to discuss with children the strategies they use.

To develop and apply word identification strategies, readers need to know how, when, and why to use them. You will find three-part strategy lessons in Chapters 4, 5, and 6. In each three-part lesson, children (1) explore with their teacher the way print represents speech and a word identification strategy to use this information, (2) then move to practice with teacher guidance, and (3) end by transferring learning to genuine reading and writing.

1. **Exploration** gives readers opportunities to (1) learn letter-sound associations, multiletter structural features or analogous letter groups, (2) observe how a particular strategy works and when to use it, and (3) develop enough understanding of the strategy to try it under supervision. This is the time when teachers explain and model, and when children and their teachers join together to learn how to use strategies to identify unfamiliar words.

2. **Guided practice** gives readers a chance to remember and use letter-sound associations, multiletter structural features, or analogous letters groups, to try strategies, make inferences, draw conclusions, and cement understanding with the guidance of their teacher. Guided practice also includes the thoughtful correction of mistakes and misapplications. It ensures that readers get knowledge of results, immediate feedback, and reinforcement. For children who need more practice than that which is included in the three-part lesson, extra practice activities are included at the end of Chapters 4, 5, and 6.

3. **Transfer** is the time when strategies are transferred, or generalized, to various reading, writing, and problem-solving activities. For example, children might work individually, in small groups, or in large groups to read books, create imaginative cartoons, solve riddles and crossword puzzles, make up tongue twisters, write descriptions of favorite fiction characters, and so on.

The readers whom I teach benefit immensely from lots of opportunities to explain in their own words what they know about letter-sound associations, multiletter structural features and analogous letters. Readers also benefit from telling why they choose different word identification strategies. When children explain in their own words how our alphabetic writing system works and give reasons for using the strategies they do, they develop a self-conscious awareness of their own knowledge, as well as an appreciation of why and when to use different strategies. Thinking analytically and critically helps children become conscious—metacognitively aware—of their own strategy use and in so doing gain greater control over word identification strategies. To help children become aware of how, when, and why they use word identification strategies, ask questions such as these:

1. Does what you just read sound like a real word?
2. Does the word make sense?
3. How did you figure out that word?
4. What other kinds of words can be figured out just the way that you figured out this one?
5. When would you use this same way to figure out another word?
6. What did you learn today that will help you be a better reader?

As children answer questions like these, they organize observations, form generalizations, change or alter information and ideas, and, perhaps most important, become sensitive to how the use of word identification strategies supports comprehension.

LOOKING AHEAD: LEARNING TO USE WORD IDENTIFICATION STRATEGIES AND DEVELOPING WORD FLUENCY

Complex processes take time and experience to develop and mature. This is just as true for learning to play the guitar and learning to write a persuasive essay as it is for developing effective, efficient word identification strategies. Word identification strategies develop over time in a reasonably predictable sequence that begins long before children read storybooks and long before they go to school. Though the exact order in which word identification strategies develop is not completely understood, we do know that readers use some strategies before others.

We know from research that awareness of written and spoken language is an important part of learning to read a language written in an alphabet. So, we begin in Chapter 2 by exploring how children learn about the form and function of written language, as well as how they develop phonemic awareness, which is the ability to consciously manipulate the words, syllables, rhymes, and sounds of language. Phonemic awareness is crucial for using word identification strategies, and so you will find in Chapter 2 teaching activities to develop rhyme and sound awareness.

Research also reveals that children go through five word identification phases—pre-alphabetic, partial alphabetic, alphabetic, consolidated, and fluent recognition phases (Ehri, 1998; Frith, 1985). These word identification phases correspond to five phases of spelling growth–precommunicative, semiphonetic, phonetic, transitional, and conventional (Gentry, 1987). As children enter each new word identification phase, they begin using a new strategy. Initially, children's knowledge of the print and speech relationships needed to use the new strategy is immature. With instruction, ample reading experiences, and many opportunities to write, children's knowledge gradually matures and their ability to use the word identification strategy improves, too. Then, when children are relatively comfortable using a certain strategy and have a good understanding of the print and speech relationships that support it, they gradually move into the next phase as they begin to use a more efficient strategy based on a more advanced understanding of print and speech relationships.

When you, the teacher, are familiar with the phases of movement toward word fluency and understand the knowledge and abilities that underpin the use of strategies, you can then make decisions that will help children move from one phase to the next. A good word identification program is balanced with other components of the literacy curriculum, to be sure, but it is also related to children's phase of movement toward word fluency and conventional spelling (Moats, 1998). From reading this book, you will be able to relate what you teach (letter-sounds, multiletter structural features like the **pre-** in **preview** and **pretest,** or analogous letter groups like the **at** in **bat** and **hat**) to children's phase of word learning. To this end, Chapters 3 through 6 explain word identification strategies and the knowledge that supports them. Chapters 3 through 6 also connect the strategies with movement toward word fluency and toward conventional spelling.

Chapter 3 explains four early strategies—the environmental cue, picture cue, incidental cue, and phonetic cue strategies—used by preschool and kindergarten emergent readers. As explained in Chapter 3, children who use environmental cues, such as the golden arches to read McDonalds®, pictures to read storybooks, and color or shape to read words are at the pre-alphabetic phase of movement toward word fluency (Ehri, 1998). These children do not understand the principle of alphabetic writing and therefore do not use alphabetic cues to identify and spell words. Children are precommunicative spellers who use scribbles, mock letters, and numbers when they write (Gentry, 1987).

Eventually children discover, or are taught, that letters are constant, intact objects that represent sounds. When this happens, children understand the alphabetic principle, and they begin to use the phonetic cue strategy to identify words (Chapter 3). In so doing, children enter into the partial alphabetic phase of movement toward word fluency. Children who use the phonetic cue strategy identify words by one (maybe two) letter-sounds or letter names (Ehri, 1998). These same children are semiphonetic spellers who use one (maybe two) letters (almost always consonants) to represent whole words (Gentry, 1987).

As children learn how our alphabet represents sound, they begin using the analogy and letter-sound strategies. When children use the analogy strategy, they use parts of words they already know how to read to identify unfamiliar words (Chapter 4). For example, on seeing **lid** for the first time, children may recognize the analogous letter group **id** from a known word (**hid**) and then combine the beginning letter-sound (the l which represents "l") with the sounds represented by **id** ("**id**") to pronounce "**lid**." Next, readers cross-check to decide whether a word makes sense in the reading context. Cross-checking (Chapter 4) is the last step in word identification, regardless of the word identification strategy used.

If there is a stereotype for decoding, surely it has to be the letter-sound strategy (Chapter 5). Readers who use the letter-sound strategy connect the sounds represented by the letters in written words with the sounds of spoken words. Children who do this have reached the alphabetic phase of movement toward word fluency (Ehri, 1998). These children have a good working knowledge of letter and sound relationships, and use this knowledge to spell phonetically (Gentry, 1987). When spelling phonetically, children represent all essential sounds in words, though words are not spelled conventionally (**cuppol** for **couple**). Because children pay attention to and use all the letter-sound relationships in words, they can identify unfamiliar words on their own and hence begin to develop the ability to read independently. Added to this, children's fluent reading vocabulary rapidly expands as they use decoding to learn the many new words they encounter in print.

The multiletter chunk strategy (Chapter 6) is the most streamlined word identification strategy described in this book, the last to develop, and a more advanced strategy than either the analogy or letter-sound strategies. Readers who use this strategy are in the consolidated phase of movement toward word fluency because they have successfully combined, or consolidated, the individual letters in words into large multiletter groups (Ehri, 1998). Children recognize many different-size chunks, or multiletter groups, in words. Many of these multiletter groups are meaningful (as the **aqua** in **aquarium** and the **re-** in **rework**), which gives readers information about pronunciation, as well as meaning. Though children in first grade use multiletter chunks, it is not until sometime in the second grade that the multiletter chunk strategy really begins to mature. And, as children move into higher grades, they continue to refine this strategy. Children who use the multiletter chunk strategy are transitional spellers (Gentry, 1987). While these children spell most words conventionally, their spelling may include inappropriate letters or alternative spellings (**nete** for **neat**).

When children are adept at using the multiletter chunk strategy and when all the words in everyday reading are in their fluent reading vocabularies, children enter into the fifth and final phase of fluency—fluent, automatic recognition. Children become conventional spellers (the last spelling phase) when they correctly spell most regular and irregular words, and use letter-sound relationships and word structure (prefixes, suffixes, syllables, and so forth) to spell unfamiliar words (Gentry, 1987). Children at the fluent word recognition phase read all sorts of material rapidly and automatically. Because attention is not distracted by a plethora of unfamiliar words in text, readers concentrate fully on comprehension. They use reading to learn the information in complex and conceptually demanding high school and college textbooks, and enjoy reading many different genres for pleasure. Though most words are automatically recognized, when readers do meet unfamiliar words, such as the technical words in the content subjects studied in high school, they have at their fingertips many effective strategies for adding words to their fluent reading vocabularies. Though accomplished readers prefer more efficient strategies, readers keep less efficient ones in reserve just in case sophisticated strategies fail. Thus, in a very real sense, every word identification strategy is always available, should a situation call for it.

Translation of Figure 1–1, Maria's Valentine
Dear Mrs. Saracho,

You are a great teacher. I am learning new things every day. I hope that you will be able to teach here next year. You are the nicest teacher in fifth grade.
Love,
Maria

REFERENCES

Adams, M. J. (1990). *Beginning to read: Thinking and learning about print.* Cambridge, MA: MIT.

Au, K. H., Carroll, J. H., & Scheu, J. A. (1997). *Balanced literacy instruction: A teacher's resource book.* Norwood, MA: Christopher-Gordon.

Bauman, J. F., Hoffman, J. V., Moon, J., & Duffy-Hester (1998). Where are teachers' voices in the phonics/whole language debate? Results from a survey of U.S. elementary classroom teachers. *The Reading Teacher, 51,* 636–650.

Carver, R. P. (1998). Predicting reading level in grades 1 and 6 from listening level and decoding level: Testing theory relevant to the simple view of reading. *Reading and Writing: An Interdisciplinary Journal, 10,* 121–154.

Chall, J. S., Jacobs, V. A., & Baldwin, L. E. (1990). *The reading crisis: Why poor children fall behind.* Cambridge, MA: Harvard University Press.

Cunningham, A. E., & Stanovich, K. E. (1997). Early reading acquisition and its relation to reading experience and ability 10 years later. *Developmental Psychology, 33,* 934–945.

Ehri, L. C. (1997). Sight word learning in normal readers and dyslexics. In B. Blachman (Ed.), *Foundations of reading acquisition and dyslexia* (pp. 163–189). Mahwah, NJ: Erlbaum.

Ehri, L. C. (1998). Grapheme-phoneme knowledge is essential for learning to read words in English. In J. L. Metsala & L. C. Ehri (Eds.), *Word recognition in beginning literacy* (pp. 3–40). Mahwah, NJ: Erlbaum.

Foorman, B. R., Francis, D. J., Fletcher, J. M., Schatschneider, C., & Mehta, P. (1998). The role of instruction in learning to read: Preventing reading failure in at-risk children. *Journal of Educational Psychology, 90,* 37–55.

Foorman, B. R., Francis, D. J., Beeler, T., Winikates, D., & Fletcher, J. M. (1997). Early interventions for children with reading problems: Study designs and preliminary findings. *Learning Disabilities, 8,* 63–71.

Freppon, P. A., & Dahl, K. I. (1998). Theory and research into practice: Balanced instruction: Insights and considerations. *Reading Research Quarterly, 33,* 240–251.

Frith, U. (1985). Beneath the surface of developmental dyslexia. In K. E. Patterson, J. C. Marshall, & M. Coltheart (Eds.), *Surface Dyslexia* (pp. 301–330). London: Erlbaum.

Gentry, J. R. (1987). *Spel . . . is a four letter word.* Portsmouth, NH: Heinemann.

Goodman, K. (1996). *On reading: A common-sense look at the nature of language and the science of reading.* Portsmouth, NH: Heinemann.

International Reading Association. (1997). *The role of phonics in reading instruction: A position statement of the International Reading Association* [Brochure]. Newark, DE: Author.

Moats, L. C. (1998). Teaching decoding. *American Educator, 22,* 42–49; 95–96.

Samuels, S. J., & Flor, R. F. (1997). The importance of automaticity for developing expertise in reading. *Reading & Writing Quarterly: Overcoming Learning Difficulties, 13,* 107–121.

Scieszka, J. (1989). *The true story of the three little pigs!* New York: Viking Penguin.

Snow, C. E., Burns, M. S., & Griffin, P. (1998). *Preventing reading difficulties in young children.* Washington, DC: National Academy Press.

Stahl, S. A., Duffy-Hester, A. M., & Stahl, K. A. D. (1998). Everything you wanted to know about phonics (but were afraid to ask). *Reading Research Quarterly, 33,* 338–355.

Strickland, D. S. (1998). *Teaching phonics today: A primer for educators.* Newark, DE: International Reading Association.

Warton-McDonald, R., Pressley, M., Rankin, J., Mistretta, J., Yokoi, L., & Ettenberger, S. (1997). Effective primary-grades literacy instruction = balanced literacy instruction. *The Reading Teacher, 50,* 518–521.

CHAPTER 2

Becoming Aware of Language

Insights into Print and Phonemic Awareness

This chapter describes how emergent readers and writers develop insight into the form and function of written language, and into the words, rhymes, and sounds of spoken language. You will find in this chapter many engaging activities to use in your classroom to increase children's ability to recognize rhyme, to separate spoken words into sounds, and to blend sounds into words. You will also learn about tests of phonemic awareness to use in your classroom.

KEY IDEAS

➤ As emergent readers and writers explore written language, they become aware of its form and function. They learn how writing is arranged on pages, the properties of words and letters, and its use and many purposes.

➤ As children explore spoken language, they develop phonemic awareness, which is the awareness and conscious manipulation of the words, rhymes, and sounds in language.

➤ Phonemic awareness develops sequentially, beginning with word awareness, then progressing to rhyme awareness, and finally to awareness of individual sounds in words.

➤ Children who are phonemically aware identify and manipulate the sounds of language. They do this by separating words into sounds, and by blending individual sounds into words.

DEVELOPING INSIGHT INTO WRITTEN LANGUAGE

James's writing includes letters, two words (**at** and **no**) copied from his kindergarten classroom, a large form that looks somewhat like a letter, and two smiley faces (Figure 2–1). He writes **at** and **no** on a line he has drawn. From his writing, we can infer that James knows that letters are important, that the words in his classroom are significant, and that writing is supposed to go on lines. Children like James become aware of the form of written language—the way writing is arranged on pages and the properties of words and letters—and the function of written language—its use and many purposes—when they experiment with writing and talk about the words, pictures, and print in storybooks read aloud to them (Cheek, Flippo, & Lindsey, 1997; Galda, Cullinan, & Strickland, 1997).

Young children are naturally curious about writing and they are inveterate experimenters. They experiment with scribble writing, drawing, mock letters, letter strings, and words. Scribble writing is easy to recognize because it looks a lot like cursive in that it has connected wavy lines and goes from left to right. The long wavy line traversing Marty's writing is an example of scribble writing (Figure 2–2). Whereas James draws while he writes, some children draw first and write later, perhaps using their drawings as an inspiration for writing (Christie, Enz, & Vukelich, 1997). Sometimes emergent writers use several forms at once—connected scribbles, mock letters, and real letters—as we see in Marty's writing (Figure 2–2). Marty will continue to use a variety of representations until he begins to read and write conventionally (Sulzby, 1996).

Children like Michelle (Figure 2–3) experiment by writing the same letters over and over again. Michelle uses capital (uppercase) and lowercase letters, and

Figure 2–1 By experimenting with writing, emergent readers and writers, like James, have opportunities to discover the conventions of written language.

copies several words from the print in her kindergarten classroom. She is sorting out in her own mind the properties that make letters and words unique. She already knows writing is arranged from left to right and from top to bottom. However, Michelle does not fully appreciate the concepts of word and letter, for she neither uses white spaces to separate the words she copies nor does she combine letters to write her own words. Michelle's, James's, and Marty's writing represent ideas, not specific words. This explains why each child cheerfully reads his or her own writing when they first share it with their teachers and why they cannot reread it a day or so later.

Their kindergarten teachers encourage James, Marty, and Michelle to write in their own way using their own knowledge of print. Without such freedom, some children worry about matching adult standards and therefore want their teachers to write for them or want their teachers to tell them how to spell all the words they write (Tompkins, 1998). Immersion in reading and writing is important, to be sure, but it is also important to let children know that their writing is valued and that they are free to write on their own in their own way.

Before James and Marty write letters conventionally, they have to learn the features that distinguish one letter from another. It takes a good bit of experimentation and experience to differentiate letters that share some of the same distinctive features, such as **b** and **d** and **p** and **q,** and words that share many of the same letters, such as **was** and **saw** and **then** and **when.** With so many relatively similar-looking letters and so many words that have several letters in common, word reversals and letter confusions are a normal part of learning to read. It is typical for

Figure 2–2 Marty, a kindergartner, uses connected scribbles, mock letters, and real letters when he experiments with writing.

kindergartners and first graders to reverse words (to write **was** instead of **saw**) and to confuse letters (to write **b** rather than **d**). The more children read and write the more sensitive they become to the features that distinguish letters and words. You can expect, therefore, to observe fewer and fewer reversals and confusions as children become more knowledgeable readers and writers. In my experience, by the time children are in second grade they may occasionally reverse and confuse letters and words, but this is an exception, not a general attribute of children's writing.

As children become aware of the alphabetic principle, they use their knowledge of the sounds in words and the letters of the alphabet to invent spelling. For example, children might use one or more consonant letters to represent whole words, as **m** for **man** and **rn** for **run.** Words spelled like this are called semiphonetic because letters that represent important sounds are left out (Gentry, 1987). When children develop more detailed concepts of sound and letter associations, they use more letters to write words and the words they write include vowels. Nadia (Figure 2–4), for instance, invents her own spelling by using letters to represent some, but not all, of the sounds in words, as in **pazz** for **pizza,** and **suy** for **Sue's.**

FiShSFiNaYesKYLLCnayonS
nnKKiiLL LLLSSKKLCrAßRno
CJKKKNttKpooooaannhrKttt
ShrimpShpppppppannhowill((((((
Book
pencils
peß

Figure 2–3   Through pieces of writing like this, learners like Michelle have opportunities to discover the ways that words and letters are formed.

Figure 2–4   Nadia uses semiphonetic spelling to write nearly all the words in her story as she writes: **I went to Sue's and ate pizza.**

Figure 2–5 Rashid's
story includes a combination
of phonetic and conventional
spelling. His story reads: **I
know how it's like to have
stitches because I have five
stitches. It hurt when I got
my stitches in.**

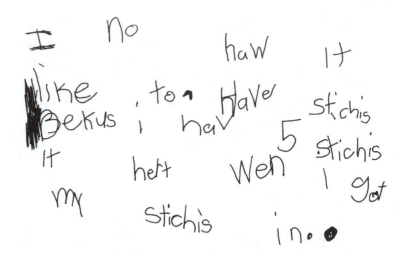

Words that can be figured out by associating sounds with letters are spelled phonetically (Gentry, 1987). Examples of this type of invented spelling are **noc** for **knock, varry** for **very, tern** for **turn,** and **bekus** for **because.** Rashid, whose story is shown in Figure 2–5, uses a mixture of phonetic (**stichis** for **stitches; hert** for **hurt**) and conventional spelling (the words **like** and **my,** for example). Rashid is developing insight into punctuation, as illustrated by his use of some capitals and periods. He has developed word and letter concepts and hence appreciates the importance of using letters to represent sounds in words. He also knows that writing is purposeful, is intended to be shared, and can tell something important about the writer.

Rashid could not write **stichis** (**stitches**) if he did not know that (1) spoken language is made up of words, (2) written words correspond to spoken words, (3) spoken words are made up of sounds, and (4) letters represent the sounds in spoken words. Thinking analytically about the segments of written and spoken language is essential, especially for children who learn to read a language such as ours that uses an alphabetic writing system.

DEVELOPING PHONEMIC AWARENESS

The language children bring to school serves many different purposes. First and foremost, it gives children a way to interact with others so as to exert some measure of control over their lives and their environment. So long as children carry on everyday conversations, they concentrate on communication, not on words, syllables, rhymes, and sounds. This changes when children learn to read. As they move toward literacy, children begin to think about spoken language in a different way. They stand back from the meaning of language in order to analyze speech. And, as they do this, emergent readers and writers discover that spoken language is composed of words, syllables, rhymes, and sounds. The children in your classroom who are aware of and consciously manipulate the words, syllables, rhymes, and sounds in language have developed **phonemic awareness.**

Phonemic awareness is the ability to think analytically about the word, syllable, rhyme, and sound segments of language and the ability to act on the basis of this analysis. Children who are phonemically aware can (1) separate spoken language into words, syllables, rhymes, and sounds; and (2) blend individual sounds together to pronounce words. These children deliberately arrange, rearrange, add, and delete the sounds in words. What's more, children use their awareness of language segments to connect the pieces of spoken language with the pieces of written language.

In the absence of phonemic awareness, children perceive speech as a continuous, undivided stream and therefore lack insight into the basic premise of written language—that print represents speech at the sound level. If children are to learn to read English, they have to understand that our writing system connects sounds and letters (Nunes, Bryant, & Bindman, 1997). Children must realize that words and syllables consist of individual sounds because without this understanding they have no basis for making the connections between letters and sounds that are at the heart of alphabetic writing.

Though phonemic awareness and phonics develop reciprocally (getting better in one results in improvement in the other) as children learn to read, phonemic awareness and phonics are not the same (Vandervelden & Siegel, 1995). Whereas phonemic awareness is insight into the words and sounds of spoken language, phonics is the relationship between sounds and letters. When children demonstrate phonemic awareness, they manipulate the words, syllables, rhymes, and sounds of language. When children demonstrate phonics knowledge, they use their understanding of letter-sound relationships to pronounce unfamiliar words while reading and to spell while writing. Children need phonemic awareness to make sense of the principle of alphabetic writing; they need phonics to identify new words, to develop a large fluent reading vocabulary, and to spell new words when writing.

Awareness of the segments of spoken language develops in a predictable sequence: Awareness of the words in everyday conversations develops first. Some children may make this discovery when they are as young as three years old, but most certainly do so by the beginning of kindergarten. When children explore nursery rhymes and poetry in day care, preschool, and kindergarten, they develop awareness of rhyme in language. As children develop awareness of rhyming sounds, they may also become aware of the beginning sounds in words. Later, when kindergartners and first graders have lots of opportunities to explore spoken and written language, they discover that words and rhymes are made up of individual speech sounds.

Word Awareness

Children show that they conceive of spoken language as a series of word-length segments when they clap or move a block for every word they hear in a sentence. Such children are consciously aware that spoken messages are put together by stringing one word after another. These children are, therefore, prepared to search for meaningful word-length segments in print that match the meaningful word-length segments they identify in speech. Words are large segments of spoken language and hence are the easiest to separate from speech. There are two reasons for this. First, the words in everyday messages are meaningful, which is a distinct advantage when listening for them in spoken language. And second, words are large bundles of sound and, as a result, are more obvious than rhymes or individual sounds.

Word awareness develops gradually as a natural consequence of experiences with language and is enhanced by reading and writing. Reading contributes to word awareness inasmuch as written words are concrete referents, which helps emergent readers form and then crystallize the abstract concept of word-length language segments. Writing experiences contribute to word awareness in that the writing process encourages children to think about the spoken word-length segments they would like to include in their messages.

One way to heighten word awareness is to point to—and have children point to—each word as it is read. Pointing to words as they are read in big books, storybooks, and poems, and on wall charts and chalkboards, has two advantages: First, this helps children discover the match between voice (spoken words) and print (written words). And second, pointing to words gives emergent readers opportunities to discover the word-length segments in spoken language that are represented by the word-length segments in written language. Other ways to enhance word awareness are to draw attention to interesting words by framing them (cupping hands around words), drawing clouds around words (drawing lacy bubbles around words), and using a word window to highlight words (using tagboard strips cut so as to reveal one word at a time).

Rhyme Awareness

Traditional nursery rhymes, jump-rope jingles, clapping games, and counting verses, such as "One Potato, Two Potato," are jam-packed with rhyme. Children tune into rhyme quite early in their lives, so it is no coincidence that the kind of language play that capitalizes on rhyme comes into its own during the elementary school years. In fact, children as young as three years may be sensitive to rhyme (MacLean, Bryant, & Bradley, 1987), and kindergartners who have experience with poetry and rhyme are generally quite good at identifying rhyming words (Treiman & Zukowski, 1991). What's more, kindergartners who are aware of rhyme are better readers later in school than kindergartners who are not sensitive to rhyme (Bradley & Bryant, 1978).

Rhyme awareness is a middle ground between awareness of words and awareness of individual speech sounds. Children who detect rhyme have enough phonemic awareness to connect speech with print at a level that is smaller than whole words but larger than single sounds. Rhyme awareness primes children to look for the letters in written words that represent the rhyme in spoken words. This, in turn, paves the way for the use of rhyme to identify unfamiliar words by analogy, which is explained in Chapter 4. Additionally, the concept of rhyme gives writers insight into ways to spell words that rhyme and to use rhyming language.

Figure 2–6 Justin's rhyming poem, "Apples," shows that he has developed an awareness of rhyming sounds in language.

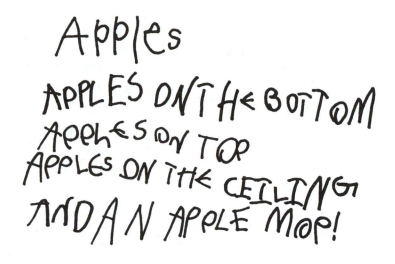

The four-year-old who says that **wall** and **fall** sound alike is aware of rhyming language. The first grader who gives examples of rhyming words, such as **car, star,** and **jar,** is paying attention to rhyming sounds. Children also show rhyme awareness when they make lists of rhyming words and when they clap for rhyming words in poetry. Likewise, children demonstrate awareness of rhyme in their writing.

Justin (Figure 2–6) has developed considerable awareness of rhyme. He wrote this poem after he and his first-grade classmates had shared books about apples. *Ten Apples Up On Top!* (LeSieg, 1961), which tells the rhyming story of animals balancing apples and being chased by an angry bear with a mop, clearly influenced Justin's thinking as he composed. Notice how Justin uses two of the rhyming words from the storybook—**top** and **mop**—to create his own special poetic mood, message, and expression.

While most emergent readers and writers develop rhyme awareness early, some of the kindergartners and first graders in your classroom may not be aware of rhyming sounds. These children may not develop rhyme awareness by simply participating in normal classroom activities with the rhyme in poetry (Layton, Deeny, Tall, & Upton, 1996). When children increase awareness of rhyme, their reading ability will also improve (Bradley & Bryant, 1983). Awareness of rhyme helps reading ability regardless of children's age, intelligence, or their mothers' education (Bradley, MacLean, Crossland, & Bryant, 1989, reported in Bradley & Bryant, 1991). So if some of the children whom you teach are unaware of the rhyming sounds in language, it will be beneficial for them to develop this awareness.

Activities for Rhyme Awareness

Bookstores and libraries offer a cornucopia of poetry collections for all ages, not to mention excellent books written in verse, such as *Lulu Crow's Garden* (Boyd, 1998) and *Sun Song* (Marzollo, 1995) for younger children, and *The Heartland* (Siebert,

1989) and *Half a Moon and One Whole Star* (Dragonwagon, 1990) for older children. Dr. Seuss books are chock full of rhyme, and a recent book, *Hooray for Diffendoofer Day!* (Seuss & Prelutsky, 1998) carries on the tradition of zany words and characters. When you select poetry books, look for traditional favorites like Mother Goose rhymes and consider, too, contemporary books such as *For Laughing Out Louder* (Prelutsky, 1995), a collection of short amusing poems sure to entertain young listeners.

As children explore rhyming words in your classroom, have fun making up rhymes for holidays, characters in favorite books, children's names, and things children are studying in science and social studies. Write rhymes with children by having them dictate to you or writing on their own. Put children's poems on bulletin boards; hang them from the ceiling; tape them to the door; write them on the chalkboard. Frame rhyming words; encourage children to think of rhyming examples; talk about why some words rhyme and others do not; make lists of rhymes; challenge children to find something in your classroom (a **book,** for example) that rhymes with another word (**look,** for instance); and put pictures in a pocket chart (or on the chalk tray) and invite children to group rhyming pictures together, such as **sun** and **bun,** and **nose, hose,** and **rose.** Use the following game-like activities to develop and enhance rhyme awareness, adapt them to your own teaching style, and enjoy exploring with children the rhyming words in our language.

Hands Up for Rhyming Words

This is a whole group activity that not only keeps every child involved but helps you quickly spot who is aware of rhyme and who is not.

Things You'll Need: Good rhyming poems; colorful squares of construction paper.

Directions for Recognizing Rhyming Words: Children listen to rhyming (**"mop-top"**) or nonrhyming (**"plum-top"**) words and hold up their hands when words rhyme. Children who hold up their hands right away, without looking at their neighbors, are aware of rhyming words. Those who copy their neighbors are not fully aware of rhyme. Another idea is to ask children to hold up colorful squares every time they hear rhyming words in a poem or a book written in verse. For instance, children would hold up a square for words like **mouse** and **house, rat** and **hat,** and **goat** and **throat** when you read *Lulu Crow's Garden* (Boyd, 1998). And to extend this spoken language activity to written language, write the rhyming words from the book on a chalkboard or wall chart, show children the rhyming language in the book, and discuss rhyming words.

Rhyming Picture Bookmark

Children use their knowledge of rhyme to make a handy bookmark with this engaging large group or center activity.

Figure 2–7 Making rhyming picture bookmarks is fun, gives children extra practice recognizing rhyming words, and results in a handy place marker for the books children enjoy at school or at home.

Things You'll Need: A bookmark pattern that has a picture in the top square and is printed on sturdy construction paper (Figure 2–7); pictures that do and do not rhyme with the picture at the top of the bookmark; scissors; paste.

Directions: Children decide which pictures rhyme with the one at the top of the bookmark, then cut them out and paste them in the bookmark squares. If children want to color pictures, ask them to color before they cut and paste. Generalize this activity to written language by taking children aside individually and having them watch as you write the rhyming words under the rhyming pictures on their bookmarks before they take them home. Laminate the rhyming bookmarks for longevity.

Figure 2–8 Sorting rhyming pictures into paper lunch sacks gives children an opportunity to analyze the rhyme in words and to differentiate one set of rhyming sounds from another.

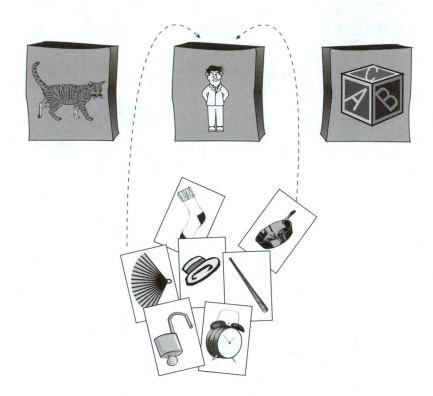

 Rhyming Picture Sack Sort

This sorting activity is effective when children work individually or with a learning partner; it makes a nice addition to a learning center.

Things You'll Need: Two to three lunch sacks for each child or set of learning partners; rhyming pictures on 3×5 cards; tape. Get ready for sorting by taping a picture to each sack and to as many 3×5 cards as children are to sort; make sure the pictures on the cards rhyme with a picture on one of the sacks.

Directions: Children sort the pictures on cards by putting them into a sack that has a rhyming picture on it, as shown in Figure 2–8. When finished sorting, children fold over the top of each sack, write their names on the back, and leave the sacks in the basket you use to collect children's work. This way you know who sorted correctly and who did not.

Picture-Rhyme Pages

In this activity, children draw their own rhyming pictures and share them with their classmates.

Figure 2–9 After Gerald drew this pair of rhyming pictures, his kindergarten teacher shared them with the class. The rhyming pictures are: **bat-cat; goose-moose; mouse-house.**

Things You'll Need: Pieces of paper folded in half; crayons.

Directions: Children draw two rhyming pictures, one picture on one side of the folded paper and one on the other, as shown in Figure 2–9. To link spoken language with written language, label the pictures children draw. Children then share their rhyming pictures with their classmates.

✹ Rhyme Collage

A rhyme collage is a wonderful addition to your classroom and a great resource for the rhyming words needed for other activities in this section.

Things You'll Need: Old magazines and catalogs; scissors; a large sheet of newsprint; tape or paste.

Directions: Children cut out rhyming pictures from magazines and catalogs, and then paste them onto a large sheet of paper you have put on a bulletin board. When the rhyming collage is complete, discuss the rhyming pictures, write the words under them, and talk about the connections between spoken and written language.

✹ Rhyme Puppet

Puppets are great teaching tools for large and small groups. This is one of the ways I use my own puppet, whom I call Tacoma.

Things You'll Need: A wonderful puppet with a very large mouth that opens and closes!

Directions: The puppet says two (or more) words and children decide if the words rhyme. For instance, the puppet might say **"bag-rag"** or **"bag-nose."** Children put their thumbs up for rhyming words, down for nonrhyming words. When the puppet's words do not rhyme, the puppet asks children to suggest rhyming words. Suggesting rhyming words gives children extra opportunities to focus on rhyming language. An additional option is to write on a wall chart or chalkboard the rhyming words the puppet says. If you do this, be sure that the words you write both sound and look alike.

✤ *Rhyme Mobiles*

Rhyme mobiles are fun to make and give children opportunities to decorate their classroom with rhyme. They are appropriate for large and small groups.

Things You'll Need: Old magazines and catalogs; scissors; several sheets of colorful construction paper cut into geometric shapes; paste; colorful yarn cut into different lengths; a coat hanger (or something similar) to hang the mobiles.

Directions: Children cut out rhyming pictures from magazines and catalogs and paste one picture each onto one side of a colored piece of construction paper. Children write, or watch you write the word for the rhyming picture on the other side. Then punch a hole in the top of each piece, thread a colorful strand of yarn through the hole and tie the yarn to a coat hanger (Figure 2–10). Integrate rhyme mobiles with mathematics by discussing the circles, triangles, squares, and rectangles that adorn the mobile.

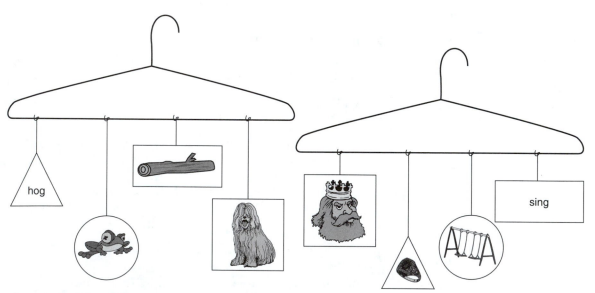

Figure 2–10   Rhyme mobiles give children opportunities to think about rhyme, make colorful decorations and, if construction paper is cut into circles, triangles, squares and rectangles, provide an opportunity to integrate language arts and mathematics.

Picture-Rhyme Game

This is a rhyming picture version of the popular game Concentration® and is a good game for children to play while visiting the centers in your classroom.

Things You'll Need: A homemade deck of cards with pairs of rhyming pictures. Laminate cards to make them durable. Use copies of the rhyming pictures from activities and lessons already described in this chapter.

Directions: Children put all the cards face down on a table. Taking turns, children turn two cards face up. Children remove cards with pictures that rhyme, such as **cat** and **hat;** those that do not rhyme are turned face down again. The player with the most rhyming cards wins.

Sound Awareness

At six years old, Melanie (Figure 2–11) already knows something that every reader of a language written in an alphabet must learn: She knows which spoken sounds to connect with which written letters. Look at the clever way she writes **ch-ch-ch-chilly, sn-snowballs, ch-chillier,** and **ah ah ah ahchooooo!** She literally separates language into sounds before her readers' eyes.

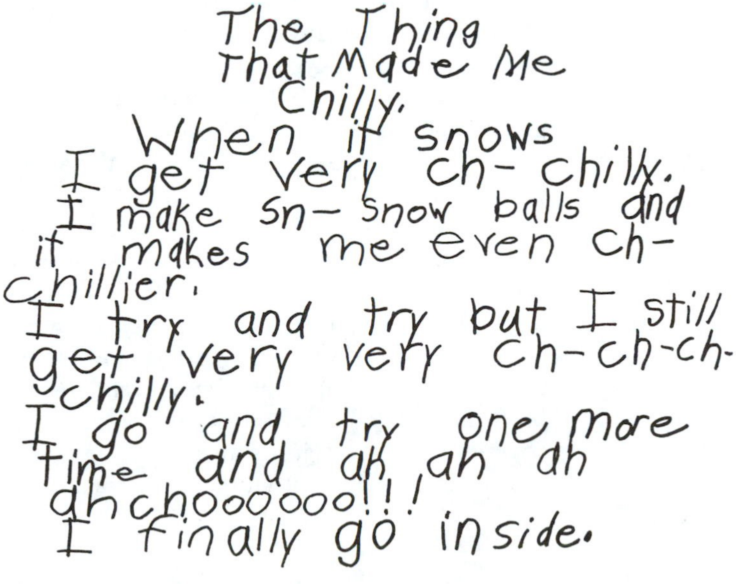

Figure 2–11   Melanie demonstrates sound awareness when she separates the beginning sounds from words in her story to help her readers experience the sensation of being cold.

The Thing
That Made Me
Chilly.
When it snows
I get very ch-chilly.
I make sn-snow balls and
it makes me even ch-
chillier.
I try and try but I still
get very very ch-ch-ch-
chilly.
I go and try one more
time and ah, ah ah
ahchooooooo!!!
I finally go inside.

Melanie, and other sound aware children, can do two things. First, they can separate words into sounds. They can, for instance, separate a word such as **lamp** into four sounds—**"l," "a," "m," "p."**[1] To do this, children disassemble words— they literally break words apart into individual sounds. Second, children blend individual sounds together to form meaningful words. When children blend, they assemble sounds into words. For example, the sounds **"l" + "a" + "m" + "p"** would be blended together into **"lamp."**

The individual sounds in spoken language are much more challenging to identify than whole words and rhymes. For this reason, I can say with certainty that the children in your classroom who are aware of sounds are also aware of rhyme. The reverse is not true: Children who are aware of rhyme are not necessarily aware of individual sounds (Barron, 1998). Over the years, I have taught many children who are keenly sensitive to rhyme, but who cannot separate words into sounds and blend sounds into words.

The sounds, or phonemes, in words are not single sounds at all. Rather, they are a whole collection of slightly different sounds called allophones. For instance, the **"p"** in **pansy** is not exactly the same sound as that heard in **strap,** nor is it the same as that heard in **leopard, suspicion, disprove,** or **lamp.** Even though these sounds are not identical, listeners perceive them to be the same and hence group all these allophones into one phonemic category—**"p".**

Sound awareness is essential to reading and writing because alphabetic writing represents speech sounds, not whole words or rhymes. Emergent readers must, therefore, understand that (1) sounds are strung together to form the words of language, (2) words can be separated into sounds, and (3) the letters in written words correspond to the sounds in spoken words. It is not surprising, then, that children who begin school with high phonemic awareness make faster reading progress in first grade than those with low phonemic awareness (McBride-Chang, Wagner, & Chang, 1997), whether children grow up in economically advantaged or poor families (Nicholson, 1997). Phonemic awareness predicts the reading ability of four- and five-year-olds (Lonigan, Burgess, Anthony, & Barker, 1998), and of children from kindergarten through fourth grade (Wagner et al., 1997). Consequently, the children in your classroom with more phonemic awareness are likely to have larger fluent reading vocabularies than children with less awareness. Though children with low sound awareness do poorly on tasks where they must use letter-sound associations (Juel, Griffith, & Gough, 1986), when given opportunities to increase sound awareness, low awareness children successfully use letter-sound associations to identify words (Fox & Routh, 1984).

Though separating words into sounds is important, children must also be able to blend sounds into words. Children who are taught to separate words into sounds and to blend are better readers throughout the early grades (Ball & Blachman, 1991). Not surprisingly, children with sound awareness are better spellers, too. The words that first and second graders correctly separate into sounds are spelled with greater accuracy than the words children incorrectly sep-

---

[1]In this book, for simplicity, rather than using a standard system of phonetic symbols, letters that typically stand for the sounds are used and are placed within quotation marks.

arate into sounds (Foorman, Jenkins, & Francis, 1993). Hence, phonemic awareness at the sound level is linked to both reading and spelling. All things considered, if some of the children whom you teach have not discovered the sounds in language, they will benefit from activities that increase sound awareness, becoming better readers and spellers as a consequence.

Guidelines for Teaching Sound Awareness

There is every reason to believe that phonemic awareness improves with instruction (Braunger & Lewis, 1997; Busink, 1997). And, of course, children differ in the level of sound awareness they bring to your classroom. Some need more explicit instruction, others less. Consistent with a balanced view of phonics (and phonemic awareness) in your classroom, provide more phonemic awareness learning opportunities to children with low awareness than to children with high awareness. The following eight guidelines will help you ensure that the children in your classroom get the most out of sound awareness activities.

1.   Teach awareness of beginning sounds first (the **"m"** in **"man"**), ending sounds second (the **"n"** in **"man"**) and middle sounds third (the **"a"** in **"man"**). This is the natural sequence in which sound awareness develops in most children (Foorman et al., 1993).

2.   Teach both sound separation and sound blending; successful readers are good at both.

3.   Teach letter and sound relationships (Chapters 4 and 5) along with phonemic awareness. Rhyme and sound awareness activities are not particularly effective without some letter-sound knowledge (Lundberg, Frost, & Petersen, 1988). The reason, says Chew (1997), is that the letters in written words help make the sounds in spoken words visible. Letters are fixed in time and space, while sounds are fleeting. When children associate sounds with letters, the sounds are more likely to be identified as separate entities. And so, teaching children letter and sound relationships enhances phonemic awareness. Better phonemic awareness, in turn, helps children learn and use the letter-sounds of phonics.

I have one cautionary note to add, however: The mutually supportive relationship between phonemic awareness and learning letter-sound associations may exist only when children reach some minimum threshold of phonemic awareness (Peterson & Haines, 1998). If children are completely unaware of the rhymes and sounds in language, teaching them how our alphabetic writing system works is not likely to result in phonemic awareness. So, you can expect the children in your classroom to benefit from the mutually supportive relationship between phonemic awareness and letter-sound (or rhyme) learning when children already have some rudimentary phonemic awareness.

4.   When emphasizing the sounds in words, say words slowly, keeping the sounds connected while at the same time stretching them out, much like you pull a rubber band from a small to a large size. "Rubber banding" calls attention to individual sounds without actually breaking words apart and helps children identify sounds in words they do not know how to spell.

5.   When saying sounds in isolation, avoid adding an extra **"uh"** unless it is absolutely necessary. For example, **"s"** can be pronounced by itself; it need not be pronounced as **"suh."** Some sounds require that we add an extra vowel, the **"uh."** For example, the sound represented by the letter **b** in **bunny** sounds like **"buh"** when said alone. This, however, is not the case with **"f," "m," "n," "r"** and **"l."** The extra **"uh"** confuses many would-be blenders. So, add an extra vowel only when necessary.

6.   When counting sounds, remember that the number of sounds is not always equal to the number of letters in spelling. For example, **sheep** has three sounds, **"sh," "ee"** (long **e**), and **"p,"** but five letters. It is the number of sounds, not the number of letters, that is important for phonemic awareness.

7.   When referring to *sounds* in words, use the sound **"m,"** not the letter name. Say something like, "Monkey begins with **'m'** (the sound)." If you wish to call children's attention to letter names, you might say, **"Monkey begins with the letter m (the name)."**

8.   Use activities children enjoy and stay away from activities that look and feel like drill. Have fun with language, use a variety of activities, and share books in which authors play with language. For example, in *Martha Blah Blah* (Meddaugh, 1996), a dog, Martha, talks when she eats alphabet soup. But when some of the letters are left out of her soup, Martha leaves those sounds out of words, which results in interesting pseudo words, like "Goo oup o." for "Good Soup." Books like *Martha Blah Blah* give children opportunities to make inferences and draw conclusions about the manner in which sounds are arranged, rearranged, and sequenced in language.

Activities for Sound Awareness

There are twelve sound awareness activities in this section—seven for separating words into sounds and five for blending. Some activities have more than one version, which makes for a total of seventeen different activities to use with the children whom you teach—ten sound awareness and seven blending activities. You will find in Chapters 4 and 5 activities that help children learn and use the associations among letters and sounds. Use the activities in these chapters along with the previously described rhyme activities and the sound awareness activities that follow.

Tapping Sounds

Tapping helps children identify sounds in words, is fun, requires very little time, and takes virtually no extra preparation or materials on your part. Though this activity could be done in a large group, my preference is to use it with a small group because this way I can immediately help children who falter.

Things You'll Need: Pencils and a hard surface to tap them on.

Directions: Say familiar words from poems, storybooks, and wall charts and ask children to tap for each sound heard. When children first begin tapping for sounds, "rubber band" words and repeat them several times. Later, when children are better at tapping, you will not need to rubber band or repeat. Begin tapping for short, two-sound words (**"me"**). When children can tap for the two sounds they hear in words like **"me,"** introduce three (**"cap"**) and four (**"soda"**) sound words.

Listening for Sounds

When children listen for sounds, they line up a tile (or tagboard square) for each sound heard in words. Listening for Sounds, like Tapping Sounds, can be a large group activity, though I prefer to keep the group small so as to observe each child and to help children when necessary.

Things You'll Need: One-inch tiles (purchased from a home improvement store), words from books shared many times. (If you cannot find tiles, use tagboard squares.)

Directions: Say a word slowly, "rubber banding" it so that all sounds are pronounced clearly. As you rubber band the word, children move one tile for each sound heard, lining up the tiles in a row from left to right. When children can move a tile for every sound heard, write letters on the tiles (or on tagboard squares). This increases awareness of the connections between the sounds in spoken words and the letters in written words.

Counting Sounds

I have found counting sounds to be a little more challenging than tapping or moving objects like tiles, so use this activity after children are successful with the first two activities. As with the above two activities, I recommend that you use Counting Sounds with small groups to afford the opportunity to monitor each individual child while teaching.

Things You'll Need: 5×8 cards with the numerals 2, 3, or 4 written on them. I suggest you use different color cards for different numbers. This way you know at a mere glance if children have selected the card with the numeral that matches the number of sounds in a word.

Directions: Slowly say a word, "rubber banding" it so that each sound is clearly heard. Children count sounds and then hold up the card that shows the number. Carefully watch to see who responds quickly, who hesitates, and who waits for a neighbor to select a card. Anyone who hesitates or copies from a neighbor needs more practice.

Sound Boxes

Variations of this activity have been used since the 1970s when a Soviet researcher, Elkonin, developed a method in which children move tokens for sounds in words. Today, a similar technique is used in Reading Recovery lessons (Clay, 1985). The two

Figure 2–12 Sound awareness increases when children move pennies into boxes for the sounds they hear in words and point to pennies representing beginning, middle, and ending sounds.

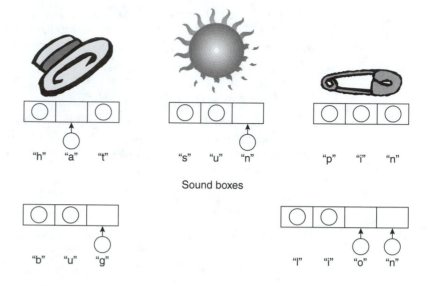

Sound boxes

versions I describe—Sound Boxes with Pictures and Sound Boxes without Pictures—focus on separating words into sounds and give children practice blending, too.

Things You'll Need: Sound boxes (Figure 2–12); several pennies (or buttons) for each child; pictures with names that are two, three, or four sounds long. (Sound boxes are connected boxes where each box represents a sound in a word.)

Directions for Sound Boxes with Pictures: Give each child a piece of paper which has several pictures with sets of sound boxes underneath each one. The number of connected boxes below each picture equals the number of sounds in the picture's name. Call attention to the picture and say its name slowly, "rubber banding" it. Then ask children to say the word slowly with you. Children then push a penny into a box for each sound heard. Count boxes and count sounds. Last, children blend sounds together.

Directions for Sound Boxes without Pictures: Give each child a piece of paper with sound boxes (Figure 2–12) for words that are two, three, or four sounds long. Say a word slowly, "rubber banding" it, as children push pennies into a box for each sound heard. Then blend sounds together. Now ask children to point to a penny that represents a single sound and to tell its position—beginning, middle, end—in the word. Learning to identify the position of sounds in words helps some children gain insight into sound segmentation (Edelen-Smith, 1997). For example, after pushing pennies for **"boat,"** you might say, "Point to the penny that stands for **'b'** in **'boat'**." When children do this, ask, "Does **'b'** come at the beginning, middle, or end of **'boat'**?" When children are comfortable moving pennies into sound boxes, write the letters in boxes (Chapter 5). Talk about beginning, middle, and ending sounds as a way of building background for the next lesson.

🦋 *Puppet Talk*

Each of the four versions of Puppet Talk—Detecting Shared (or the Same) Sounds, Detecting Different Sounds, Deleting Sounds, and Blending Sounds—teach either sound segmentation or sound blending with the help of a lively puppet. I have found this activity to be very successful with groups of up to ten children.

Things You'll Need: A puppet with a mouth that opens and shuts.

Directions for Detecting Shared Sounds: The easiest version is for the puppet to say two words—**"mile"** and **"mop,"** or **"mile"** and **"bed"**—and the children tell whether the words begin alike. A slightly more challenging version is for the puppet to say three words, two that share a sound and one that does not, and children tell which two words have the shared sound. For example, the puppet might say something like, "Which words begin alike—**milk-map-dog.**" After children say **"milk"** and **"map,"** the puppet asks them to say the shared sound. For variety, have the puppet ask children to think of other words that begin with the same sound. Be sure the puppet "rubber bands" words. To focus on letter sounds and names, write words in a list, underline the letter **m** (in the example of **milk** and **map**) name the letter, and talk about the sound the letter **m** represents. After children develop awareness of beginning sounds, introduce ending sounds and then middle sounds.

Directions for Detecting Different Sounds: Follow the same procedure as above, but this time the puppet asks children to listen for a word that does not begin alike. For instance, the puppet might say, **"Map, sun, mine.** Which word has a different beginning sound? **Map, sun, mine**?" As a follow-up, the puppet might ask, "What sound comes at the beginning of **sun**? What sound comes at the beginning of **map** and **mine**?" And, of course, move to ending and middle sounds after children develop awareness of beginning sounds.

Directions for Deleting Sounds: Children tell what is left when the puppet asks them to take a sound away from a word. For instance, the puppet might say, "Say **meat** without the **'m'**." Or the puppet might say, "Say **meat** without the **'t'**." In the first example, children would say **"eat,"** in the second they would say **"me"** (long e).

Directions for Blending Sounds: The puppet says the sounds of a word separately and children tell the word the puppet is trying to say. For example, if the puppet says, **"s" "e"** (long **e,** as indicated by a double **e** in spelling—ee) **"d,"** children say **"seed."**

🦋 *Graphing Sounds*

Use this sound segmentation activity with children who are successful with the Counting Sounds activity. It works equally well for large and small groups.

Things You'll Need: Familiar pictures; scissors; tape; a large piece of newsprint. Beforehand draw a series of two, three, four, or more connected boxes on a large piece of newsprint, spacing boxes fairly far apart. Fasten newsprint to a bulletin board.

Figure 2–13

Graphing sounds gives children practice identifying the number of sounds in words, and the finished graph is a wonderful resource for rhyming words and for integrating language arts with mathematics.

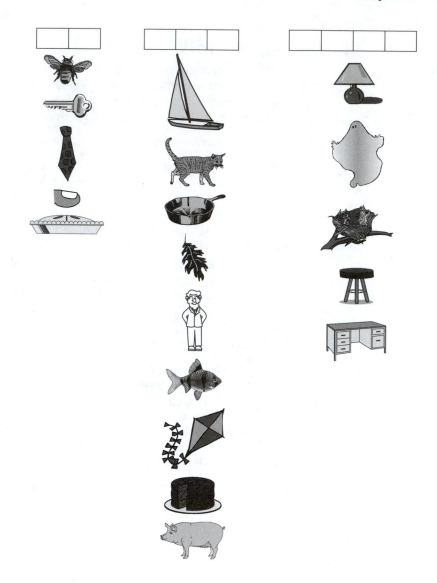

Directions: Children cut out pictures from magazines and old workbooks, count the sounds in the picture names, and tape the pictures below the connected boxes that match the number of sounds, thereby making a giant bulletin board graph showing the distribution of words with different numbers of sounds (Figure 2–13). It will take several days to make the graph. During that time, review picture names and count sounds with children and, should a picture be misplaced, put it under the correct number of boxes. Integrate this activity with mathematics by adding up the words under each set of connected boxes, as well as the total number of pictures found. Talk about the concepts of distribution and proportion (most, least).

Sound Sack Sort

This is the sound awareness analog of the rhyme awareness sorting activity (Rhyming Picture Sack Sort) described earlier. It makes a great center activity for individuals or groups of two children.

Things You'll Need: Two or more sacks for each individual or group; pictures on 3×5 cards. Tape a picture to each sack. The pictures on cards should have a beginning, middle, or ending sound in common with one of the pictures on a sack.

Directions: Focus on one position in a word—beginning, middle, or ending sounds—for each sorting activity. Children sort pictures by putting them into the sack that has a picture with a shared sound. For example, children might sort for the same beginning sound by putting pictures of a **bus, bee, bear, banana,** and **balloon** in a sack with a picture of a **ball** on the front; pictures of a **doll, doughnut, duck,** and **drum** are put in a sack with a picture of a **dog** on front.

To extend this activity to written language, focus first on beginning letter-sounds because these are the easiest for children to identify and, coincidentally, are typically consonant letters that predictably represent sound. Write the beginning letter under the picture on each card. In so doing, it is probable that some children will sort visually, only by letter, not by sound. However, if children are comfortable sorting by beginning sound, adding a visual cue (letters) helps children build from phonemic awareness (ear) to phonics (letter-sound knowledge using both the ear and the eye). And, of course, be sure to talk with children about beginning sounds (and sounds in other positions in words) and the letters that represent those sounds.

Arm Blending

Year after year I successfully teach beginning readers and struggling readers to blend this way. Arm blending is a tactile, kinesthetic approach to blending that is easy to teach to large and small groups. The children I teach use arm blending on their own when reading all sorts of materials in all sorts of places. You and the children whom you teach will be impressed with the results!

Things You'll Need: Nothing special.

Directions for Arm Blending: Children imagine that they place sounds on their arms and then blend by saying sounds as they slide their hands from shoulder to wrist. To blend **"m," "a,"** and **"n,"** children put their right hand on their left shoulder (reverse for left-handed children) and say **"m,"** their hand in the crook of their arms and say **"a,"** and their hand on their wrists and say **"n."** Then children slide their right hands down their left arms from shoulder to wrist blending the sounds together as their hands sweep down their arms. When finished, ask children what word they pronounced. The motion of the sweeping hand sliding down the arm is a kind of tactile analog for what the voice does when sliding sounds together during blending. And, when the children I teach mentally "place" sounds on their arms, they are able to remember the right sounds in the right order during blending.

 ## *Finger Blending*

When Finger Blending, children use their fingers to anchor sounds in memory and to guide blending. This activity requires more dexterity than Arm Blending and is therefore more appropriate for older children. I describe two versions of Finger Blending—Five Finger Blending and Single Finger Blending.

Things You'll Need: Nothing extra.

Directions for Five Finger Blending: Children use their forefinger (index finger), middle finger, ring finger, and little finger to blend by tapping these fingers to the thumb. Suppose children are going to blend **"b," "a," "b," "y."** They touch their forefinger (index finger) to their thumb while saying **"b,"** middle finger to the thumb saying **"a,"** ring finger to the thumb saying **"b,"** and little finger to thumb saying **"y."** To blend, children place each finger on the thumb as they pronounce sounds, thereby blending sounds into **"baby."** Obviously, this type of finger blending works for words that have four sounds or less.

Directions for Single Finger Blending: Some children, especially older children, feel self-conscious using four fingers to blend. They prefer to single finger blend, which is less obvious to onlookers. To do this, children use their right forefinger to place sounds on the knuckles of their left forefinger (reverse for left-handed children). To blend **"bat,"** children touch the innermost knuckle with their right forefinger while saying **"b,"** the middle knuckle while saying **"a,"** and the outer most knuckle while saying **"t."** Children blend by sweeping their right finger over the left finger as they say sounds. For words with more than three sounds, distribute sounds between knuckles.

 ## *Picture Blending*

This activity uses pictures of familiar objects to help children develop the concept of blending (Catts & Vartiainen, 1993). I have found it to be especially successful with young children.

Things You'll Need: Large pictures of familiar objects; scissors.

Directions: Show children a picture, say its name, and then cut it into as many equal parts as there are sounds in the word. For example, you might show children a **boat,** say the word **"boat,"** and then cut the picture into three parts. (Cut the picture horizontally, not vertically.) Now, point to each piece and say the sound it represents. In the example of **boat,** you would point to the first part of the picture while saying **"b,"** to the second part saying **"o"** (long **"o"**), and to the third part

Figure 2–14   Picture
Blending gives children a
concrete visual reference to
illustrate the idea of
blending sounds into words.

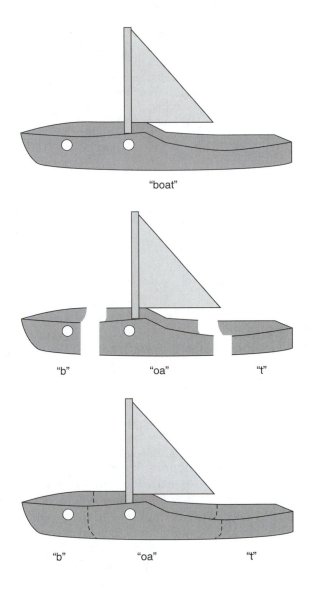

when saying **"t."** Explain that the pieces of the picture can be put together just like
sounds can be put together to make a word. Demonstrate by moving the pieces together while you blend the sounds to pronounce **"boat."** Let the children try it,
pushing picture parts and blending sounds. Figure 2–14 is an example of Picture
Blending for the word **boat.** Extend this activity to written language by writing the
letters under each picture segment. When you do this, be sure to select pictures that
are spelled like they sound (such as **cat** and **pig**). And, after children blend, talk
about the sounds in words and the letters the sounds represent.

Figure 2–15 The slide in the activity Sliding Sounds Together gives learners a visual cue for blending. After sounds are blended, the whole word is written at the bottom of the slide.

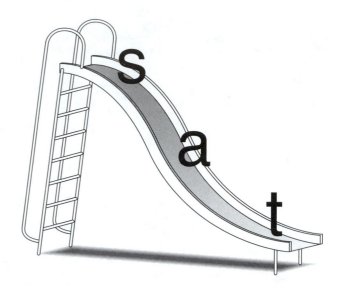

 ## Sliding Sounds Together

The children I teach enjoy this blending activity a great deal, perhaps because it uses a picture of a slide to graphically depict the blending process (Figure 2–15). I have found this to be a successful activity for large or small groups.

Things You'll Need: No special material is needed.

Directions: Draw a large slide on the chalkboard. Write a word on the slide, distributing letters from the top to near the bottom. To demonstrate blending, pronounce each sound as you slide your hand under each letter, adding sounds one after the other until you reach the bottom of the slide. Ask children to tell you the word and then write the word at the bottom of the slide. Be sure to slide in a fluid motion and keep your voice aligned with your sliding hand. Then invite a volunteer to be the slider—the person who moves his or her hand down the slide. Ask the whole group to blend the sounds as the "slider" slides toward the bottom. Ask the slider to pronounce the whole word when he or she gets to the bottom.

Mystery Bag Blending

In this large or small group blending activity, children use the individual sounds of a word as clues to the identity of something hidden in a paper bag.

Things You'll Need: One medium-size paper bag; many small items to put in the bag.

Directions: Put your hand in the bag and grab something, such as a small plastic **pig.** Keeping the object inside the bag, say, "I have something. It is a **'p' 'i' 'g'.** What is it?" When children say **"pig,"** show them the plastic pig, put it beside the bag and grab another object, perhaps a toy **spoon.** I sometimes play this guessing game thematically by putting things in the bag that are related, such as farm animals or food, and telling children a short story about a trip or adventure where all the items were found. To extend this to written language, after all the mystery words are identified, write each one on the chalkboard. Then talk about the letters, say the sound each represents. This helps make the sound "visible" in that children see the letters as visual representations of sounds. End by pointing to each letter, saying its sound, and blending the sounds together into the word.

ASSESSING PHONEMIC AWARENESS

You now have many different rhyme and sound awareness activities from which to choose. But before using these activities (sound identification and sound blending), you need to know which children in your class would benefit from increased rhyme awareness, increased sound awareness, and increased blending ability. One way to judge children's word, syllable, rhyme, and sound awareness is to observe their behavior as they read and write every day in your classroom. If you wish to go beyond classroom observation, you will want to use an assessment tool designed specifically to determine phonemic awareness. There are a number of assessment tools from which to select. With a single exception, all require that you test children individually.

One of the most enduring measures is the *Lindamood Auditory Conceptualization Test*, Revised Edition (Lindamood & Lindamood, 1979), which has been used since the early 1970s. It has a range from kindergarten to adult and requires that children arrange colored blocks to show sequences of sounds in nonsense strings and syllables. The results are reported in minimum levels of performance indicative of success reading and spelling at or above grade level. *Sawyer's Test of Awareness of Language Segments* (Sawyer, 1987) also uses colored blocks which young children position to indicate words, syllables, and sounds. Results indicate whether a child is ready to profit from basal instruction, which makes this test appropriate for beginning readers. The *Test of Auditory Analysis Skills* (Rosner, 1979) has thirteen items that require children to delete sounds from words. It is appropriate for children from kindergarten through third grade, and expected levels of performance are listed for each grade. Children whose performance is below expectation are candidates for phonemic awareness training, according to this tool.

If you prefer a group paper and pencil test, consider the *Test of Phonological Awareness* (Torgesen & Bryant, 1994). This test has two versions that assess children's ability to identify same and different sounds. The kindergarten version assesses beginning sounds; the first- and second-grade version assesses ending sounds. Percentile ranks and standard scores are reported. The *Comprehensive Test of Phonological Processes* (Wagner, Torgesen, & Rashotte, 1999) is a norm-referenced individually administered instrument that measures phoneme awareness, blending, memory, and rapid naming. Scores include percentile ranks, age and grade equivalents, and quotients for phoneme awareness, memory, and naming. There are two forms, one for five- and six-year-olds and one for ages seven through eighteen years. With its dual focus on phonemic awareness and rapid naming, this instrument is appropriate for assessing learning disabled and struggling readers.

In 1995, Yopp published the *Yopp-Singer Test of Phoneme Segmentation,* intended for kindergartners and beginning first graders (Yopp, 1995). The twenty-two items on this test measure children's ability to separate into individual sounds words that are two or three sounds long. The *Roswell-Chall Auditory Blending Test* (Roswell & Chall, 1997) assesses children's ability to blend from two to three sounds. First published in 1963, this individually administered test consists of thirty items and classifies blending as adequate or inadequate. *The Phonological Awareness Test* (Robertson & Salter, 1997) is intended for five- through nine-year-olds and includes awareness of rhyme, sound segmentation, deletion, isolation and substitution, blending, phonics, decoding nonsense words, and invented spelling (optional). Age equivalents, percentile ranks, and standard scores are given.

The Phonological Awareness Profile (Robertson & Salter, 1995), a criterion-referenced test for children ages five through eight, assesses essentially the same areas as the *Phonological Awareness Test* (Robertson & Salter, 1997). The authors suggest that the profile can be used as a pre- and post-teaching measure. The *Phonological Awareness Handbook for Kindergarten and Primary Teachers* (Ericson & Juliebo, 1998) includes pre- and post-teaching measures for rhyme, blending, segmenting, and invented spelling. You will also find tests for classroom use in *Phonemic Awareness for Young Children: A Classroom Curriculum* (Adams, Foorman, Lundberg, & Beeler, 1998). Part of a larger teaching program, these tests measure rhyme detection, syllable and sound counting, matching beginning sounds, comparing word length, and representing sounds with letters. *SPARC for Phonological Awareness and Listening Comprehension* (Thomsen, 1997) is a spiral-bound book with pictures and activities that can be used for informal assessment or for teaching. Appropriate for children from four to ten years old, this resource includes rhyming; blending; segmenting sentences into words and words into syllables; awareness of beginning, ending, and vowel sounds; and contrasting beginning and ending sounds.

PHONEMIC AWARENESS IN A BALANCED READING PROGRAM

When considering the proper place of phonemic awareness in a balanced reading program, the first question to ask is *when* to use the activities in this chapter. My advice is to (1) teach phonemic awareness early, beginning in kindergarten; (2) teach phonemic awareness along with letter and sound relationships using the activities in Chapters 4 and 5; and (3) continue teaching until children have enough phonemic awareness to use the alphabetic principle to identify unfamiliar words while reading, to spell words when writing, and to build a large fluent reading vocabulary.

The rhyme and sound awareness activities in this chapter will help you decide *how* to teach phonemic awareness. *How much* phonemic awareness to teach depends on children's insight into the rhymes and sounds of language. You can find out how much insight children have into the rhymes and sounds of language by observing them as they read and write every day in your classroom, or you can use one of the assessment instruments designed to measure awareness. The low awareness children in your classroom will need more time and energy devoted to explicit instruction in phonemic awareness than average awareness children. You may even find that some of the children in your class have such high awareness that they do not need any explicit instruction at all.

As for the question of *under what circumstances* to teach phonemic awareness, you will want to differentiate instruction if there is a broad range of awareness among the children in your classroom. By using small group (or flexible skill group) instruction you can teach exactly what children need to learn to help them progress in reading. Should it turn out that your whole class needs help in a specific area, say blending, then blending would be an excellent choice for large group instruction.

Phonemic awareness in a balanced reading program is in proportion to individual children's needs. In other words, there is no one-size-fits-all answer when it comes to deciding *how, how much,* and *under what circumstances* to teach phonemic awareness. You need to know children's level of awareness—rhyme or sound—and then use this knowledge to decide which of the activities in this chapter best meet children's needs. When planning instruction consider the children whom you teach, the materials you have on hand, and your own teaching style. Follow the teaching guidelines offered in this chapter when you use phonemic awareness activities. Use classroom observation or one of the previously described assessment tools (or other tools at your disposal) to judge how much and under what circumstances to teach phonemic awareness so as to keep phonemic awareness in balance with other aspects of your classroom reading program.

REFERENCES

Adams, M. J., Foorman, B. R., Lundberg, I., & Beeler, T. (1998). *Phonemic awareness in young children: A classroom curriculum.* Baltimore: Brooks Publishing.

Ball, E. W., & Blachman, B. A. (1991). Does phoneme segmentation training in kindergarten make a difference in early word recognition and developmental spelling? *Reading Research Quarterly, 26,* 49–66.

Barron, R. W. (1998). Proto-literate knowledge: Antecedents and influences on phonological awareness and literacy. In C. Hulm & R. M. Joshi (Eds.), *Reading and spelling: Development and disorders* (pp. 153–173). Mahwah, NJ: Lawrence Erlbaum.

Boyd, L. (1998). *Lulu crow's garden.* Boston: Little, Brown and Company.

Bradley, L., & Bryant, P. E. (1978). Difficulties in auditory organization as a possible cause of reading backwardness. *Nature, 271,* 746–747.

Bradley, L., & Bryant, P. E. (1983). Categorizing sounds and learning to read: A causal connection. *Nature, 301,* 419–421.

Bradley, L., & Bryant, P. E. (1991). Phonological skills before and after learning to read. In S. A. Brady & D. P. Shankweiler (Eds.), *Phonological processes in literacy* (pp. 85–96). Hillsdale, NJ: Lawrence Erlbaum.

Braunger, J., & Lewis, J. P. (1997). *Building a knowledge base in reading.* Portland, OR: Northwest Regional Educational Laboratory.

Busink, R. (1997). Reading and phonological awareness: What we have learned and how we can use it. *Reading Research and Instruction, 36,* 199–215.

Catts, H. W., & Vartiainen, T. (1993). *Sounds abound: Listening, rhyming and reading.* East Moline, IL: LinguiSystems.

Cheek, E. H., Flippo, R. F., & Lindsey, J. D. (1997). *Reading for success in elementary school.* Madison, WI: Brown & Benchmark.

Chew, J. (1997). Traditional phonics: What it is and what it is not. *Journal of Research in Reading, 20,* 171–183.

Christie, J., Enz, B., & Vukelich, C. (1997). *Teaching language and literacy preschool through the elementary grades.* New York: Longman.

Clay, M. M. (1985). *The early detection of reading difficulties* (3rd ed.). Portsmouth, NH: Heinemann.

Dragonwagon, C. (1990). *Half a moon and one whole star.* New York: Alladin Books.

Edelen-Smith, P. J. (1997). How not brown cow: Phoneme awareness activities for collaborative classrooms. *Intervention in School and Clinic, 33,* 103–111.

Ericson, L., & Juliebo, M. F. (1998). *The phonological awareness handbook for kindergarten and primary teachers.* Newark, DE: International Reading Association.

Foorman, B. R., Jenkins, L., & Francis, D. J. (1993). Links among segmenting, spelling, and reading words in first and second grades. *Reading and Writing: An Interdisciplinary Journal, 5,* 1–15.

Fox, B., & Routh, D. K. (1984). Phonemic analysis and synthesis as word attack skills: Revisited. *Journal of Educational Psychology, 76,* 1059–1064.

Galda, L., Cullinan, B. E., & Strickland, D. E. (1997). *Language, literacy and the child* (2nd ed.). Fort Worth, TX: Harcourt Brace College Publishers.

Gentry, J. R. (1987). Spel . . . is a four-letter word. Portsmouth, NH: Heinemann.

International Reading Association. (1997). *The role of phonics in reading instruction: A position statement of the International Reading Association* [Brochure]. Newark, DE: Author.

Juel, C., Griffith, P. L., & Gough, P. B. (1986). Acquisition of literacy: A longitudinal study of children in first and second grade. *Journal of Educational Psychology, 78,* 243–255.

Layton, L., Deeny, K., Tall, G., & Upton, G. (1996). Researching and promoting phonological awareness in the nursery class. *Journal of Research in Reading, 19,* 1–13.

LeSieg, T. (1961). *Ten apples on top!* New York: Random House.

Lindamood, C. H., & Lindamood, P. C. (1979). *Lindamood auditory conceptualization test,* (Rev. Ed.) Austin, TX: Pro-Ed.

Lonigan, C. J., Burgess, S. R., Anthony, J. L., & Barker, T. A. (1998). Development of phonological sensitivity in 2- to 5-year-old children. *Journal of Educational Psychology, 90,* 294–311.

Lundberg, I., Frost, J., & Petersen, O. (1988). Effects of an extensive program for stimulating phonological awareness in preschool children. *Reading Research Quarterly, 23,* 263–284.

MacLean, M., Bryant, P., & Bradley, L. (1987). Rhymes, nursery rhymes, and reading in early childhood. *Merrill-Palmer Quarterly, 33,* 255–282.

Marzollo, J. (1995). *Sun song.* New York: Harper Collins.

McBride-Chang, C., Wagner, R. K., & Chang, L. (1997). Growth modeling of phonological awareness. *Journal of Educational Psychology, 89,* 621–630.

Meddaugh, S. (1996). *Martha blah blah.* Boston: Houghton Mifflin.

Nicholson, T. (1997). Closing the gap on reading failure: Social background, phonemic awareness, and learning to read. In B. Blachman (Ed.), *Foundations of reading acquisition and dyslexia: Implications for early intervention* (pp. 381–407). Mahwah, NJ: Lawrence Erlbaum.

Nunes, T., Bryant, P., & Bindman, M. (1997). Spelling and grammar—The necsed move. In C. A. Perfetti, L. Rieben, & M. Fayol (Eds.). *Learning to spell: Research theory and practice across languages* (pp. 151–170). Mahwah, NJ: Lawrence Erlbaum.

Peterson, M. E., & Haines, L. P. (1998). Orthographic analogy training with kindergarten children: Effects on analogy use, phonemic segmentation, and letter-sound knowledge. In C. Weaver (Ed.), *Reconsidering a balanced approach to reading* (pp. 159–179). Urbana, IL: National Council of Teachers of English.

Prelutsky, J. (1995). *For laughing out louder.* New York: Alfred A. Knopf.

Robertson, C., & Salter, W. (1995). *The phonological awareness profile.* East Moline, IL: LinguiSystems.

Robertson, C., & Salter, W. (1997). *The phonological awareness test.* East Moline, IL: LinguiSystems.

Rosner, J. (1979). *Test of auditory analysis skills.* Novato, CA: Academic Therapy Publications.

Roswell, F. G., & Chall, J. S. (1997). *Roswell-Chall auditory blending test.* Cambridge, MA: Educators Publishing Service.

Sawyer, D. J. (1987). *Sawyer's test of awareness of language segments.* Rockville, MD: Aspen Publishers.

Seuss, Dr., & Prelutsky, J. (1998). *Horray for diffendoofer day!* New York: Alfred A. Knopf.

Siebert, D. (1989). *The heartland.* New York: Harper Trophy.

Snow, C. E., Burns, M. S., & Griffin, P. (Eds.). (1998). *Preventing reading difficulties in young children.* Washington, DC: National Research Council.

Sulzby, E. (1996). Roles of oral and written language as children approach conventional literacy. In C. Pontecorvo, M. Orsolini, B. Burge, & L. B. Resnick (Eds.), *Children's early text construction* (pp. 25–46). Mahwah, NJ: Lawrence Erlbaum.

Thomsen, S. (1997). *SPARC for phonological awareness and listening comprehension.* East Moline, IL: LinguiSystems.

Tompkins, G. E. (1998). *Language arts: Content and teaching strategies* (4th ed.). Columbus, OH: Merrill.

Torgesen, J. K., & Bryant, B. R. (1994). *Test of phonological awareness.* Austin, TX: Pro-Ed.

Treiman, R., & Zukowski, A. (1991). Levels of phonological awareness. In S. A. Brady & D. P. Shankweiler (Eds.), *Phonological processes in literacy* (pp. 85–96). Hillsdale, NJ: Lawrence Erlbaum.

Vandervelden, M. C., & Siegel, L. S. (1995). Phonological recoding and phoneme awareness in early literacy: A developmental approach. *Reading Research Quarterly, 30,* 854–875.

Wagner, R., Torgesen, J. K., & Rashotte, C. (1999). *Comprehensive test of phonological processes.* Austin, TX: Pro-Ed.

Wagner, R. K., Torgesen, J. K., Rashotte, C. A., Hecht, S. A., Barker, T. A., Burgess, S. R., Donahue, J., & Garon, T. (1997). Changing relations between phonological awareness abilities and word-level reading as children develop from beginning to skilled readers: A 5-year longitudinal study. *Developmental Psychology, 33,* 468–479.

Yopp, H. K. (1995). A test for assessing phonemic awareness in young children. *The Reading Teacher, 49,* 20–29.

CHAPTER
3

Early Strategies

Using Pictures, Smudges, and Letter-Sound Associations to Identify Words

This chapter describes the four early word identification strategies that begin the development of a fluent reading vocabulary. You will learn how emergent readers and writers use cues in the environment and in pictures to make sense of print. You will find out how children use incidental cues to identify words. You will discover the way that emergent readers and writers use one or two letter-sound associations to identify words and why this is important. You will also learn how the use of early strategies corresponds to the movement toward word fluency, and how this connects with movement toward conventional spelling, and what you can do to support it.

KEY IDEAS

➤ The earliest word identification strategies develop long before children go to school and long before they actually learn to read.

➤ Emergent readers and writers often associate meaning with cues in the environment, such as logos and the designs of product packages. In doing this, they are using the environmental cue strategy.

➤ Children who use the picture cue strategy infer meaning from illustrations.

➤ Emergent readers and writers who use the incidental cue strategy rely on colored ink, word shape, letter shape, and other visual reminders like smudges to identify words.

➤ When children turn their attention to the properties of our alphabetic writing system, remembering an association between a letter-sound (or a letter name) and a written word, they are using the phonetic cue strategy.

The four word identification strategies explained in this chapter develop early, either before children go to school or when they start school. The first three strategies—environmental cue, picture cue, and incidental cue—do not use letter and sound cues. The fourth strategy—the phonetic cue—takes only minimal advantage of our alphabetic writing system. Though these early strategies are not reliable ways to figure out the identity of unfamiliar words, emergent readers and writers use them, and hence it is important that you understand how they work. With insight into these early strategies, you are in a position to guide children so that they move toward the use of dependable word identification strategies which, in turn, support the development of a large fluent reading vocabulary.

ENVIRONMENTAL CUES: MAKING SENSE OF THE WRITING IN EVERYDAY SURROUNDINGS

Five-year-old John copied **California, October, no, stop,** and **soap** from the wall chart in his kindergarten classroom (Figure 3–1). At three years old, Vitterica already knows she can find a hamburger, drink, fries, and a small toy at every fast food restaurant with golden arches on the sign. Why do these young children connect meaning with the print and illustrations they see on signs, product labels, billboards, and food packages? The answer, say Harste, Burke, and Woodward (1982), lies in children's need to make sense of their environment. Children who associate the meaning of print with familiar features in the environment use the **environmental cue strategy.**

Making sense of print in the environment gives preschoolers a measure of control over their lives. The preschooler who can recognize the box of Raisin Yum Yum cereal on the grocery shelf might be able to talk her mother into buying that particular breakfast food. Though she quickly recognizes the cereal box, this same child cannot read the word **raisin** on the package of raisins her mother buys for midday snacks. While this preschooler might not be able to tell what the writing **Raisin Yum Yum** actually "says," in all likelihood she can give an approximation that is both meaningful and contextually acceptable. Shown a box of Raisin Yum Yum, she might say something like "cereal," "breakfast," or "eat breakfast." The reason emergent readers give feasible approximations is that they connect meaning with the everyday settings in which print appears, not with specific words.

It is not surprising, then, that preschoolers who use environmental cues generally do not notice misspellings, like **Xepi** for **Pepsi,** nor do they recognize words when logos are removed or when the words are written outside their normal environmental contexts (Masonheimer, Drum, & Ehri, 1984). However, by associating meaning with the environmental context in which print appears, children are taking an important step toward developing the concept that writing is supposed to make sense.

Figure 3–1 John enjoys copying the words he sees displayed in his kindergarten classroom.

PICTURE CUES: SHARING IDEAS THROUGH ILLUSTRATIONS

Children who infer the meaning of written messages from illustrations use the **picture cue strategy.** Long before children know enough words to read storybooks on their own and well before going to school, many read their favorite books by inferring and predicting meaning from pictures. Emergent readers who connect illustrations with meaning use a picture cue strategy. These children expect writing to label pictures and therefore look for cues to meaning in illustrations. For instance, four-year-old Thomas used picture cues when he proudly held up a poster of a race car his father brought from a business trip to Detroit and announced that the poster said: "Gentlemen, start your engines." The fact that the words on the poster bore not the slightest resemblance to the message Thomas read was of little consequence to him; Thomas focused entirely on the rich picture context.

The adults in Thomas's life read to him regularly, which has a positive affect on his interest in books. The interactions during story reading appear to be influenced by children's age (Martin, 1998) and the characteristics of the storybooks themselves (Elster, 1998). Children who have been read to at home and in day care expect pictures to signal meaning. Turning the pages and cueing on pictures, emergent readers say words that could have been written by the author but are not necessarily on the page.

Like the print in our everyday surroundings, the pictures in storybooks are an avenue to meaning that does not call for knowing specific words, remembering letters, or understanding the principle of alphabetic writing. It follows, then, that emergent readers who use cues from the environment to read signs and labels are also likely to use pictures to read storybooks. To successfully use the environmental and picture cue strategies, emergent readers need only associate meaning with easy-to-recognize features like the McDonald's® Golden Arches and the illustrations in books. And, of course, because these strategies bypass print, children do not need phonemic awareness, letter-sound knowledge, or the ability to identify individual words and letters to use them.

Emergent readers who use the cues in pictures to "read" their favorite storybooks may also use pictures when they write stories on their own. Kesha, a beginning kindergartner, drew the picture story in Figure 3–2 after hearing her teacher read and reread *Arthur's Halloween* (Brown, 1982). Notice that Kesha faithfully renders the big scary house that is so prominent in *Arthur's Halloween*, including a smiley face on the door to show the house is not frightening. Kesha clearly understands the picture-meaning connection. She also knows that writing is an important feature of books, and therefore, in her picture story, she includes letters and a word copied from the print in her classroom. In some ways, the **O**s are part of Kesha's picture story. If the children whom you teach write stories like Kesha's, rest assured that such stories represent a normal stage in becoming literate. When Kesha read her picture story to her teacher, she described the house that she drew, and she described the events that she remembered from *Arthur's Halloween*. From Kesha's writing, we can infer that she is searching for a medium

Figure 3–2 As children like Kesha begin to pay attention to written language, they may draw pictures to represent the events in familiar storybooks, and they may include pictures, letters, and words copied from their classroom.

through which she might effectively communicate with her audience, as yet unaware of the manner in which our alphabetic writing system represents speech.

INCIDENTAL CUES: LOOKING FOR SMUDGES, COLOR, WORD SHAPE, AND LETTER SHAPE

In their search for more trustworthy strategies, emergent readers look beyond cues in the environment and in pictures. In so doing, they discover a group of cues that include colored ink, word shape, letter shape, and visual reminders like smudges and dog-eared pages. These cues are incidental to alphabetic writing inasmuch as they do not reveal the specific sounds that the letters in words represent. The use of these cues, called the **incidental cue strategy,** is another step toward the development of word fluency. You can safely assume that the children in your classroom who use incidental cues also know how to use environmental and picture cues. The opposite is not necessarily true: Children who use the environmental and picture cues do not necessarily use incidental cues to identify words.

The use of incidental cues is a low-level uncomplicated way to identify words. It requires no attention at all to the specific letter sequence of words or to letter and sound cues. However, identifying a word by its unique shape or the presence of a unique letter (the **q** in **quick**) does require a rudimentary under-standing of the function of the white spaces between words and, if words are written in sentences, left-to-right and top-to-bottom progression. You can expect the emergent readers whom you teach to use incidental cues before they use letter and sound cues. This is so regardless of how easy or difficult words are to identify (Gough, 1993).

Jesse, whose story is shown in Figure 3–3, uses a combination of picture and incidental cues. He looks for smudges, word shape, letter shape, and color cues. And, if he knows something about the story, he uses his background knowledge and picture cues to tell the story from memory. When he writes, Jesse puts one letter after another across the page. He writes his name and copies the words **yellow** and **me,** as well as the letters of the alphabet, from the print in his kindergarten classroom. He also includes numbers and a picture.

What Jesse does not do is link the letters in written words to the sounds in spoken words. Jesse does not yet understand the basic premise upon which alphabetic writing rests, and therefore he writes strings of random letters (when he is not copying). Jesse is interested in print, however, for his careful copying suggests that he attends to some of the words he sees in school and is aware of the importance of the words in his classroom.

Because incidental cues are not tied to the way the alphabet represents speech, they have no predictable, logical association with the written language. As a consequence these cues are very fragile and nontransferable. Hence, four- and five-year-olds who use incidental cues may remember a word on a flash card when the card has a thumbprint, but not when there is no thumbprint. It is the smudge, not the spelling, that these children select as a cue (Gough, Juel, & Griffith, 1992). Even so, the children in your classroom who look for incidental cues are thinking about print, looking for features that set one group of letters apart from another, and generating hypotheses about writing.

Figure 3–3 Jesse knows that words and letters are important, and he explores written language by copying the many different types of print that he sees in his classroom.

Color is the most obvious of the four incidental cues. I was reminded of this one morning as I watched a group of kindergarten children reading a wall chart of daily activities. The wall chart had the following seven sentences that children read each morning at the beginning of the school day: "We will read a book together. We will talk about the story. We will have centers. We will have lunch. We will listen to a story. We will drop everything and read. We will write." As one little boy read the familiar sentence, **We will write,** he stopped when he came to the word **write.** Without a moment's hesitation his friend, Jacob, came to the rescue. "You know it's **write** because it's (written in) green," Jacob announced helpfully. While **write** was written in green on the chart, the other words in the sentence were in black. Jacob knew that colored ink set **write** apart from other print on the wall chart and therefore he was using color to identify this word.

Word shape, or configuration, is a third type of incidental cue. Emergent readers who use word shape to identify unfamiliar words look for the overall contour formed by letters. The word **hat,** for example, has two ascending letters separated by a letter that stays on the line, so its configuration looks like:

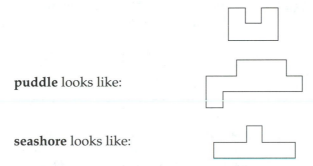

puddle looks like:

seashore looks like:

Word shape is not completely irrelevant to our writing system, since shape is determined by whether letters in a word are on the line or extend above and below the line. While word shape does not give emergent readers cues to sound, it does provide some information emergent readers can use to narrow down word choices, though this information is frequently unreliable.

Because so many words have virtually identical patterns of upward and downward sloping letters, identifying words by their configuration alone makes reading more difficult than it should be. Children who use configuration to recognize the word **hat** are bound to be confused when they try to read other words with a similar shape, such as **bat, tub,** and **hot.** For this reason, it makes no sense at all to ask children to guess a word by its shape, draw an outline around a word to highlight its shape, or match a written word to its shape (Dechant, 1991).

In addition to word shape, emergent readers may also use a fourth cue, letter shape. It seems that emergent readers do not think of individual letters as a special class of objects with constant shapes and forms (Adams, 1990). When these children look at letters, they focus on such properties as circles, arcs, humps, and lines. Children might, for instance, remember the word **nail** because the letter **n** has one "hump"; **took** because it has two circles in the middle that look like eyes; **banana** because it begins with a stick and ball (the lowercase **b**). Paying attention to circles, arcs, humps, and lines creates all sorts of confusion. Take **g** and **j,** as an example. Both **g** and **j** have "tails," so children may not think of **g** and **j** as different letters. Emergent readers who identify the word **game** because it has a "tail" may misread **juice** because the letter **j** has a "tail" too.

You may find that some of the children in your classroom associate word meaning (not sounds) with the incidental cues in words. When they do this, children focus on an incidental cue and associate it with word meaning. For example, a child who recognizes **doll** by its double **ll** may freely interchange the words **baby** and **toy** for the word **doll.** Rather than associating the specific spoken word **"doll"** with the unique sequence of letters in the written word **d-o-l-l** the child associates word meaning with the **ll,** which in turn results in substitutions that are synonyms or near synonyms. A major drawback to incidental cues is that the cues that are helpful under one reading condition are frequently not helpful under another condition. So long as words appear on pages with smudges, are written in color, have unusual characteristics like a double **oo,** a distinctive letter, or a unique shape, children may identify words with ease. But the use of these cues can lead to a great many misidentifications, as well as to confusion and frustration.

THE PRE-ALPHABETIC PHASE OF MOVEMENT TOWARD WORD FLUENCY AND THE PRECOMMUNICATIVE PHASE OF SPELLING

The children in your classroom who use environmental, picture, and incidental cues to identify words are in the **pre-alphabetic** phase of movement toward word fluency (Ehri, 1998). The pre-alphabetic phase begins in preschool and usually ends some time during the kindergarten year. Emergent readers at this phase cannot name the letters of the alphabet or, at best, can name only a few letters. They do not know the letter-sounds of phonics and lack phonemic awareness. Children cannot tell you, their teacher, that **"man"** and **"monkey"** begin alike, nor can they identify **man** and **monkey** by the **"m"** sound associated with the beginning letter, **m.** These children do not understand how our English alphabetic writing works and hence do not remember words by their unique letter sequences and do not use letter and sound cues. Not surprisingly, pre-alphabetic emergent readers have difficulty reading words that are outside the context of environmental cues and rich picture cues or that cannot be identified by incidental cues. And, not surprisingly, these children cannot read their own writing after a day or so because their writing does not systematically represent speech.

The children in your classroom who are pre-alphabetic emergent readers are also precommunicative spellers. Warren (Figure 3–4), a pre-alphabetic reader, is a precommunicative speller whose writing shows no relationship between sounds and letters (Gentry, 1987). Warren strings letters together, unaware of speech and print connections. To recognize the precommunicative spellers in your classroom, look for writing with no white spaces, inconsistent use of white spaces (Jesse, Figure 3–3), mock letters sprinkled among real letters, pictures that are at least as prominent as

Figure 3–4 A pre-alphabetic reader and precommunicative speller, Warren combines mock letters with real letters, stringing them across the page, unaware of speech and print connections.

writing (Warren, Figure 3–4; James, Figure 2–1), the same letter written over and over again (Kesha, Figure 3-2), and writing that wanders randomly around the page (Jesse, Figure 3–3). You will also observe that, though precommunicative spellers use upper case and lower case letters, they have a decided preference for upper case letters.

Pre-alphabetic emergent readers and precommunicative spellers move farther toward word fluency when reading and writing experiences help them develop phonemic awareness, letter name knowledge, and letter-sound knowledge. And, as children develop sound awareness and letter-sound knowledge, they will begin to identify words by connecting one or two letters with sound. When children do this, they use the phonetic cue strategy.

THE PHONETIC CUE STRATEGY

When emergent readers begin to use letter and sound cues, they typically take a rather simplistic and marginally effective route to word learning, the **phonetic cue strategy** (Ehri, 1998). With this strategy, children connect a single letter-sound cue (maybe two) or a letter name with the pronunciation of a whole word. For example, if a child sees the word **sandwich** in a storybook and if that child knows the sound associated with the letter **s,** the child may then identify **sandwich** by associating the sound represented by the letter **s** with the **"s"** sound heard in **"sandwich."**

A letter name may be used as a cue to identify a word if the name includes a portion of the sound the letter represents. For instance, a child who knows the name of the letter **s** may associate a portion of the sound heard in the letter name—the **"sss"** that is part of the name—with the **"s"** sound heard in **"sandwich."**

Once emergent readers and writers link a letter-sound or letter name with a written word, they may assume that the same cue always represents the same word. As a consequence, if emergent readers use the sound represented by the letter **s** (**"s"**) as a cue to identify **sandwich,** then every word that has an **s** in spelling is read as **"sandwich."** Hence, **sofa** and **see** are read as **"sandwich"** because each shares the same cue—the letter **s** that represents **"s."**

At a *minimum,* children are aware of at least one sound in the spoken words they hear in everyday conversations, though their phonemic awareness may well be greater than this. You can expect these children to be aware of the beginning sounds and to be able to separate the beginning sound from the vowel and remaining consonants—separate the **"s"** from the **"at"** in **"sat"** (Stahl & Murray, 1998). Children also know the features that distinguish one letter from another and therefore identify individual letters consistently and reliably. They know that words are made up of letters, and they know the sounds or names of some letters. It is especially important at this time in children's development as readers and writers to teach them letter names. Letter names help children develop awareness of sounds inasmuch as the letters themselves become concrete visual referents and reminders of the individual speech sounds in words. Additionally, and also importantly, knowing letter names can, with proper support from teachers, help children develop knowledge of letter-sounds when sounds are partially present in letter names. While children's knowledge may not go beyond a handful of letter-sounds or letter names, this is all it takes to identify words with the phonetic cue strategy.

To better understand the phonetic cue strategy, consider how Estiban uses a phonetic cue to identify the word **potholder** in the storybook *Oma and BoBo* (Schwartz, 1987). On page 20 of the book, the author writes, "Oma looked at her old red potholder hanging on the wall." The picture on page 20 depicts other sentences on the page far better than the ideas in this sentence. Consequently, the picture cue strategy is not very helpful. Hence, Estiban turns to the phonetic cue strategy and he uses it as follows:

1. Estiban notices that **potholder** begins with a letter he recognizes: **p.**
2. He then associates the sound **p** represents (**"p"**) with the spoken word **"potholder."**
3. The next time Estiban comes across **potholder** in the story, he thinks of the sound **p** represents (**"p"**) and then uses this combination to identify **potholder.**

If Estiban did not know the sound associated with the letter **p** (or any other letter in **potholder**), he could still use the phonetic cue strategy, provided that he knows the name of such letters as **p, t, l,** or **d.** Most consonant letters give clues to letter sounds, and the names of the vowels (**a, e, i, o,** and **u**) are helpful when vowels represent long sounds, as in **came, sleep, tide, road,** and **tube.** Therefore, even if the only thing Estiban knows about letters happens to be their names, he can link the sound cue in a letter name to pronunciation.

Since so many different words share letters, the strategy Estiban uses is obviously very ineffective. Perhaps the greatest advantage of this strategy is that it gives children opportunities to develop, test, and revise hypotheses about how alphabetic writing works. As emergent readers and writers experiment with even a single cue, they refine their phonemic awareness and extend their letter-sound knowledge. The more children know about the words, rhymes, sounds, and letters of spoken and written language, the more they absorb, internalize, and generalize about letter and sound relationships. Increased phonemic awareness and greater letter-sound knowledge, in turn, provide a platform for developing more reliable and more streamlined word identification strategies. Though the phonetic cue strategy is relatively short-lived, it eases emergent readers and writers into strategically using alphabetic writing and as such is the precursor to the development of more advanced word identification strategies.

THE PARTIAL ALPHABETIC PHASE OF MOVEMENT TOWARD WORD FLUENCY AND THE SEMIPHONETIC PHASE OF SPELLING

Lexi (Figure 3–5) has reached the **partial alphabetic** phase in movement toward word fluency, which usually occurs in kindergarten and for some children in early first grade (Ehri, 1998). Lexi (and other partial alphabetic emergent readers) writes

Figure 3–5 Lexi conventionally spells words in her fluent reading vocabulary and uses the beginning consonant to spell other words. Lexi often struggles when identifying new words because she does not know enough letter-sound associations to fully translate words into speech. Her story reads: I want to go to the park. I want to swim. I want to play on the playground.

from left to right, uses white spaces to separate words, fluently recognizes a few often-used words, and can read and write her own name. Lexi's approach to word identification is systematic in that she uses one or two letter-sounds to figure out a word's identity. The advantage of beginning and ending letters is that they convey considerable information about a word's identity when combined with the reading context. However, because Lexi does not remember words by their complete letter sequence, she is likely to confuse words that begin and end alike, such as **seed** and **salad** or **many** and **monkey.**

Children like Lexi who are partial alphabetic emergent readers know more letter-sounds and have more phonemic awareness than children like James, Jesse, and Warren who are at the pre-alphabetic phase. Lexi has enough phonemic awareness and knows enough about letter names and letter-sounds to use one or two alphabetic cues when she reads. However, Lexi often struggles when identifying new words because she does not know enough letter-sounds and does not have enough phonemic awareness to fully translate words into speech. She has difficulty learning words by analogy (relating parts of known words to parts of unknown words) and sounding out words.

While children like Lexi may know the sounds of high frequency single consonants, like **m, n, p,** and **s,** they do not have much, if any, knowledge of vowel letter patterns, consonant blends like **bl, tr,** and **st,** or consonant digraphs (two letters representing one sound, as **th, sh,** and **ch**). Because Lexi attends to only part of the letter-sound associations in words, she is likely to misidentify words that share the same letters. Lexi, and the children like her whom I teach, frequently guess at words using the context, picture cues, and beginning and/or ending letter-sounds. I find that so long as context and picture cues are robust, children are usually successful reading unfamiliar words. I also find that these same children may accurately read a word on one line or in one book only to misread the very same word on another line or in another book. This type of miscuing occurs because children lack the ability to fully decode unfamiliar words. Context has a strong affect on the word identification of these children: High context, including excellent, descriptive pictures is most conducive to accurate word identification; weak context and picture cues may result in guesses that do not make sense in the story. While the partial alphabetic emergent readers in your class do add words to their fluent reading vocabulary, vocabulary growth is slow. Reading may be peppered with miscues, and many of the words children spell may not be readable because important sounds are omitted.

Just as Lexi uses partial alphabetic cues to read, so too does she use partial alphabetic cues when spelling. She spells semiphonetically—she uses letters to represent some, but not all, of the important sounds in words (Gentry, 1987). From Lexi's writing we observe that she uses consonant letters to represent sounds when she spells. She uses a **w** to represent **want** and **swim,** and **p** to represent **park.** Lexi conventionally spells words in her fluent reading vocabulary (**I, to, go, the, play**). Notice how she spells **playground: Play** is among the words she recognizes fluently. The portion of this compound word that is not fluent, **ground,** she represents with the letter **g,** resulting in **playg.**

Figure 3–6 Alecia is phonemically aware of beginning and ending sounds, and she uses letters to represent the beginning and ending sounds in words, some middle sounds, as well. She is moving into the use of more sophisticated letter and sound relationships than simple phonetic cues. Her story reads: I have green and blue eyes. I have brown hair. I have a twin sister. My favorite color is pink. My favorite food is corn. My favorite restaurant is Chick-Fil-A®. I love my dog. I like to see my friends.

Alecia (Figure 3–6) has moved farther toward word fluency than Lexi. Alecia writes about her favorite things using a blend of conventionally spelled words and semiphonetically spelled words that are not yet in her fluent reading vocabulary. In comparing Lexi and Alecia's writing, we see that Alecia has more known words in her story (**I, have, green, and, blue, a, my, is, love, dog,** and **see**), and she typically uses two or three consonants for words she spells unconventionally (some examples are **bn** for **brown, sdr** for **sister,** and **lk** for **like**). We can infer from Alecia's use of letters to represent sounds in words (for example, **clr** for **color, fd** for **feed, rt** for **restaurant**) that she is carefully thinking about alphabetic cues. Further evidence comes from her use of the vowel letter **i** in **pink** (spelled **pik**). In contrast to Lexi who uses only beginning consonants to spell, Alecia frequently writes both beginning and ending sounds, and includes some middle sounds as well (**sdr** for **sister** and **clr** for **color**). We have additional evidence Alecia is looking carefully at print in the way she uses hyphens to spell her favorite restaurant, **Chick-Fil-A**®—spelled as **C-F-a.** From her story we can infer that Alecia is phonemically aware of beginning and ending sounds, and she is developing awareness of the middle sounds in words. When spelling, Alecia connects this phonemic awareness with the sounds letters represent. Alecia shows us through her writing that she is moving into the use of more sophisticated letter and sound relationships than simple phonetic cues.

WHAT YOU CAN DO TO HELP PARTIAL ALPHABETIC READERS AND SEMIPHONETIC SPELLERS MOVE TOWARD WORD FLUENCY

The five- and six-year-olds in your classroom who are at the partial alphabetic phase will use phonetic cues to identify words when reading and spell words semiphonetically when writing. In order to use more effective strategies, children must go beyond dependence on beginning and ending consonant letter-sound associations. While children have a working knowledge of frequently occurring single consonants, they lack vowel letter-sound knowledge. Since English words cannot be pronounced without a vowel sound, this knowledge is crucial for the growth of children's reading vocabulary. So teach these children more about letter-sound associations, including vowel letter combinations, and develop their phonemic awareness.

Children at this phase of word fluency should write every day for all sorts of purposes. As they write, children have opportunities to think analytically about the sound-letter relationships in words they wish to spell and, coincidentally, you have opportunities to help them gain insight into consonant and vowel letter-sound associations. The activities in Chapter 2 are highly beneficial for teaching these children how to identify the individual sounds in words and how to blend. My experience with partial alphabetic readers is that they especially benefit from practice blending. If you observe children omitting, adding, or rearranging sounds during blending, then the blending activities in Chapter 2 will help these children move further toward word fluency. As you help children refine blending, look to see if they quickly and confidently identify the middle sounds in words. Vowels often occur in the middle of English words, sandwiched between consonants. Beginning and ending letters are easier to connect with sounds than letters in the middle of words, which explains why children like Lexi and Alecia most often use first and last letters to identify and spell words.

The children whom I teach frequently benefit from a combination of activities to help them learn vowel letter-sound combinations (assuming, of course, that children know the consonant sounds) and phonemic awareness activities that focus on middle sounds. Refer to Chapter 2 for teaching suggestions and combine them with activities in Chapters 4 and 5. When children can identify words by associating all the letters with sounds, they have become full alphabetic readers and phonetic spellers (discussed in Chapter 5). And, as children analyze spoken and written words, they naturally look for cues in unfamiliar words that are present in familiar words. When readers do this, they use existing information to construct and acquire new knowledge by dividing words (or syllables) into sound and letter patterns. This is the key to identifying words with the analogy strategy, which is the topic of the next chapter.

REFERENCES

Adams, M. J. (1990). *Beginning to read: Thinking and learning about print.* Cambridge, MA: MIT.

Brown, M. (1982). *Arthur's halloween.* Boston: Little, Brown.

Dechant, E. (1991). *Understanding and teaching reading: An interactive model.* Hillsdale, NJ: Lawrence Erlbaum.

Ehri, L. C. (1998). Grapheme-phoneme knowledge is essential for learning to read words in English. In J. L. Metsala & L. C. Ehri (Eds.), *Word recognition in beginning literacy* (pp. 3–40). Mahwah, NJ: Lawrence Erlbaum.

Elster, C. A. (1998). Influences of text and pictures on shared and emergent readings. *Research in the Teaching of English, 32,* 43–77.

Gentry, J. R. (1987). *Spel . . . is a four-letter word.* Portsmouth, NH: Heinemann.

Gough, P. B. (1993). The beginning of decoding. *Reading and Writing: An Interdisciplinary Journal, 5,* 181–192.

Gough, P. B., Juel, C., & Griffith, P. L. (1992). Reading, spelling and the orthographic cipher. In P. B. Gough, L. C. Ehri, & R. Treiman (Eds.), *Reading acquisition* (pp. 35–48). Hillsdale, NJ: Lawrence Erlbaum.

Harste, J. C., Burke, C. L., & Woodward, V. A. (1982). Children's language and world: Initial encounters with print. In J. Langer & M. Smith-Burke (Eds.), *Bridging the gap: Reader meets author* (pp. 105–131). Newark, DE: International Reading Association.

Martin, L. E. (1998). Early book reading: How mothers deviate from printed text for young children. *Reading Research and Instruction, 37,* 137–160.

Mason, J. M. (1980). When do children begin to read: An exploration of four-year-old children's letter and word reading competencies. *Reading Research Quarterly, 15,* 203–227.

Masonheimer, P. E., Drum, P. A., & Ehri, L. C. (1984). Does environmental print identification lead children into reading? *Journal of Reading Behavior, 16,* 257–271.

Schwartz, A. (1987). *Oma and BoBo.* New York: Harper & Row.

Stahl, S. A., & Murray, B. (1998). Spoken vocabulary growth and the segmental restructuring of lexical representations: Precursors to phonemic awareness and early reading ability. In J. L. Metsala & L. C. Ehri (Eds.), *Word recognition in beginning literacy* (pp. 65–87). Mahwah, NJ: Lawrence Erlbaum.

CHAPTER

4

The Analogy Strategy with Onsets and Rimes

Using Familiar Words to Identify Unfamiliar Words

This chapter describes two strategies: the analogy strategy and the cross-checking strategy. As you read this chapter, you will learn how syllables consist of onsets and rimes, how the analogy strategy—in which readers use parts of known words to read unfamiliar words—works, and how to help readers use familiar words to identify unfamiliar words. You will also find out how readers cross-check for meaning and why this strategy is important for word identification.

KEY IDEAS

➤ Syllables have a two-part structure, consisting of an onset, which is the consonant(s) at the beginning of syllables, and a rime, which is the vowel and any subsequent consonants at the end of syllables.
➤ Readers who use the analogy strategy connect an onset and a rime in words they already know how to read with the same onset and rime in a word they do not know.
➤ The cross-checking strategy helps readers make sure that the words they identify fit the reading context.
➤ Successful word identification depends on cross-checking, regardless of the strategy used to identify the word.

Look at the following sets of words:

rain	wish	more
train	swish	shore
obtain	finish	ignore
terrain	publish	explore
maintain	astonish	omnivore
constrain	embellish	commodore
bloodstain	accomplish	underscore

A quick glance is all it takes to recognize that the same patterns of letters and sounds occur in many different words. Once readers discover that the seven words in each of these three word mountains share a letter pattern, they have a way to organize their thinking so as to use parts of known words to identify unknown words. When using the analogy strategy, readers find a shared letter pattern in words, such as the **ain** in **rain** and **train,** and then use the similarity to identify unfamiliar words that have the same pattern, such as **maintain** and **constrain.**

LOOKING INSIDE SYLLABLES

Lucy sets a decidedly lighthearted tone as she ruminates about school in the poem in Figure 4–1. Lucy repeats words, rhymes words, and, what's more, all the words she uses have only one syllable.

Looking inside the syllables in Lucy's poem reveals a two-part structure that consists of an **onset** and a **rime** (Goswami, 1997). **Onsets** are the consonants that

Figure 4–1 Some of the one-syllable words in Lucy's poem consist of an onset and a rime; others consist of a rime only.

come at the beginning of syllables, as the **sch** in **school.** Similarly, the **s** in **sit,** the **sl** in **slit** and the **spl** in **split** are onsets. Onsets are always consonants, and there can be as many as three clustered together at once (**sch** and **spl,** for example). **Rimes** are the vowel(s) and consonant(s) at the end of syllables. The rime in **school,** for example, is **ool.** Correspondingly, the **ent** in **tent** is a rime consisting of the vowel (**e**) and the consonants that follow it (**nt**); the rime in **scream** is **eam;** in **black,** it is **ack.**

Rhyming words like **school** and **cool** share a rime, in this case the rime **ool.** When rime is common to two or more words, the words usually share a rhyming sound.

In rimes, consonants do not have to follow the vowel: sometimes the vowel ends the syllable, as in **my** (onset = **m** + rime = **y**) and **be** (onset = **b** + rime = **e**). Some syllables have only a rime, no onset, as in **an** and **it.** Table 4–1 shows the onset-rime structure of the one-syllable words in Lucy's poem.

TABLE 4–1   *Onsets and Rimes in Lucy's Poem*

Onset	+	Rime	=	One-Syllable Word
sch	+	ool	=	school
c	+	ool	=	cool
	+	is	=	is
l	+	ike	=	like
f	+	un	=	fun
n	+	eat	=	neat

TABLE 4–2   *Onsets and Rimes in Multiple-Syllable Words*

Onset	+	Rime	+	Onset	+	Rime	+	Onset	+	Rime	=	Word
p	+	ump	+	k	+	in					=	pumpkin
m	+	et	+		+	al					=	metal
p	+	oul	+	tr	+	y					=	poultry
c	+	al	+	c	+	u	+	l	+	ate	=	calculate
sk	+	el	+		+	e	+	t	+	on	=	skeleton
r	+	e	+	pl	+	en	+		+	ish	=	replenish

Words with more than one syllable are analyzed in just the same way. The only difference is that syllables are combined, as shown in Table 4–2.

In Appendix A, you will find lists of rimes and examples of words in which the rimes appear. Rimes with an asterisk are used in literally hundreds of words (Cheek, Flippo, & Lindsey, 1997; Fry, 1998). Beginning readers and expert readers alike use onsets and rimes to identify words (Bowey, 1990). So Appendix A includes examples of one-syllable words, like **skate** and **late,** as well as longer words like **calculate, elevate,** and **mutate.** The onsets and rimes in syllables provide tremendous insight into our alphabetic writing system. And when readers develop knowledge of onsets and rimes, the stage is set to move beyond the phonetic cue strategy and into use of the analogy strategy.

USING THE ANALOGY STRATEGY WITH ONSETS AND RIMES

Readers who use the analogy strategy connect onsets and rimes in words they already know how to read with the same onsets and rimes in words they do not know how to read. The basic premise is that if words share onsets or rimes, then words must also have similar pronunciations. When generalizing the rime in one word to the pronunciation of another word with the same rime, readers look for shared letter patterns. It turns out that even young readers are sensitive to the shared patterns, or the rime, in written language and use this knowledge to identify words (Goswami, 1997).

What Readers Know About Phonemic Awareness

Children who use the analogy strategy are aware of the beginning sounds and the rhyming sounds in words. They know, for instance, that **"fun"** begins with **"f"** and can give examples of words that begin with the same sound, such as **"fun," "fat,"** and **"five."** Readers can also identify words that share rhyming sounds, such as **"fun,"** **"run,"** and **"spun,"** and, if asked by their teachers, can give examples of words that rhyme, **"sun,"** **"gun,"** and **"bun,"** for instance. And, of course, these readers can separate words into onsets and rimes. For example, they know that **"fun"** consists of an **"f"** and **"un,"** and therefore separate each part—onset and rime—from the whole word, **"fun."** Furthermore, readers know how to blend beginning sounds (onsets) and the sounds of vowels and ending consonants (rimes) together to form recognizable words. They can, for instance, blend **"f"** and **"un"** together to pronounce **"fun."** It is not surprising, then, that awareness of rhyming sounds in language is significantly related to the children's ability to use the analogy strategy (Goswami, 1998).

What Readers Know About the Sounds Associated with Onsets and Rimes

To use the analogy strategy with onsets and rimes, readers need only remember the sounds associated with onsets, such as the **"f"** in **fun,** and whole rimes, such as the **"un"** in **fun.** Because readers do not need to analyze the individual letter-sound combinations inside rimes, they may not necessarily know the sounds associated with the individual vowels and consonants in rimes. For example, though **"un"** represents the two sounds **"u"** and **"n,"** readers may conceptualize **un** as one complete unit not as the two letter and sound combinations **u–"u"** plus **n –"n."** So, when readers see the words **fun** and **sun,** they will tell you, their teacher, that the **un** represents **"un"** in each one. However, they may not associate the sound of **"u"** with the letter **u** in **un** or in other rimes consisting of the same letter-sound combination, like **ug** and **ut.** Children will tell you instead that **ug** represents **"ug"** in **tug** and **ut** says **"ut"** in **cut.**

What Readers Do with Their Knowledge

Suppose for the sake of illustration that Tamara, who is a first grader, does not automatically recognize the word **tent** in the sentence **Jane saw a large tent in the camp ground.** Suppose further that Tamara cannot figure out **tent** from picture cues, syntactic cues, semantic cues, or background knowledge. However, Tamara brings to reading the knowledge of onsets and rimes in words she knows how to read. Here is how Tamara uses the analogy strategy:

1. Tamara notices a familiar onset and a familiar rime in **tent.** She recalls that the **t** in **tell** represents **"t,"** and that the **ent** in **went** represents **"ent."**
2. Tamara exchanges the **"w"** for the **"t,"** which leaves **"t"** + **"ent."**
3. She then blends **"t"** + **"ent"** to pronounce **"tent."**
4. Last, Tamara checks to make sure **"tent"** is a good fit for the sentence. She asks herself: Does **tent** sound and look right? Does **tent** make sense in the passage? Do I know what the author means? If the answers to these questions are yes, Tamara continues reading. If the answers are no, Tamara tries once again to figure out **tent.**

THE CROSS-CHECKING STRATEGY

In the example, the last thing Tamara did was to verify that **tent** made sense in the sentence. When readers make sure that the words they identify fit the reading context, it is called **cross-checking.** Cross-checking is a strategy all by itself and the last step in word identification. Good readers always cross-check, regardless of whether they identify words with the analogy strategy or some other strategy.

Cross-checking ensures that word identification supports comprehension. When cross-checking, readers actively think about meaning, taking into account the overall sense of the surrounding phrases, sentences, and paragraphs, as well as sentence structure, print and speech relationships, and their own personal reasons for reading. Once satisfied that the newly identified word makes sense in the context, readers immediately focus their attention back on reading and understanding the text.

Cross-checking gives readers valuable feedback on their own decoding efforts. Thus, one consequence of cross-checking is a metacognitive, or conscious, awareness of the success of word identification. Readers know whether an identified word is acceptable or unacceptable for the reading passage. An acceptable outcome is a real, meaningful word that makes sense in the context; an unacceptable outcome is either a nonsense word or a word that does not fit the context.

Readers who cross-check put only as much mental energy into word identification as is necessary to identify a word as consistent with the author's message. These readers know when to stop word identification and proceed with textual reading and when to give word identification another try. When a word makes sense, identification stops and comprehension moves forward unimpeded by the confusion created by an unknown word. On the other hand, if an identified word does not make sense, then cross-checking lets readers know that they have not constructed a meaningful message.

Readers who use the cross-checking strategy are guaranteed of a good fit between identified words and authors' messages. Readers who do not cross-check accept the results of word identification even if those results are nonsense. For these reasons, cross-checking is absolutely essential and must be used every time readers identify an unfamiliar word.

RIMES, PHONOGRAMS, AND WORD FAMILIES

Some popular teaching materials in the 1960s grouped words into "families" where every family member shared a common letter pattern or phonogram. When these materials were first published, they were dubbed "linguistic" because their authors were linguists, not educators, and the materials themselves were supposed to reflect linguistic principles. The Merrill Linguist Reading Program (1986) and Programmed Reading (Phoenix Learning Resources, 1994) are contemporary examples of this approach. Linguistic materials emphasize recurring letter patterns consisting of a vowel and one or more consonants. These vowel-and-consonant patterns are called phono-

Figure 4–2 When Anna's teacher asked her to write as many words as she could, Anna wrote twenty words using only four rimes–op, ox, ad, and am.

top bop pop
had flop mop
fox bad
box cop jam
ox Sam
pad mad
chop am hop
dad bad

grams and, in most instances, phonograms corresponded to rimes. Anna (Figure 4–2), for instance, uses the **op** phonogram to write **bop, top, pop, mop, cop, chop,** and **flop.**

The sentences in linguistic materials are jam-packed with words sharing a common phonogram, like **The man has a tan pan in the van.** There is minimal variation among words, with many differing only in the onset, as we see in Anna's list. Though the objective of linguistic materials is to teach word identification, children do not learn the "rules" of phonics. Words are taught by sight, not by sounding and blending as in traditional synthetic phonics programs. Children abstract their own generalizations about letter-sound correspondences as a consequence of reading words from the same families. All things considered, onset-rime is not a new idea. Yet, our understanding of why onsets and rimes are important and how onset-rime contributes to word identification is new. As a result, teachers now understand why it is important to encourage readers to look for onsets and rimes in words. Today's teachers are therefore better able to provide readers with appropriate opportunities to learn and use the analogy strategy.

Why Onsets and Rimes?

Readers who use analogous onsets and rimes put less mental effort into word identification than do readers who decode words letter-sound by letter-sound. First, learning that **ent** represents **"ent"** is far less challenging than learning that the **e** represents the sound of **"e,"** **n** the sound of **"n,"** and **t** the sound of **"t."** Second, blending onsets and rimes is much easier than blending individual sounds because with onsets and rimes there are only two items. In the example of **tent,** analogy users would blend only **"t"** + **"ent"** in comparison with the four sounds—**"t"** + **"e"** + **"n"** + **"t"**—associated with individual letters. Fewer items to blend, in turn, reduces the probability of reversing sounds, deleting sounds, or adding sounds. Consequently, readers who might not be successful sounding out and blending **tent** as **"t"** + **"e"** + **"n"** + **"t"** may be able to decode **tent** when it is divided into **"t"** + **"ent."** Fewer demands on phonemic awareness make word identification with onsets and rimes more accessible to young, inexperienced, and less phonemically aware readers. For this reason, the analogy with onsets and rimes strategy is a good place to begin with children who have difficulty decoding words letter-sound by letter-sound.

Onsets and rimes are reasonably dependable visual maps to sound, and so readers can justifiably place a certain amount of confidence in them. Onsets are reasonably dependable because they consist exclusively of consonant letters. As it turns out, the consonant letters in our writing system are far more reliable representations of sound than are the vowels. When combined with rich context cues, onsets give readers considerable insight into a word's identity. Upon seeing the word **track** for the first time in the sentence, **The train rolled down the track,** a reader who knows the onset, **tr,** and who is sensitive to context cues might logically assume that this never-seen-before word is **track.**

Though consonants are relatively dependable visual maps, this is not so for vowels. Each vowel represents more than one sound, as with the **a** in **track, bake, saw,** and **car.** When syllables, in this example the one-syllable word **track,** are divided into onsets and rimes, the trick vowels are not quite so troublesome. The explanation is that the vowels in rimes are learned as part of a chunk of letters and sounds. For this reason, readers who learn rimes do not have to understand why the **a** in **track** is pronounced one way and the **a** in **brake** another way. Instead, children remember that the **ack** in **track** represents **"ack"** and the **ake** in **bake** represents **"ake."** No further analysis is called for. Anna wrote the word list in Figure 4–2 when her teacher asked her to write as many words as she could in a short period of time. We can infer from Anna's list that she thinks about the rime in words, for the twenty words are made up of only four rimes, **op, ox, ad,** and **am.** Anna thinks of rimes as intact multiletter units. She knows how to substitute onsets to make new words, so we would expect her to also read and write words like **drop, stop, sad, lad, ram,** and **ham** (provided that she knows the letter-sound associations for the onsets in these words).

Remembering rimes sidesteps the need to learn exceptions to the conventional way letters represent sounds in English words. Take the **old** in **told,** for example. The **o** in **told** should represent the same sound as the **o** in **rock,** since there is only one vowel (the **o**) in these short words and both vowels are followed by two consonants. This is not so, of course. Children would be confused if they tried to read **told** as though the **o** represented the sound in **rock.** However, the sound represented by the **o** in **told** is not at all troublesome when remembered as part of the whole rime **old.** Children who know how to read the rime in **told** have a cue to the identification of any word that shares this rime, for example, **gold, behold,**

scold, and **enfold.** The net effect is that even vowels that stand for a variety of sounds are easily remembered and decoded when learned as part of frequently recurring rimes.

Onsets, Rimes, and Word Fluency

As Lilly (Figure 4–3) writes about her pet cat she conventionally spells words in her fluent reading vocabulary and spells other words by adding different onsets to the **at** rime. We can infer from her story that Lilly is thinking carefully about speech-to-print relationships, resourcefully combining her knowledge of onsets and rimes with her memory for known words and her understanding of letter-sound associations. When Lilly reads, she uses frequently occurring rimes, as well as letter-sound relationships, to identify new words. It is quite typical for readers like Lilly to use both the analogy and letter-sound strategies, for children develop them at more or less the same time. For this reason, children's progress toward word fluency in light of their use of alphabetic cues and spelling is explained in detail in the next chapter (Chapter 5) when we consider the letter-sound strategy.

Children like Lilly look for consistency in written and spoken language relationships. They learn and remember words by paying attention to recurring letter patterns, and hence they can write and read words that are made up of

Figure 4–3   When writing, Lilly uses her knowledge of rimes and her ability to substitute beginning consonants (onsets).

the letter combinations (onsets and rimes) they already know. Significantly, children are able to figure out the identity of some words that have known onsets and rimes without their teachers' help, though they continue to need guidance from their teachers and structure in learning. If you teach children like Lilly, you can expect them to learn more and more about onsets and rimes through reading, writing, and learning activities like those described later in this chapter.

LESSONS TO HELP READERS LEARN AND USE ANALOGOUS ONSETS AND RIMES

Whenever you point out shared onsets and rimes among known and unknown words, you help children use the analogy strategy. For example, if a child does not automatically recognize **tent** and if picture and context cues are not strong enough to help the child figure out this word, then you might say something like, "Look at this word (pointing to **tent**). Now, look at this word (pointing to **went** in another sentence). If this (pointing to **went**) is **"went,"** what do you think this word (pointing to **tent**) might be?" Or you might point to **tent** and say, "Can you think of another word that begins with **t**? Can you think of another word that ends with **ent**? How can you use this to help you figure out **tent** (spell the word aloud)?" And, of course, you would take this opportunity to model how to substitute beginning consonants (onsets). You might do this by saying, "I know the word **went.** So to read this word (pointing to **tent**), I will change the **w** to a **t,** which makes **"tent."** Now you try it with me." As readers use the analogy with onsets and rimes strategy, give them opportunities to reflect on their own strategy use by asking questions like those in Chapter 1. Ask, too, questions that specifically help readers develop sensitivity to analogous onsets and rimes. For example, you might ask, "What word do you already know that can help you figure out this new one?" Or you might ask, "Can you think of a word that begins with the same letter(s)? How about one that ends with the same letters?"

Use the six lessons that follow to help children learn and use the analogy with onsets and rimes strategy. These lessons follow the exploration, guided practice, and transfer format described in Chapter 1 and are flexible enough to be part of all kinds of listening, reading, and writing experiences in your classroom. They are a basic framework for teaching. You, the teacher, can use them to teach any onset or rime that is worthwhile for children to learn and use. And, as with any lesson or activity in this book, adapt them to be compatible with your own teaching style and use them with children who will benefit from developing greater ability to strategically use the onsets and rimes in known words to identify unknown words. Along with these lessons, give children opportunities to read books with words that share rimes, compare and contrast the onsets and rimes in words, make onset and rime wall charts and put them up in your classroom, and use the extra practice activities described in the next section.

Building Words with Onset and Rime Tiles

In this lesson, readers build words by lining up small tiles that have onsets or rimes written on them. The lesson, which gives children the opportunity to use onsets and rimes to spell words, is appropriate for small groups of children in any grade.

Things You'll Need: One set of onset-rime cards that combine to build often-seen and often-used words; as many sets of onset-rime tiles as there are cooperative groups or individuals in your class; a pocket chart. Onset-rime cards are unlined index cards that have an onset or rime written on them. Onset-rime tiles are ceramic tiles with an onset or rime written on them. Look for small tiles in home improvement stores. Use a black permanent marker to write onsets on some tiles, rimes on others. Store tiles in a plastic container with many small compartments. If you do not have a plastic container, store tiles in locking bags and put the bags in a sturdy shoe box.

Exploration: Use a pocket chart and onset-rime cards to demonstrate word building, as shown in Figure 4–4. Put an onset and a rime card side by side in a pocket chart (**s** and **at,** perhaps) and explain the sounds the onset and rime represent. Then push the cards together to build a word (**sat**), again pointing out the onset and rime. Use a different onset and the same rime to build another word (**fat,** for instance). Explain the sounds represented by the onset and rime and push the cards together to build a second word. Now, there are two words in the pocket chart— **sat** and **fat.** Build several more words, and by all means have children participate in word building. Last, review the words by having children read them and find the common rime. (For children who understand the way many words can be built from the same rime, I suggest that you go beyond word building with one rime and introduce another onset-rime combination (perhaps **m** and **an**). Build different

Figure 4–4 The use of a pocket chart to build words helps readers gain insight into the sound that analogous onsets and rimes represent in words.

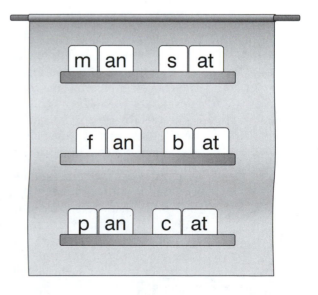

words with the new rime (**fan, can,** and **pan,** perhaps). Line up words with the same rimes in columns, thus creating opportunities to compare and contrast the rimes in words.)

Guided Practice: When I teach children who are just beginning to use onset-rime tiles to build words, I give them tiles with different onsets and only one rime. For example, children might use tiles with **f, c, m, r,** and **p,** and the **at** rime tile to build **fat, cat, mat, rat,** and **pat.** I give children who are veterans at word building several onset tiles (such as **f, c, m, r,** and **p**) and two (or more) rimes tiles (**at** and **an,** for example). Children then work individually or with a learning partner to build as many words as they can think of that are spelled with the onset-rime tiles. Children write the words as they build them, and then count the number of different words they build.

Transfer: Challenge children to read everything on the walls, windows, and doors of your room—wall charts, posters, bulletin boards, and stories they have read, dictated, and written. Children can read individually or together in pairs. Make sure children point to each word as it is read. Ask them to write down words that are spelled with a particular onset or rime. Then, when everyone has read everything in the room and made lists of words that are spelled with the same onset or rime, have children compare lists, talk about words, find words in the room, and read sentences in which words are written.

 Rime Wordplay

In this lesson readers in second grade and up create fanciful adjective-noun word pairs that share a rime. In so doing, children have opportunities to learn how some words that are spelled similarly also sound similar. And, additionally, readers have an opportunity to learn more about the adjectives and nouns in language.

Things You'll Need: Paper, pencils, crayons.

Exploration: Begin by reviewing nouns and adjectives, which are typically taught in second grade. Ask children to suggest nouns and make a long list of them. Then, one-by-one look at the nouns and ask children to think of adjectives that share a rime. For example, children might suggest **brown** to describe the **clown.** Talk about the shared rime and how combining adjectives and nouns makes for unlikely and humorous rhyming pairs, such as **red Fred** and **brown clown.** Write examples on a wall chart; discuss ways in which words that share a rime sound alike and look alike. (Sometimes two-word rimes are called Hinky Pinks.)

Guided Practice: Challenge children to create and illustrate their own imaginative, and perhaps unconventional, adjective-noun word pairs that share a rime. Interesting characters, places, and things children find in familiar books are especially good to use as one of the words in a rhyming pair. And, of course, the words on lists created by the group are fair game. Figure 4–5 shows rime pairs and pictures created by a multiage group of second and third graders. Put pictures of Rime Wordplay on the bulletin board, thus setting the stage for the transfer activity that follows.

Figure 4–5 Learners think about rime and about word meaning when they create and illustrate pairs of words that share the same rime.

Transfer: Invite children to work collaboratively to write definitions for the adjective-noun word pairs they created, such as defining a **soggy doggy** as **"a drippy dog"** or **"a wet pet."** Ask children to write definitions on tagboard strips. Then (1) fasten word pairs and pictures on a bulletin board, (2) prop definitions written by different cooperative groups on the chalk tray, and (3) invite children to match word pairs with definitions. This is lots of fun and offers many opportunities for children to talk about rimes, words, adjectives, nouns, and definitions. Combinations of word pairs, pictures, and creative definitions make a great bulletin board.

Writing Tongue Twisters

Children's natural attraction to alliteration makes creating tongue twisters fun, a great way to explore onsets, and an imaginative way to transfer learning. Use this activity with small groups of first, second, and third graders who need practice paying attention to onsets and practice reading words fluently; give more support to younger children, less support to older children.

Figure 4–5   (*Continued*)

Things You'll Need: Tongue twisters remembered from childhood or a good book with lots of twisters, such as *World's Toughest Tongue Twisters* (Rosenbloom, 1986) and Charles Keller's *Tongue Twisters* (1989).

Exploration: Say a tongue twister and then ask children to say it with you. Next, challenge children to say the twister on their own and ask them to identify the repeated sound. Call attention to alliteration by asking children to discover the quality that makes twisters unique.

Guided Practice: Share books that highlight alliteration, such as the zany *Aster Aardvark's Alphabet Adventure* (Kellogg, 1992) and the captivating *Animalia* (Base, 1987) for younger readers, and the hilarious story of *Princess Prunella and the Purple Peanut* (Atwood, 1995) for older readers. To further explore alliteration, write a tongue twister on the chalkboard and ask children to read it with you in chorus. Ask a volunteer to underline all the instances of the same onset; count how many times words begin with the same letter and the same sound; reread the twister until children read fluently and accurately; then invite the whole group to write a tongue twister together.

Transfer: The playful, engaging, and alliterative language in books such as *Aster Aardvark's Alphabet Adventure* (Kellogg, 1992), *Animalia* (Base, 1987), and *Princess Prunella and the Purple Peanut* (Atwood, 1995) invite children to create their own alliterative tongue twisters. First graders may enjoy making up twisters as a small group activity, dictating as you write on chart paper. Second graders and up may like to work cooperatively to write their own tongue twisters. Share the alliterative tongue twisters children write (as shown in Figure 4–6), read twisters aloud in chorus, put them on wall charts, ask children to tape-record tongue twisters and make tapes available for everyone's listening pleasure! Or follow the example of authors like Kellogg, Base, and Atwood. Fasten together children's alliterative sentences and illustrations to make a book of playful, alliterative language created by the readers and writers in your classroom.

Mystery Words and Riddles

With its focus on mystery words and riddles, this lesson is a favorite of children who enjoy word games and puzzles. In this lesson, children use onset and rime clues to figure out mystery words, which are then written on mini-chalkboards; they also use rime clues to solve riddles. Mystery Words and Riddles calls for everyone in a large or small group to respond. It is suitable for first, second, and third graders.

Things You'll Need: As many mini-chalkboards as there are children in your classroom, chalk, old socks, a book with rhyming words. Mini-chalkboards are lap-size chalkboards that can be purchased in most teacher supply stores. Old socks make great erasers. Put a piece of chalk in the toe of each and store socks right along with the mini-chalkboards. This way children have an eraser (the sock) and chalk all rolled into one.

Figure 4–6 Writing and illustrating tongue twisters gives children opportunities to identify the onsets in words and to creatively use this knowledge.

Horribal Harry hits hippos on a hill on a happy holiday in Hairballville.

Exploration: Explain that children are to use clues to figure out mystery words. Demonstrate by writing two clue words on a large chalkboard in your room (**rice** and **bug,** perhaps). Then say something like, "The mystery word starts with the sound at the beginning of **rice** and rhymes with **bug.** What is the mystery word?" Show children how to add the onset from one word (the **r** in **rice**) to the rime from the other word (the **ug** in **bug**) to write the mystery word, **rug.** Introduce two or three other examples, encouraging children to solve the riddle on their own. Discuss how and why clues are used; encourage children to share how they discover mystery words from clues.

Guided Practice: Give each child a mini-chalkboard, a piece of chalk, and a cloth (old sock) to use as an eraser. Use the same procedure just described, only now ask children to write the mystery word on their own mini-chalkboards and hold up chalkboards when finished. Everyone in the group responds, which gives you valuable insight into how children use their knowledge of onsets and rimes. Relate practice to social studies, science, health, and mathematics vocabularies by using words from these content areas.

Transfer: Read a book written in rhyme like *Antarctic Antics* (Sierra, 1998). This book includes riddles in the text, which gives you the opportunity to explain that children are going to solve riddles just like the ones in *Antarctic Antics* and that children will use rime clues to find solutions. For example, you might make up riddles using **fish, wish, gliding,** and **sliding** (which are part of the rhyming language of the book) as cue and solution words:

I live in the water.
I have fins and gills.
Penguins eat me for dinner.
What am I?
Clue: wish

Penguins think this is fun.
They go very fast.
They do this on a glacier.
What is it?
Clue: gliding

To solve the first riddle, challenge children to think of a word that ends like **wish,** begins with a different sound and is a sensible solution. Erase the **w** from **wish** and write **f** in its place. To solve the second riddle, ask children to think of a solution that ends like **gliding.** Erase the **gl** and write **sl** to make **sliding.** Make up all sorts of riddles using the words on the bulletin boards and wall charts in your classroom. Once children are familiar with solving riddles, many will enjoy creating their own riddles and sharing them with their classmates.

Rime Find

The focus in this lesson is on recognizing the rime in words that appear in the books children read during shared or guided reading. It is appropriate for first and second graders, and struggling third graders, and is best when taught to small groups.

Things You'll Need: Books with words that share rimes, a large piece of tagboard cut into a circle to make a beginning letter wheel, a brad, a marker, a large piece of chart paper, sticky paper, cards with words that have often-used rimes on them. To make a beginning letter wheel, which is used in the practice portion of this lesson, cut a piece of tagboard into a circle, divide the circle into three to six sections, and write an onset in each. Then make a "pointer" out of tagboard and use a brad to fasten it to the center of the wheel.

Exploration: Write a rime on the chalkboard, **ook** for example, and explain that this rime is part of many different words. Demonstrate how to add an onset to the **ook** rime to make a word like **cook.** Write a list of consonants (onsets) that might be combined with **ook,** making sure to include a few that do not make a real word. For example, you might write, **t, b, l, h,** and **m.** Then ask children to think of words that can be made by combining the beginning consonants with **ook** to make a real word, such as **took, book, look, hook** and so forth. Make a list of words with **ook** and ask everyone to read it in chorus while you point to each word. For combinations that do not make real words, such as **mook,** pronounce the nonsense word and have children determine that it is not a real word. I have found that children get lots of practice this way and enjoy figuring out which are real words and which are not.

Guided Practice: Show children the beginning sound wheel and review the sound each onset represents, in this example the wheel might have the letters **f, s, m, t, l,** and **d.** Then write a rime on the chalkboard, perhaps **old.** Explain that you are going to spin the pointer (or ask a child to spin the pointer). When it lands on a beginning letter, children are to look at the rime on the chalkboard to see if it can be combined with the beginning sound to make a real word. Children then say (or write) the onset-rime combination. Ask children if the combination makes a real word. If so, write the word on the chalkboard. Once all the beginning letters on the wheel have been tried, write another rime, **ip** for instance, on the chalkboard and begin again. Do this for several rimes. In this example, real word combinations consist of **fold, sold, mold, told, sip, tip, lip,** and **dip.**

Transfer: Read a book with lots of rhyming words, such as *Just Open a Book* (Hallinan, 1995). At the top of a very large piece of chart paper, write the title and author. Below and to the far left, write short sentences (or phrases) from the book that contain a word with an often-used rime. Leave plenty of blank space to the right of each sentence (or phrase). For example, you might write several sentences and phrases from *Just Open a Book,* such as **You can go to the moon.** (page 4) and **on an old pirate ship** (page 2). Read each sentence (or phrase) and discuss the often-used rime in a word (in this example, **moon** or **ship**). Challenge children to think of other words with the same rime and write the words in the blank space to the right of the sentence (or phrase) that contains the word. The finished product is a chart with several short sentences and phrases from *Just Open a Book,* plus many different words that share the same rimes. For variety, children might read the sentences (or phrases) and discuss the rime in words as a group activity. Then children might work individually or with a partner to think of words that share rime, write the words on sticky paper, and stick the words on the chart. After a day or two, gather the group together around the chart, read the words on the sticky paper, and talk about shared rime.

Predicting and Writing Rhyme

In this large or small group lesson, children predict words that share rimes in familiar poems, and, as a transfer activity, add new and creative endings to poems. Children of every age, from the youngest to the oldest, can predict words that share rimes (the rhyme) and add new endings to rhyming poems, provided that poems have been shared in class.

Things You'll Need: Pieces of sticky paper, familiar poems like traditional nursery rhymes, longtime favorites such as *Oh, A-Hunting We Will Go* (Langstaff, 1989), humorous poems such as those found in Sendak's *Chicken Soup with Rice* (1962), thoughtful and fanciful poems such as the ones in Silverstein's *Where the Sidewalk Ends* (1974), or poetry that tells a story such as *Everett Anderson's 1, 2, 3* (Clifton, 1977).

Exploration: Share poetry. Read poems, write them on wall charts, and have children read and reread them in chorus. Make lists of the words in poems that share rimes.

Guided Practice: Select a familiar poem and put it on a wall chart in your classroom. Use a sticky piece of paper to cover up a word that shares a rime with another word. For example, if the word **train** appears on one line and then the word **rain** appears in the next line or two, cover up **rain.** Ask children to read the poem aloud, and, when they come to the covered-up word, to predict the word under the paper. Once children make their prediction, take off the sticky paper to reveal the written word. Discuss spoken rhyme and written rime, point out words on wall charts and bulletin boards, and ask children to find rimes in books and poems.

Transfer: Challenge children to write their own versions of a familiar, favorite poem by adding a new ending.

For first and second graders, begin by writing a new ending as a whole-group activity. As the group writes, point out how to preserve the poet's sense of rhyme and rhythm. When the new ending is written, read the poem in chorus with the class, sweeping your hand under the words as they are read aloud. When children understand what they are to do, invite younger ones to create their own personal endings for the same poem that the group wrote an ending for. The endings in Figure 4–7 were written by first graders after their teacher shared the big book *Oh, A-Hunting We Will Go* (Langstaff, 1989). When finished, ask younger children to illustrate their work. Then ask them to read their poems with the new endings and to share their illustrations.

Third graders and up enjoy writing new endings (either individually or in groups) for poems that are their own personal favorites. For example, poems such as "The Toucan" in *Where the Sidewalk Ends,* (Silverstein, 1974), is particularly suited for older learners. Not only does "The Toucan" have an easy-to-follow rhyme and rhythm, but Silverstein literally invites learners to add to this poem. Have children illustrate the ending they write.

Once older children have written and illustrated endings for their personal favorites, ask them to trade their poems with a classmate. To do this, children give a classmate the original poem and the new ending they have written. (Tell children to hold on to the illustration they made for the ending; the illustration will be needed later.) Now, challenge classmates to read the original poem, to read their classmate's new version, and to illustrate the new ending. This way each new ending has two artistic interpretations: one made by the author of the new ending and one by a classmate. Now have children compare artistic interpretations, discuss the feelings poems convey, and contrast points of view as expressed in words and in pictures.

Figure 4–7 Writing new endings for familiar poems helps readers gain insight into words that share letter and sound patterns.

Figure 4–7   (*Continued*)

EASY-TO-DO AND EXTRA PRACTICE ACTIVITIES

Here are six easy-to-do activities and eight extra practice activities for children whose use the analogy strategy is limited by their lack of onset-rime knowledge. Once you have decided who will benefit from extra practice, you may want to create flexible skill groups. Dissolve the flexible skill groups when children demonstrate that they successfully and strategically use onsets and rimes.

Easy-to-Do Activities

Here are six easy-to-do extra practice activities that you and the children whom you teach will find enjoyable and beneficial. The activities require no special materials and little, if any, preparation on your part.

1. *Make Lists:* Challenge children to think of words that rhyme with food names, holidays, animals, community places, games, and toys. Make lists of these words and fasten them to walls, bulletin boards, and doors. For example, children might think of words that rhyme with **book,** such as **look, cook, hook, took, brook,** and **shook,** or words that rhyme with **school,** such as **stool, cool, pool, fool, spool,** and **tool.** Compare and contrast words; use words for writing, in games, and in poems.

2. *Celebrate Onsets:* Explore onsets with an old-fashioned celebration, an alliterative feast with all sorts of things that begin alike, such as popcorn, pizza, potatoes, pineapple, pretzels, and pie. Then write poems and stories about the experience, using lots of words with shared onsets.

3. *Alliterative Shopping Lists:* Create an alliterative shopping list of all sorts of things—real and imagined—that a store might sell. Make a game of it, saying "I went to the store and I found a **banana** to buy." Then ask each child to add something to the list that begins with the same letter and sound as **banana—basket, bread, book, balloon, bean.** Make a list on the chalkboard. Discuss onsets and the sounds they represent, and then invite children to create their own imaginative shopping lists.

4. *Personalized Onset and Rime Lists:* Support children as they make their own personalized lists of words with shared onsets or rimes. They can put the lists in folders to be used as references for all sorts of reading and writing occasions.

5. *Class Roll:* Use children's names to develop a knowledge of onsets. Say something like, "I am thinking of someone in our class whose name begins with the same sounds as **bug** and **bear.** Who is it?" When children say, **Bobby,** ask them what letter **Bobby** begins with. Write the upper and lower case letter on the chalkboard. Use this activity, or your own personal adaptation of it, to line up children for lunch, for recess, or to go home at the end of the school day.

6. *Onset Houses:* Write a word on the chalkboard, draw a rectangle around it, and say something like, "Today, we are going to build a house of bricks. Each brick has a word inside. I will draw the first brick; it has **big** written in it." Then draw another brick, explaining that this empty brick needs a word inside, too. Ask, "Who can think of another word that begins like **big** and is spelled with a **b**?" Encourage children to find words in the room that begin with **b.** The child who finds (or thinks of) a word on a wall chart or bulletin board, such as **baby,** comes to the chalkboard and writes that word inside the brick. Continue building until the house is complete. For variety, put the bricks in different arrangements; for example, an igloo, a log cabin, a teepee, a fanciful castle, a strong fort.

Extra Practice Activities
 ### Egg Words

This is a matching activity where children put together two halves of colorful plastic eggs—one half with an onset written on it and the other with a rime. This activity is most suitable for first graders who have some experience reading. It is a good activity for centers and is best done when children work individually.

Things You'll Need: Many colorful plastic eggs, a permanent marker. To make egg words, write an onset on one half of a colorful plastic egg and a rime on the other half. Make matching easy by writing the onset and rime for a word on the same color egg halves; more difficult by mixing colors. Keep the eggs in a basket when they are not being used.

Practice: Egg words are formed when two halves of plastic eggs, each with an onset and a rime written on them, are locked together. To build egg words, children put together two halves of colored plastic eggs that have a rime and an onset (Figure 4–8). Put the eggs into a basket, separate them into halves, scramble the halves, and then challenge children to put egg words together.

Figure 4–8
Children build words by putting the halves of plastic eggs with onsets on them together with the halves that have rimes written on them.

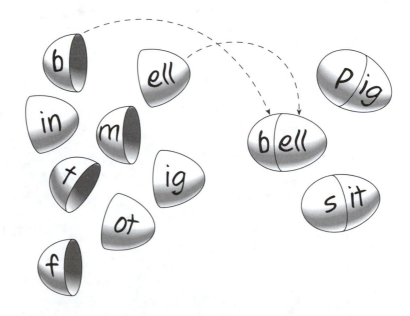

Word Chains

In this activity, first graders make brightly colored paper chains with words that either have the same onset or the same rime, depending on which aspect of print (onsets or rimes) you wish to emphasize. And, of course, such a large undertaking is a project that is best accomplished by groups working together cooperatively.

Things You'll Need: Many colorful pieces of construction paper cut into strips about an inch wide, markers, tape or a stapler.

Practice: Explain that children are to make a chain by writing words that begin alike (or words that end with the same letter pattern) on construction paper strips. Tape or staple the ends of strips into a circle, linking the circles with one another to form a giant chain that makes an engaging display. Of course, the more words children write, the longer the chain, so there is great incentive for them to think of a lot of words to make the chain as impressive as possible. Before you hang chains, make a wall chart list of words and count the number of words children chain together. Drape chains over bulletin boards; hang them from one corner of the ceiling to the other; tape them to desks, windows, and walls.

Rime (or Onset) Pick-Up

In this game-like extra practice activity, children pick up sticks—either the kind found in popsicles or used as tongue depressors—with rimes on them, think of a beginning sound, and then say the word. This center activity is best when two or three children play together.

Things You'll Need: Many sticks with rimes written on them. Using a permanent marker, write often-used rimes on sticks (Figure 4–9). Purchase sticks by the box

Figure 4–9
Children get lots of practice thinking of the recurring rime in words when they pick up craft sticks with rimes written on them and then think of a beginning sound to make a word.

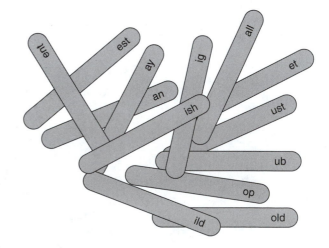

in the craft section of a variety store or buy tongue depressors. Look in Appendix A for rimes and use rimes that make many different words (identified by an asterisk), as well as other rimes children read in storybooks. Sometimes I write the same rime on several different sticks to give children practice making more than one word with the same rime. (**Note:** Turn this into a game of Onset Pick-Up by writing beginning letters on the sticks rather than rimes.)

Practice: Scatter sticks on a table or floor. Explain that each stick has a rime (or onset) on it. Taking turns, children pick up a stick, read the rime, and think of a beginning sound to make a word. If the beginning sound and rime together make a word, the child puts the stick in his or her own personal pile. Each stick is worth one point. The player who gets the most sticks (the most points) wins. Sometimes I ask players to write the words they make so as to give them practice seeing the words from the game and to help me check to make sure that players are making real words, not nonsense words.

Rime Tic-Tac-Toe

This old standby is played much like the original version of the game, except words sharing rimes are used instead of **X**s and **O**s. It is useful for children who are in the first grade and up.

Things You'll Need: Laminated Tic-Tac-Toe playing cards made of tagboard or heavy paper, erasable markers. To make tic-tac-toe cards, draw the traditional nine-box design on tagboard or heavy paper (Figure 4–10). Above the design, write two words with different onsets or two words with different rimes, such as **sat** and **ran**. Underline the onset or the rime in each word (**sat, ran**). Laminate cards and ask players to use erasable markers when they play. This way the same cards may be used many times.

Practice: Any child who knows how to play Tic-Tac-Toe needs only cursory guidance to use this practice and reinforcement activity. Two children play; each writes a word with the same rime (or onset) as that at the top of the playing card (Figure 4–10). The traditional rules hold—any three words joined in a horizontal, vertical, or diagonal direction win. **Note:** This game can be used for letter-sounds (Chapter

Figure 4–10   Tic-Tac-Toe challenges children to think of words that share the same rime. This activity can also be adapted for words that have specific letter-sound associations, such as short or long vowels or r-controlled vowels, and meaningful chunks, like prefixes and suffixes.

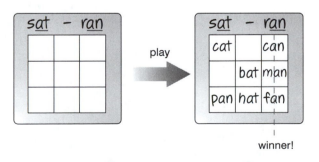

5), prefixes (Chapter 6), or suffixes (Chapter 6) by writing two words with different letter-sounds, prefixes, or suffixes at the top of the Tic-Tac-Toe cards.

 ## Onset-Rime Tachistoscopes

A tachistoscope is a device through which a strip of tagboard is drawn to reveal one word at a time. Tachistoscopes challenge children to read words made of different combinations of onsets and rimes. They are suitable for children of any age and are particularly helpful for children who need to practice substituting one onset for another.

Things You'll Need: Several tachistoscopes, as shown in Figure 4–11. While tachistoscopes can be purchased, they are extremely easy to make. To make a tachistoscope, write onsets on a strip of tagboard. Then cut a medium-size shape out of tagboard to serve as the body of the tachistoscope. Use all sorts of shapes—airplanes, panda bears, ice cream cones, telephones, cereal boxes, valentines, the sky's the limit. Next write a rime on the tachistoscope and cut a window (two horizontal slits) beside the rime. Make the window large enough so that the strip with onsets can be threaded through. When the strip is pulled through the tachistoscope, different words are formed.

Practice: Show children (1) how to thread the tagboard strip through the slits that form the window on the body of the tachistoscope and (2) how to line up onsets with rimes so as to form words. Tachistoscopes are used for individual practice,

Figure 4–11
Tachistoscopes give children practice identifying words that are formed when different onsets are combined with the same rime.

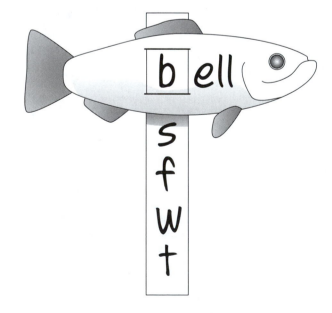

which means they fit nicely into learning centers. Ask children to write the words they make, and use the words in the Building Words with Onset and Rime Tiles activity described earlier.

Rime (or Onset) Train

To ride the rime train, children make their own tickets by writing words with rime on cards and then putting the cards inside train cars that have the same rime written on them. This gives children practice noticing the rime in words, finding rime in print and writing words with a common rime. **Note:** Focus on onsets by writing them on the envelopes fastened to train cars.

Things You'll Need: Four to six large envelopes with a rime (or an onset) written on each, a colorful train engine and cars, unlined index cards, and pencils. To make the rime train, cut colorful construction paper into an engine, cars, and a caboose. Staple a large envelope, flap side out, to each car. Fasten everything to a bulletin board, making sure the train is low enough for children to open envelope flaps to put word cards inside, as shown in Figure 4–12.

Practice: Explain that this riming train has many different cars, each with a special rime. To ride the riming train, children make their own tickets by writing on an index card a word with the same rime as they see on a train car and then putting it inside the car. Demonstrate how to lift the flap on an envelope to put a ticket (card) inside. Ask children to write their name on each ticket (card) so you know who rides the train (who contributes words). When the train is ready to leave the station, take out the tickets (cards), read the words, discuss the rimes, and return tickets to their makers so children can take them home to share.

Muffin Tin Words

This is a particularly good activity for learning centers and yields a permanent record of the words children build.

Things You'll Need: A muffin tin, onset-rime tiles, muffin word guides. Look for old muffin tins at yard sales and secondhand shops. Put an assortment of onset and rime tiles in each compartment of the muffin tin. Tape a small label above each

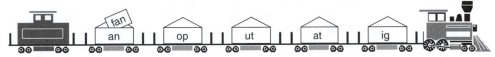

Figure 4–12   Getting on board this train calls for writing words with rimes and putting them inside the proper car. When the train leaves the station, all the cards are read and returned to the children, who then take them home for additional practice.

Figure 4–13 The muffin word guide that children fill in when they combine onset tiles with rime tiles placed in a muffin tin is a permanent record of the words that children build.

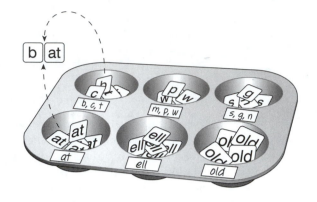

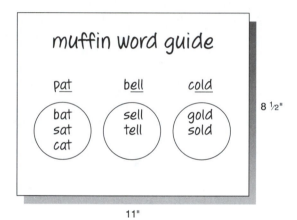

compartment to tell which onset or rime tile is inside. To make a paper guide for muffin words (Figure 4–13), draw several circles on a sheet of blank paper to simulate a row on a muffin tin. Then write a word above the simulated muffins. Underline a rime or an onset in the word. Children then build words that share the underlined onset or rime, and write the words in the "muffins."

Practice: Explain that the muffin tin has small labels that tell which onset-rime tiles are inside each compartment. Give children a muffin word guide, which has sample words with underlined onsets or rimes and several blank muffin circles underneath them (Figure 4–13). Children read the underlined words on the guide sheet and use onset-rime tiles to build other words that share the same onset or rime. As they build words with onset-rime tiles, children write words in the blank "muffin" circles under each underlined word. Ask children to count how many words they build. If they build more words than fit in the blank muffins on the guide, ask them to write the extra words underneath the muffins. Have the children add the words they build to their personal word lists.

✸ *Fish for Onsets*

This is a version of the fishing game in which children fish for words in a bucket "pond" and read the words they catch. Rather than simply reading words, as is the procedure in the traditional version, children substitute one onset for another in order to figure out words. Fish for Onsets is suitable for small groups of first graders and second graders who need extra help learning how to exchange onsets.

Things You'll Need: A plastic bucket to serve as a pond, a pole (a ruler works well), string, paper clips, a magnet, fish made of laminated construction paper, a marker. To make the fishing pole, tie a string to a ruler and fasten a small magnet to the end of the string. To make the fish, cut colored construction paper into fish shapes. Write a word on one side of each fish—the word **band** for instance. On the other side, write an onset that creates a word when substituted for the beginning letter in the word on the reverse. For example, you might write an **s** because it makes the word **sand** when substituted for the **b** in **band.** Last, fasten a large paper clip to each fish and dump all the fish in the pond (the plastic bucket).

Practice: Explain that children are going on a fishing trip. Each fish has a word on one side and an onset (beginning letter[s]) on the other. When children catch a fish, they are to read the word on one side and exchange the beginning sound written on the reverse side (Figure 4–14). If the child who is fishing correctly figures

Figure 4–14
Children exchange one beginning sound (onset) for another to discover the words they catch in a "pond" made from a bucket or pail.

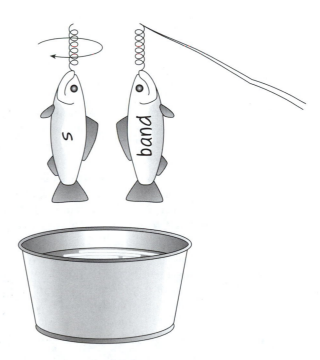

out the word, that fish is removed from the pond. If the word is not correctly identified, the fish is thrown back into the pond for another try later in the game.

To demonstrate, ask a child to catch a fish and then to read the word on one side—**band,** for example. Then show everyone the onset **s** written on the reverse side. Write the word **band** and the onset **s** on the chalkboard. Erase the **b** and replace it with **s** saying, "What new word is made when we take off the **b** and put the **s** in its place?" Repeat several times. Once children understand how to play Fish for Onsets, continue by having one child at a time be the "fisher." As each fish is caught, ask the children who are not fishing to write the word on a sheet of paper, and to hold up the word as soon as they figure it out. Not only is this a good quick check to see who can and who cannot substitute beginning consonant onsets, but it also gets everyone involved in an active way.

USING ONSETS, RIMES, AND LETTER-SOUND ASSOCIATIONS

The number of words children can identify with the analogy strategy using onsets and rimes is limited (1) by the onsets and rimes children remember in words, and (2) by the frequency with which rimes occur in often-read words. For example, if children do not have a word spelled with **ent** in their reading vocabulary, such as **went,** then the analogy strategy is useless for identifying **tent.** As a consequence, children need a reasonably large pool of words in memory from which to make comparisons. With a decent size pool of remembered words, children have a firm basis for making analogies between familiar and unfamiliar words. The more words with varied rimes children have in their reading vocabularies, the more useful the analogy strategy.

As already explained, readers who use the analogy strategy do not have to look inside rimes to figure out the sounds letters represent (they do not have to know the sound the **a** represents in **at** and **ack,** for instance). Some readers seem to gain insight into vowel and consonant letter-sound associations by learning rimes (Peterson & Haines, 1998). However, not all readers do this, perhaps because teaching rimes does not include teaching the letter-sound associations inside rimes. Should readers consider only intact rimes, they may not think carefully about the letter-sound structure of our alphabetic writing system. This may explain why beginning readers who use rimes to make analogies are less proficient at decoding than their classmates who consider letter-sounds (Bruck & Treiman, 1992). As a consequence, overemphasis on the analogy strategy with onsets and rimes may well result in readers who have limited insight into the letter-sound associations within rimes. These readers may be hampered in their attempts to identify unfamiliar words, since they may not be able to make sense of unknown words that do not have overlapping onsets and rimes. Consequently, a combination of experiences with *both* rimes and letter-sounds holds the most promise for developing word fluency.

Finally, though the analogy strategy with onsets and rimes is a helpful and productive tool for children to use to identify unfamiliar words, it is not entirely suited to unlocking the complete range of words in our alphabetic writing system. Our alphabet is basically a written map for the sounds in words, not the rimes or syllables in words. Anyone who reads and writes a language written in an alphabet must understand how letters represent sounds. Since children develop the analogy strategy and the letter-sound strategy about the same time, and since both are beneficial, I recommend that you use the activities in this chapter to increase children's strategic use of onsets and rimes, and the activities in Chapter 5 to increase their strategic use of letter-sound combinations. After all, word identification is more than one strategy. It is a whole collection of different strategies; the more strategies readers have at their fingertips, the better.

REFERENCES

Atwood, M. (1995). *Princess Prunella and the purple peanut.* New York: Workman Publishing.

Base, G. (1987). *Animalia.* New York: Henry N. Abrams.

Bowey, J. A. (1990). Orthographic onsets and rimes as functional units of reading. *Memory and Cognition, 18,* 419–427.

Bruck, M., & Treiman, R. (1992). Learning to pronounce words: The limitations of analogies. *Reading Research Quarterly, 4,* 374–388.

Cheek, E. H., Flippo, R. F., & Lindsey, J. D. (1997). *Reading for success in elementary schools.* Dubuque, IA: Brown & Benchmark.

Clifton, L. (1977). *Everett Anderson's 1, 2, 3.* New York: Henry Holt & Company.

Fry, E. (1998). The most common phonograms. *The Reading Teacher, 51,* 620–622.

Goswami, U. (1997). Rime-based coding in early reading development in English: Orthographic analogies and rime neighborhoods. In C. Hulme & R. M. Joshi (Eds.), *Reading and spelling: Development and disorders* (pp. 69–86). Mahwah, NJ: Lawrence Erlbaum.

Goswami, U. (1998). The role of analogies in the development of word recognition. In J. L. Metsala & L. C. Ehri (Eds.), *Word recognition in beginning literacy* (pp. 41–63). Mahwah, NJ: Lawrence Erlbaum.

Hallinan, P. K. (1995). *Just open a book.* Nashville, TN: Ideals Children's Books.

Keller, C. (1989). *Tongue twisters.* New York: Simon & Schuster.

Kellogg, S. (1992). *Aster Aardvark's alphabet adventure.* New York: William Morrow.

Langstaff, J. (1989). *Oh, a-hunting we will go.* Boston: Houghton Mifflin.

Merrill Linguistic Reading Program, Fourth Edition. Columbus, OH: Merrill.

Peterson, M. E., & Haines, L. P. (1998). Orthographic analogy training with kindergarten children: Effects on analogy use, phonemic segmentation, and letter-sound knowledge. In C. Weaver (Ed.), *Reconsidering a balanced approach to reading* (pp. 159–179). Urbana, IL: National Council of Teachers of English.

Programmed Reading, Third Edition (1994). New York: Phoenix Learning Resources.

Rosenbloom, J. (1986). *World's toughest tongue twisters.* New York: Sterling Publishing.

Sendak, M. (1962). *Chicken soup with rice.* New York: Scholastic.

Sierra, J. (1998). *Antarctic antics: A book of penguin poems.* NY: Gulliver Books.

Silverstein, S. (1974). *Where the sidewalk ends.* New York: Harper Collins.

CHAPTER 5

The Letter-Sound Strategy

Identifying Words by Their Letters and Sounds

This chapter explains the letter-sound strategy. Here you will learn how readers use the letter-sound strategy, the letter-sound relationships of phonics, why the left-to-right sequencing of letters in words is important for word identification, why grouping letters into neighborhoods is important, and ways to support readers as they use this strategy.

KEY IDEAS

➤ Letters that routinely appear right next to one another in words and signal pronunciation make up a neighborhood. Our alphabetic writing system has many different letter neighborhoods.

➤ Readers who use the letter-sound strategy associate sounds with the letters in neighborhoods and then blend sounds together to pronounce words that make sense in reading contexts.

➤ Letter neighborhoods can be grouped into three categories: those that are less challenging, more challenging, and most challenging.

Unlike the turtles in Wen Ting's drawing (Figure 5–1), the alphabet is not a jumble of topsy-turvy letter-sound combinations. Readers do not tumble aimlessly as they learn about our alphabetic writing system, nor do they stand on their heads to use letter-sound combinations to unlock the pronunciation of unfamiliar words. For readers who do not automatically recognize **topsy, turvy,** and **turtles,** the letter-sound strategy is a quick and sure route to pronunciation. Readers who use the letter-sound strategy take advantage of the most basic units of our alphabetic writing system—the letters of the alphabet and the sounds they represent.

Figure 5–1 Unlike the jumbled turtles in Wen Ting's drawing, letters represent sounds in predictable ways and are, therefore, a useful pathway to word identification.

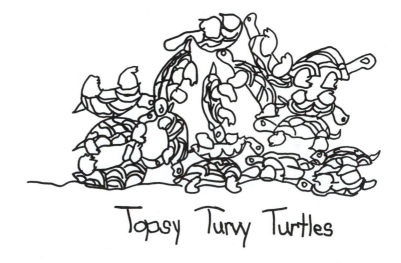

LETTERS AND THEIR NEIGHBORS

The twenty-six letters in our alphabet are a hardworking bunch. The same small group of twenty-six is systematically arranged, rearranged, and sequenced to build literally tens of thousands of words. With all this arranging and sequencing, it is inevitable that certain letters routinely appear right next to one another in spelling. This creates a type of spelling context—a neighborhood—in which certain letters are frequently and predictably the neighbors of other letters. With many fewer letters (only twenty-six) than sounds (as many as forty-three or so), English spelling contains a host of letter neighborhoods that signal pronunciation.

Letter-sound neighborhoods are pronounceable letter sequences that represent one or more sounds in words, such as the **s** in <u>s</u>at, the **sh** in <u>sh</u>aft and the **ow** in c<u>ow</u>. The way letters are sequenced from left-to-right in neighborhoods affects the sounds they represent in words. For example, the letter **a** represents one pronunciation when followed by a consonant and an **e** in the word **bl<u>ade</u>** (the vowel-consonant-e long vowel neighborhood, or **VCe** for short), another pronunciation when followed by one or more consonants in **c<u>at</u>** and **sh<u>aft</u>** (a vowel-consonant neighborhood, described as the **VC** short vowel neighborhood), yet another pronunciation when preceded by the letter **o** in c<u>oat</u> and t<u>oast</u> (a vowel-vowel neighborhood, expressed as the **VV** long vowel neighborhood), and still another when followed by an **r** in c<u>art</u> and f<u>arm</u> (an **r-controlled** neighborhood, or **Vr** for short). Table 5–1 summarizes the letter neighborhoods; Appendix B gives detailed explanations and lists of words that include neighborhoods.

Once readers understand the sounds represented by the letters in neighborhoods, they can use this information to pronounce any word that is spelled like it sounds. For example, readers may generalize their knowledge of the **VC** short vowel neighborhood to identify the short vowel sounds in **clasp, bet, lift, stop,** and **luck.** Though the underlined vowels and consonants are different, all of them form a **VC** short vowel neighborhood. It is the neighborhood—the vowel-consonant (**VC**) sequence—that signals the sounds these five different vowels represent. The letters in neighborhoods signal pronunciation at the letter and sound level, which is the same level used by our English alphabet to connect speech with print. Consequently, a small amount of letter neighborhood knowledge, in this example the **VC** short vowel neighborhood, is generalizable and transferable to a great many different letter combinations in words.

Because there is almost always more than one way to group the letters in an unfamiliar word, readers must consider which left-to-right letter sequences form pronounceable neighborhoods and which do not. For example, readers know that **sta** forms a pronounceable **CV** long vowel neighborhood in **stable.** They also know that this same sequence (**sta**) does not constitute a neighborhood in **stamp** because the **a** belongs to the **VC** short vowel neighborhood (**amp**). As children gain reading experience, they become sensitive to the letter neighborhoods that recur in many different words. Sensitivity increases as readers move up in the elementary

TABLE 5–1 *Summary of Letter Neighborhoods*	
Consonant Neighborhoods	**Examples**
Single Consonant Usually represents the sounds associated with the underlined letters in the examples.	boat, cat or city, dot, fish, game or gem, hat, jet, kite, lamp, monkey, nut, pan, queen, rain, seal, toad, valentine, wag, fox, yell, zoo
Twin (Double) Consonant Generally represents the same sound as the single consonant neighborhood.	rabbit, riddle, raffle, wiggle, hammer, mitten
Consonant Blend Sounds that are blended together when pronounced.	black, clam, flag, glad, place, sleep, brave, crab, drag, fry, grape, prize, train, scale, skate, small, snack, space, stone, swim, twig, scrap, splash, sprain, squirrel, strap, chrome, school, three
Consonant Digraph Two or more letters that represent a sound different from the sounds letters represent individually.	chair, phone, shade, thank, then, wheat, catch
Qu Represents **"kw"** as an onset and in the middle of some words, and **"k"** when it is a final sound.	queen, frequent, antique
S as a Next-Door Neighbor As an onset, **s** represents **"s."** In the middle or at the end of words, **s** represents either **"s"** or **"z."**	Onset **"s"** in sack and save Middle **"s"** in person and tassel Middle **"z"** in resent and closet End **"s"** in toss and bus End **"z"** in close and dresses
***C* or g plus a, o, and u** **Ca, co,** and **cu** usually represent **"k."** **Ga, go,** and **gu** usually represent **"g."**	**"k"** in camel, color, and Cuba **"g"** in game, got, and gum
***C* or g plus e, i, and y** **Ce, ci,** and **cy** generally represent **"s."** **Ge, gi,** and **gy** generally represent **"j"** as in jelly.	**"s"** in cedar, city, cypress **"j"** in gem, gist, energy

[1]Look at Appendix D for more detailed explanations and examples.

TABLE 5–1 *Continued*	
Vowel Neighborhoods	**Examples**
VC Short Vowel Vowels generally represent the short sound when the following next-door neighbor is a consonant.	m<u>an</u>, p<u>eg</u>, m<u>ix</u>, j<u>ob</u>, g<u>um</u>
A consonant neighborhood before the vowel forms a CVC (**cat**), CCVC (**brat**), CVCC (**back**), CCVCC (**black**), or CCVCCC (**stitch**) sequence and does not affect the sound the vowel in the VC neighborhood represents.	l<u>ast</u>, b<u>ent</u>, r<u>ock</u>, d<u>ust</u>, m<u>yth</u>, w<u>inch</u>, bl<u>end</u>, spl<u>it</u>, sl<u>ick</u>, m<u>ess</u>, d<u>epth</u>, thr<u>ust</u>
VCe Long Vowel A vowel with a consonant and a final **e** as next-door neighbors usually represents a long sound and the **e** is silent. A consonant neighborhood before the vowel forms a CVCe (**save**) or CCVCe (**slave**) sequence, and does not affect the sound the vowel in the VCe neighborhood represents.	s<u>ave</u>, th<u>eme</u>, d<u>ime</u>, b<u>one</u>, c<u>ube</u>, t<u>ype</u>
VCCe Short Vowel A vowel with two consonants and a final **e** as next-door neighbors usually represents the short sound and the **e** is silent. A consonant neighborhood before the vowel forms a CVCCe (**dance**) or a CCVCCe (**prance**) sequence and does not affect the sound the vowel in the VCCe neighborhood represents.	d<u>ance</u>, b<u>adge</u>, ch<u>ance</u>, inv<u>olve</u>, br<u>onze</u>, d<u>ense</u>, h<u>inge</u>, imp<u>ulse</u>, s<u>ince</u>, w<u>edge</u>, f<u>udge</u>

(Continued)

grades (Juel, 1983) and is significantly related to reading ability (Massaro & Hestand, 1983). And so, the more opportunities children have to strategically use letter neighborhoods as they read and write, the more children will know about the manner in which the letters in neighborhoods represent sound.

UNLOCKING PRONUNCIATION WITH THE LETTER-SOUND STRATEGY

Children who use the letter-sound strategy have the full strength and power of the alphabet at their fingertips. Thanks to their constant self-monitoring with the cross-

TABLE 5–1 *Continued*

Vowel Neighborhoods	Examples
VV Long Vowel In the combinations of **ai, oa, ay, ee, ey,** and **ea,** the first vowel generally represents a long sound and the second vowel is silent.	ch<u>ai</u>n, fl<u>oa</u>t, cl<u>ay</u>, b<u>ee</u>f, hon<u>ey</u>, b<u>ea</u>ch
Double oo Usually represents sounds heard in **cool** or **cook**	f<u>oo</u>d, m<u>oo</u>n, sh<u>oo</u>k, st<u>oo</u>d
Vowel Diphthongs **Ow** and **ou** often represent the sounds heard in **cow** and **out**, while **oi** and **oy** represent the sounds heard in **oil** and **boy**.	br<u>ow</u>n, d<u>ow</u>n, cl<u>ou</u>d, l<u>ou</u>d, c<u>oi</u>n, s<u>oi</u>l, dec<u>oy</u>, t<u>oy</u>
Vr **R** affects pronunciation so that vowels cannot be classified as short or long.	<u>ar</u>m, f<u>er</u>n, sh<u>ir</u>t, c<u>or</u>n, b<u>ur</u>n
CV The vowel may represent the long sound.	l<u>a</u>ter, b<u>e</u>long, p<u>i</u>lot, banj<u>o</u>, b<u>u</u>gle, cr<u>a</u>zy, pr<u>e</u>dict, ch<u>i</u>na, pr<u>o</u>gram, br<u>u</u>tal
Y When **y** is the only vowel in a final syllable, it generally represents the long **e** sound.	Final syllable: cand<u>y</u>, tin<u>y</u>, bab<u>y</u>, lad<u>y</u>
When **y** is the only vowel in a word, it generally represents the long **i** sound.	Only vowel: sk<u>y</u>, fl<u>y</u>, m<u>y</u>, tr<u>y</u>
Au and Aw Usually represent the sound in **fault** and **straw**.	h<u>au</u>l, exh<u>au</u>st, l<u>aw</u>n, j<u>aw</u>
Ew and Ue Usually represent the sound in **blew** and **blue**.	ch<u>ew</u>, gr<u>ew</u>, tr<u>ue</u>, val<u>ue</u>

[2]V = vowel, C = consonant

checking strategy, the words readers identify and pronounce are both understandable and contextually sensible. However, using the letter-sound strategy requires a sizable amount of mental attention, phonemic awareness, and letter neighborhood knowledge. Like so many things in life, the extra time and energy invested in something worthwhile is more than offset by the rewards. One reward is that readers can identify a large number of written words with a relatively small amount of letter-sound knowledge. This, in turn, helps children build large fluent reading vocabularies and become independent readers. And, of course, as a pathway to the identification of a large number of unfamiliar words, the letter-sound strategy supports the comprehension of increasingly more challenging text.

What Readers Know about Phonemic Awareness

Children who use the letter-sound strategy are skilled at (1) separating words into individual sounds and (2) blending individual sounds together to form spoken words. Readers use their well-developed phonemic awareness to separate words into sounds and delete sounds from words. Whereas phoneme segmentation is a good predictor of reading ability, awareness of onsets and rimes is not (Nation & Hulme, 1997). This makes sense when we consider that our English alphabetic writing system requires that readers manipulate the sounds in words—not the rime—while decoding. These same readers take it for granted that blended sounds form sensible words. Accordingly, they are perpetually on the lookout for meaning as they blend, are quick to discover when a group of blended sounds is gibberish, and do not tolerate the creation of meaningless mumbo jumbo.

What Readers Know about the Letter-Sound Neighborhoods

Children know that letters represent sounds, and they have teachers who make sure they develop in-depth knowledge of letter-sound relationships (Adams, 1990; Scanlon & Vellutino, 1997; Snow, Burns, & Griffin, 1998). While readers may not be able to re-cite the "rules" of phonics word-for-word, they have a mental representation—a mental image—of the way the letters in neighborhoods are sequenced in the words in their fluent reading vocabularies. Their in-depth knowledge of letter-sound neighborhoods gives them a powerful resource which, when combined with the cross-checking strategy, enables them to pronounce any word that is spelled like it sounds.

What Readers Do with Their Knowledge

Suppose that Leslie comes across the word **shaft** in the sentence **A shaft of moonlight fell across the rabbit's cage and spilled onto the floor below,** as she reads Deborah and James Howe's tale of a vampire rabbit named *Bunnicula* (1979, p. 20). Leslie uses the letter-sound associations of our English alphabetic writing system just exactly the way they are intended, as a sound-based representation of speech. In so doing, she reaps the full benefit of reading a language written in an alphabet, and here is how she does it:

1. Leslie groups the letters in **shaft** into pronounceable letter-sound neighborhoods. She recognizes that **s** and **h** (**sh**) belong in one neighborhood (the consonant digraph neighborhood) and that **a + f + t** is an example of the **VC** short vowel neighborhood.
2. Leslie then associates **sh** with **"sh"** and **a, f, t** with the sounds **"a" + "f" + "t."**
3. Now she blends **"sh" + "a" + "f" + "t"** to pronounce **"shaft."**
4. Last, Leslie cross-checks to make sure that **"shaft"** fits the reading context. She asks herself: Does **shaft** sound and look right? Does **shaft** make sense in

the passage? If the answers are yes, Leslie stops decoding and turns her full attention to *Bunnicula*, finishing the page and reading the rest of the chapter. If the answers are no, she returns to decoding.

Leslie's phonemic awareness is well-developed. Yet, readers do not have to be a segmenting and blending expert like Leslie in order to begin to use the letter-sound strategy. All readers need is just enough phonemic awareness to separate and blend the sounds in short words. Likewise, readers need just enough knowledge of letter-sound neighborhoods to associate sounds with the letters in short, uncomplicated words.

Sounding out a short word like **big,** which has only three sounds and a predictable **VC** short vowel neighborhood, is far less taxing than sounding out a long word like **insignificant,** which has thirteen sounds, many letter-sound neighborhoods, and five syllables. For this reason, it is quite possible, and indeed highly likely, that some children who have no difficulty whatsoever sounding out short words like **big** will have trouble using the letter-sound strategy to identify longer words like **insignificant.**

The letter-sound strategy Leslie used (as well as all other strategies explained in earlier chapters) works when, and only when, readers connect the meaning of printed words with the meaning of spoken words. In the example with Leslie, **shaft** is among the words she recognizes in conversation. So, as soon as Leslie pronounces **"shaft,"** she knows what it means. As Leslie connects the written word (**shaft**) with the meaning of a familiar spoken word (**"shaft"**), she adds a new word to her reading vocabulary. But what would happen if **shaft** was not among the words Leslie recognizes in everyday conversation?

If the words children sound out are not in their speaking vocabularies, sounding out will help with pronunciation, but not with meaning. So when you explore the letter-sound strategy (and previously described strategies) with children, make sure that the words they identify are already in their speaking or listening vocabularies. If you suspect that children do not know the meaning of the words they are to identify while reading, help them build enough background knowledge so as to add the words to their speaking vocabularies before they decode them.

Correcting Misidentifications

Readers who use the letter-sound strategy are experts at correcting their own misidentifications. Given the complexity of our English alphabetic system, there is no guarantee that the first try will always result in a meaningful word. If the sounds Leslie blends together do not make a sensible word, cross-checking brings the misidentification to light. She then draws on her considerable storehouse of letter-sound associations (and well-developed phonemic awareness) to fix mistakes and correct misidentifications. There are three ways Leslie might make a correction:

1. Reblend the same sounds, perhaps gliding sounds together more smoothly or changing the order of sounds, and then cross-checking for meaning.
2. Associate different sounds with the same letters and then reblend to form a new word that is cross-checked for meaning.

3. Redo the entire process—regroup letters into pronounceable letter-sound neighborhoods and associated sounds with the letters in neighborhoods, blend, and cross-check all over again.

The readers whom you teach are bound to prefer easier, less attention-demanding ways to correct misidentifications over energy-draining alternatives. So you will notice that successful word identifiers often try reblending as their first attempt to correct mistakes. Then, if reblending does not work, they may try different letter-sound combinations. Only when all else fails do readers typically redo the entire process of reidentifying letter-sound neighborhoods.

Readers may take minor mistakes in stride. Minor mistakes may not derail decoding because readers actively look for sensible connections between the words they recognize in everyday language and the words authors write. Accordingly, as readers cross-check, they find words in their speaking vocabularies that sound similar to minor decoding mispronunciations. When this happens, readers associate minor mispronunciations with real words that make sense in the reading context. Once plausible words are identified, readers automatically adjust mispronunciations so that the sounds in the words they decode match the words in their speaking vocabularies. The net effect is that slight letter-sound association mistakes and blending miscalculations do not require a lot of extra special effort to repair.

Interestingly, not all misidentifications interfere with comprehension, so not all misidentifications need correction. Readers have greater tolerance for misidentifications when they read a novel for pleasure than when they read a content subject textbook to learn new information. In this example, Leslie is reading *Bunnicula* for pleasure, so she is less concerned with absolute accuracy than when she reads a chapter in her science book to complete an assignment. As a consequence, the misidentifications Leslie chooses to ignore as she reads *Bunnicula* may well be, and in some cases absolutely ought to be, corrected if she were reading for technical information in a content subject.

STRICT AND LENIENT LETTER-SOUND NEIGHBORHOODS

Just as strict zoning codes limit the types of buildings developers are permitted to construct in certain areas of your community, so too do strict letter-sound neighborhoods limit the sounds readers associate with the letters in words. Readers place a lot of confidence in strict letter-sound neighborhoods because these neighborhoods offer few, if any, choice as to the sounds represented. For instance, the **sh** (a consonant digraph neighborhood) is completely restricted. **Sh** is pronounced **"sh"** in words like **shelf, trash, shepherd, admonish,** and **eggshell;** there are no other possibilities from which to choose. Under ideal conditions, every neighborhood would be completely restricted, and therefore readers could depend on the letter-sound associations in neighborhoods 100 percent of the time.

However, zoning codes, like letter-sound neighborhoods, are not always restrictive. When your city council or county commissioners pass lenient zoning codes, developers are free to build anything they desire. As a consequence, you cannot predict from one building to the next whether you will find a home, store, factory, hospital, or school. The same is true for letter-sound neighborhoods. Lenient neighborhoods put fewer restrictions on pronunciation than do strict neighborhoods. Because of this, readers have more than one pronunciation from which to choose. Not surprisingly, there are many more moderately lenient than strict neighborhoods. For example, **oo** is a moderately lenient neighborhood in that readers have two sounds to choose from—the sound heard in **moon** or the sound heard in **book.** The **ough** neighborhood is very lenient. Readers who come across this neighborhood have several different pronunciations to consider: The **ough** might sound as it does in **bough,** or **ough** might correspond to the sounds heard in **cough, though,** and **enough.** Toss in the letter **t** at the end—thus creating **ought**—and **though** becomes **thought!**

Strict letter-sound neighborhoods are easier to learn and easier to use than lenient neighborhoods because they limit the pronunciations readers need to remember and apply while identifying words. When readers come across strict neighborhoods in spelling, they do not have to think about several possible pronunciations. This makes decoding faster, more effective, and less attention consuming.

WHAT ABOUT PHONICS RULES?

If our writing system was a parcel of land, we could rezone it. Moderately lenient and very lenient neighborhoods could be made to be more restrictive and hence more predictable maps for sound. Since it has not proven to be feasible to revise our spelling system, researchers have put tremendous energy into finding out which letter sequences in spelling are dependable maps for pronunciation and which are not. In their quest, researchers have investigated forty-five different phonics rules that are supposed to describe the laws governing letter-sound relationships (Bailey, 1967; Clymer, 1963; Emans, 1967).

Take the rule that says, "A vowel in the middle of a one-syllable word represents the short sound." Let us think about this "rule," which is a way of explaining the **VC** short vowel neighborhood. We would agree that words like **tan** and **fed** are examples of the **VC** short vowel neighborhood and, coincidentally, follow the rule. Surprisingly, researchers find this rule to be relatively unreliable. In a sample of primary grade reading material, Clymer (1963) and Emans (1967) report the middle vowel rule applies only 62 and 73 percent of the time, respectively. Examining materials for grades one through six, Bailey (1967) reports that this rule is useful a mere 71 percent of the time.

Some of the examples these authors cite as exceptions to the middle vowel rule reflect a narrow interpretation of this "rule." Narrow interpretations make our alphabetic system seem more complicated than it really is. In this example, a narrow interpretation overlooks the fact that some vowels in the middle of one-syllable words do not reside in a **VC** short vowel neighborhood. Emans (1967) cites the word **hew** and Bailey (1967) the word **her** as examples of exceptions to the middle vowel rule. It is not reasonable to consider either word—**hew** or **her**—as an exception because the vowels in these words reside in two different neighborhoods: The sound represented by the **e** in **hew** resides in the **ew** neighborhood which is found in words like **jewel, chew,** and **threw** (as explained in Appendix B). The **e** in **her** is perfectly regular, too, for the **e** in this word resides in an **r-controlled** neighborhood (**Vr**), and so the sound it represents is characteristic of this neighborhood, as in **fern, germ, clerk,** and **berth** (as described in Appendix B).

Perhaps you are wondering whether you should teach children the "rules." Just because readers recite rules does not mean they know when and how to apply them. Children who memorize rules without connecting them to reading and writing may not be able to use them to support word identification or spelling. In fact, some children are quite skilled at reciting rules yet do not have the foggiest notion of how to use the rules they put so much effort into remembering. Some children learn to "parrot" rules—they recite the wording of rules but do not analyze the sequence of letters in written words and do not relate rules to the words they read and write. When rule-based knowledge is not connected to real words, children do not create images in their minds of the pronounceable letter sequences in words. Creating a strong and robust image in memory for the letter-sound neighborhoods in words is an absolute necessity, for this is one of the foundations upon which word fluency rests and is the bedrock for using the letter-sound strategy.

Rather than focus on the rules themselves, a more beneficial approach is to sensitize children to the way neighborhoods affect pronunciation and to ground neighborhoods in the spelling of words children encounter as they read and write. Does this mean that you should never say a rule? Of course not. I have found that it is sometimes quite helpful to tell children about a rule, especially when children need some clarification. In fact, explaining a rule from time to time can speed learning along, provided that the rule is used to help children understand the relationship of letter sequences to sound and that the rule is solidly related to the words children read and spell. Encourage children to analyze left-to-right letter sequences and how these sequences affect letter-sound relationships. As a result, children will learn how letter sequences form neighborhoods, develop mental images of how neighborhoods look and sound in real words, and create mental pictures of words in which neighborhoods appear. This, in turn, contributes to automatic word recognition and supports the development of a large fluent reading vocabulary.

THE ALPHABETIC PHASE OF MOVEMENT TOWARD WORD FLUENCY AND THE PHONETIC PHASE OF SPELLING

Children who understand how letters represent sounds and who use this knowledge to identify unfamiliar words are in the **alphabetic** phase of movement toward word fluency (Ehri, 1998). Whereas children in the partial alphabetic phase look mainly at beginning and ending letters, children in the alphabetic phase analyze all the letter-sound relationships in words. As a consequence, these children can identify any word that is spelled the way it sounds.

Children enter into the alphabetic phase toward the end of kindergarten or, more typically, the beginning of first grade. The children in your classroom who have reached the alphabetic phase have good phonemic awareness. They can tell you the number of sounds in spoken words and can blend multisound sequences into recognizable words. They understand how the consonants and vowels in letter neighborhoods represent sound, and they use this knowledge to unlock the pronunciation of words that are not already in their fluent reading vocabularies. Children with good phonemic awareness and an understanding of letter-sound neighborhoods learn words faster than other children (Stuart, 1995). Hence, it is not at all surprising that children at the alphabetic phase are independent readers whose fluent vocabularies are growing by leaps and bounds. Because they can identify unfamiliar words on their own, their reading level increases even when they are out of school on summer vacation, provided, of course, that they read over the summer break. These children learn many, many words, and they learn most of them on their own. This is, of course, one of the ways the alphabet is intended to assist beginning readers.

IMPLICATIONS FOR TEACHING

Awareness of the single consonant letter-sound neighborhood emerges early, as we see in the note Roger taped to the gerbil cage in his first-grade classroom (Figure 5–2). Roger, who is just beginning to make the transition into the alphabetic phase, wrote this note to tell his classmates about the feisty habits of the resident pet, Biscuit. Roger's warning reads: "Biscuit Bites. Don't bother Biscuit because he bites." Roger uses invented spelling when he writes. That is, he spells words the way he hears them rather than the way letters are conventionally sequenced. He begins words with single consonants and ends words with consonant letters, too. Roger even includes consonants in the middle of words, as in Biscuit (spelled **Bekst**) and bother (spelled **brtr**). And, when we look closely at Roger's note, we can infer that he is beginning to discover the manner in which vowel letters represent sound. It is, in fact, this emerging use of vowels that tells us that Roger is moving out of the partial alphabetic phase and into the alphabetic phase.

Figure 5–2 The invented spelling in Roger's note shows that he thinks carefully about the relationship between the letters in written words and the sounds in spoken words.

Though Roger seems to know that vowels are important, he is far from understanding all the vowel letter neighborhoods. This is quite natural because vowels reside in many different neighborhoods and hence offer many choices for pronunciation. It certainly stands to reason, then, that children need more time and more reading experience to develop sensitivity to vowel letter-sound neighborhoods and to use this knowledge to learn words (Fowler, Shankweiler, & Liberman, 1979; Zinna, Liberman, & Shankweiler, 1986). Of the forty-five phonics rules researchers use to explain letter-sound correspondences, fully two-thirds pertain to vowels (Bailey, 1967; Clymer, 1963; Emans, 1967). Perhaps this explains why children misidentify the sounds represented by vowels far more frequently than the sounds represented by consonants.

As knowledge of letter neighborhoods develops and as children move farther into the alphabetic phase, they become increasingly adept at learning words on their own and spelling words in ways that others can read. Logan's (Figure 5–3) story shows greater understanding of letter-sound associations than does Roger's note. We can infer from the way Logan spells that he understands how many different letter neighborhoods represent sound, including vowel letter-sound neighborhoods. While Roger is just moving into the alphabetic phase, Logan is solidly at this phase of word fluency (Ehri, 1998). He has enough phonemic awareness and letter-sound knowledge to completely pronounce many unfamiliar words; his vocabulary is rapidly expanding; he enjoys reading and can read easy books by himself without help from anyone else.

Logan conventionally spells words in his fluent reading vocabulary. And when he spells unconventionally, you and I can easily read what he writes. This type of spelling, called phonetic spelling (Gentry, 1987), represents all essential sounds in words, even though there may not be a correct match between letters and sounds (**drest** for **dressed,** for example). Logan thinks carefully about the sounds in words and has enough phonemic awareness to associate letters with the sounds he wants to spell, as shown by **shuse** for **shoes.** Logan's writing illustrates many characteristics of alphabetic readers and phonetic spellers: Sometimes Logan uses letter names to spell (the **e** in **storey**), substitutes incorrect letters for correct ones (**scholle** for **school**), adds incorrect letters after correct ones (**dide** for **did** and **worke** for **work**), and uses the letter-sounds he hears to represent past tense (**drest** for **dressed** and **lisend** for **listened**).

Logan's teacher observes that sometimes Logan seems to move slowly through text as he focuses on the words. Relatively slow reading may be a consequence of dedicating a good bit of attention to identifying unfamiliar words and to making sure he reads exactly what the author wrote. This kind of slow, almost plodding, reading is frequently observed in children like Logan who are just beginning to develop some measure of competence using the letter-sound strategy to figure out words on their own. As Logan's fluent reading vocabulary grows and his ability to use the letter-sound strategy improves, his reading will become quite fluent. The more Logan reads, the more opportunities he has to combine the letter-sound strategy with comprehension. This is extremely important, for the whole point of becoming a skillful letter-sound strategist is to be able to efficiently decode

Figure 5–3 Logan thinks carefully about letter-sound neighborhoods when writing. As he considers which letters represent sound, he sometimes substitutes incorrect letters for correct ones, adds incorrect letters after correct ones, and uses the letter-sounds he hears to represent past tense.

new words so as to comprehend text and to develop a large fluent vocabulary by anchoring words in memory by their letter and sound sequences.

Movement toward word fluency is gradual. There is no line in the sand where the children in your classroom are on one side—readers whose full understanding of letter-sound neighborhoods allows them to use the letter-sound strategy and to spell phonetically—or the other side—readers who are at an earlier phase (the partial alphabetic phase) or at a later phase (the consolidated phase). And, as is to be expected with any complex learning process, sometimes children will use strategies to read and spell words that are characteristic of more than one phase.

WHAT YOU CAN DO TO HELP CHILDREN MOVE TOWARD WORD FLUENCY

A balanced reading program includes a wide variety of reading and writing activities that are specifically selected to meet children's needs. Children in the alphabetic phase of word fluency and the phonetic phase of spelling benefit from opportunities to use the letter-sound strategy so as to expand their fluent reading vocabularies; develop a mental image of the letters and sounds in words; and begin to consolidate, or combine, single letter-sound neighborhoods into large multiletter groups, which is necessary for movement to the next phase (the consolidated phase), as described in Chapter 6. Here are eight things you can do in your classroom to support children as they move toward word fluency.

1. Create many and varied opportunities for children to learn the letter-sound neighborhoods. And, when you teach letter neighborhoods, anchor knowledge in the real words children read and spell every day in your classroom.

2. Give children opportunities to explain what they know about the sounds of the letters in neighborhoods and how this knowledge might help them in the future. When children do this, they reflect on how they use letter neighborhood knowledge and, in so doing, become more metacognitively (consciously) aware of how, when, and why to use the letter-sound strategy.

3. Make sure that the children whom you teach develop a "set for diversity," a flexible orientation to decoding where readers know to try one sound and, if that does not work, to try another. Examples of flexible decoding include knowing to try: (a) the short vowel sound for the **VC** neighborhood and, if that does not work, to try the long vowel sound, (b) the long vowel sound for a **VCe** neighborhood and the short vowel sound as a backup, (c) two sounds for **oo,** and (d) the long vowel sound for the **CV** neighborhood with the short vowel sound as a backup. While our alphabetic writing system is not perfect, choices (when they exist) are finite and limited. Good readers know this and act accordingly.

4. Continue to teach phonemic awareness, when needed. As children enter into the alphabetic phase, they may not be highly skilled at separating words into sounds and blending. Should children need more phonemic awareness, combine some of the activities in Chapter 2 with lots of opportunities to learn letter-sound neighborhoods and to use the letter-sound strategy.

5. Make spelling an integral part of your balanced classroom reading program. When children spell, they think about the sounds in words so as to match the sounds they hear with the letters they write. This process taps into letter neighborhood knowledge and, coincidentally, helps children gain insight into the letter-sound associations.

6. Set aside lots of time for reading a variety of materials and writing for a variety of purposes. Because children at the alphabetic phase can figure out many of the unfamiliar words they see in books, they add words to their fluent reading vocabularies as they read. And when children write, they use their knowledge of our writing system to create meaningful messages. In so doing, they have opportunities to develop mental images of the letter sequences in words, thereby helping them develop a fluent reading vocabulary.

7.   Give children opportunities to read some decodable books—books with many words that are spelled like they sound and hence can be sounded out using letter-sound neighborhood knowledge. Decodable books give children practice using the letter-sound strategy while reading connected text and, because many of the words are decodable, help convince the children whom I teach that the letter-sound strategy is worth using. When you use decodable books, remember that their purpose is to give children practice using letter-sound neighborhood knowledge. These books should never replace good quality literature in your classroom. And their presence in your classroom should not limit children's choices of the books they read. If you remember that decodable books serve a very specific purpose and then use them in the service of that purpose, you can be assured that these books will be used just the way they are intended and that children will reap the benefits of practice using their letter neighborhood knowledge.

8.   Make sure the books children read for instruction are on their instructional reading level. Instructional level books are not so easy that children read them effortlessly, not so hard as to be frustrating. Because instructional level books have a few words children do not automatically recognize, children have opportunities to use the letter-sound strategy (and other strategies) to identify words while reading. And when they do this, they also have the benefit of your guidance. And, since the reason children are reading during classroom lessons is to comprehend, their use of the letter-sound strategy is meaning driven. That is, children use this strategy to identify words that, if ignored or misidentified, would disrupt children's understanding of text.

Good readers use their in-depth knowledge of letter-sound neighborhoods with planful flexibility and resourcefulness. They *think* while using the letter-sound strategy; they apply their in-depth knowledge of letter-sound neighborhoods to identify unfamiliar words and to build a large fluent reading vocabulary; and they always focus on meaning. One way you can help children develop an in-depth letter neighborhood knowledge is to introduce neighborhoods sequentially, which is the topic of the next section.

A TEACHING AND LEARNING SEQUENCE

A good working knowledge of letter-sound associations contributes to comprehension and vocabulary alike, particularly in the early grades (Rupley & Wilson, 1997). Though we know it takes more reading and writing experiences to develop a working knowledge of vowel letter-sound neighborhoods than consonant letter-sound neighborhoods, you may be surprised to learn that research does not support the use of any one particular teaching sequence over another. There is no prescribed order in which neighborhoods have to be taught, no immutable learning hierarchy, no sequence chiseled in stone. You are free to teach letter-sound neighborhoods in any order whatsoever, so long as children are successful learning and using neighborhoods. All things being equal, I find it useful to group letter-sound neighborhoods into those that are less challenging, more challenging, and most challenging for the children whom I teach. I begin with the less challenging neighborhoods and then gradually move toward those that are the most challenging to learn and apply when reading and writing.

Less Challenging Letter-Sound Neighborhoods

Single Consonant Letter-Sound Neighborhood

The single consonant neighborhood at the beginning of words (the onset) is the easiest for children to learn and use. Beginning consonants are especially obvious and can be readily combined with syntactic and semantic cues, which keeps word identification meaning driven (refer to Appendix B for an explanation). It is not surprising, then, that many readers first pay attention to the single consonants at the beginning of words. Then, as children gain more experience reading and writing, they notice this neighborhood at the end of words.

VC Short Vowel Letter-Sound Neighborhood

The children whom I teach find the **VC** short vowel neighborhood (explained in Appendix B) to be the least challenging of all the vowel letter-sound neighborhoods. The vowels in this neighborhood usually represent the short sound, as in **at** and **in.** Should one or more consonants precede the **VC** neighborhood in a short word or a syllable, such as in **tan, chin,** and **split,** the **VC** neighborhood still represents the short sound. Likewise, even when more than one consonant follows the vowel, thus creating a **VCC** or **VCCC** sequence as in **soft** and **pitch,** the vowel typically represents a short sound. Once children know a few rimes, I encourage them to look inside the rimes they know to discover how the **VC** short vowel neighborhood represents sound. Looking inside rimes requires that children focus on the individual letters in the **VC** short vowel neighborhood, think analytically about the **VC** sequence, and use this knowledge to pronounce many different combinations of vowels and their next-door consonant neighbors.

Consonant Blend Letter-Sound Neighborhood

Letters that form a consonant blend neighborhood (as the **cl** in **clam** or the **st** in **step**) are also in the easier-to-learn category. When letters reside in a consonant blend letter-sound neighborhood, they represent the same sounds as those of the single consonant neighborhood. The only difference is the blended neighbors are pronounced by sliding sounds together rather than saying sounds separately. The consonant blend letter-sound neighborhood is a strict neighborhood, and, as a result, readers have practically no new information to learn in order to effectively use this letter sequence. Since two-letter blends are less challenging than three-letter blends, I focus first on blends in a neighborhood made of two letters (**st**) and then move to blends in a neighborhood made of three letters (**str**). I leave any blend neighborhood that includes a digraph (as the **ch** portion of **chr** in <u>**chr**</u>**ome**) until after children have developed knowledge of how the letters in a digraph neighborhood represent sound.

More Challenging Letter-Sound Neighborhoods

Consonant Digraph Letter-Sound Neighborhood

The children whom I teach usually find the consonant digraph neighborhood, such as the **ph** in **ph**ase and the **th** in **th**is, harder to learn and apply than the single consonant or consonant blend neighborhoods. Perhaps this is because the digraph letter-sound neighborhood represents a totally different sound than the letters represent separately. Hence, readers cannot generalize, or transfer, what they already know about the sounds represented by single consonant neighborhoods to the consonant digraph neighborhood.

Vowel-Consonant-e (VCe) Long Vowel Neighborhood

The **VCe** neighborhood, as in **save** and **life**, is, in my teaching experience, usually the easiest of the long vowel neighborhoods (refer to Appendix B). Though the final **e** is a good visual reminder of the **VCe** long vowel neighborhood for the vast majority of children, some readers overlook the final **e**, hence treating letters as if they are in a **VC** short vowel neighborhood. Additionally, there are some obvious exceptions to the **VCe** neighborhood (see Appendix B for an explanation). My advice is to tell children that when they see a **VCe** neighborhood, try the long vowel sound first and, if that does not make a sensible word that fits the reading context, try a short sound.

Vowel-Vowel (VV) Long Vowel Letter-Sound Neighborhood

The **VV** neighborhood is formed when the following two vowels are next-door neighbors: **ai (s**ai**l), ea (cr**ea**m), ee (s**ee**d), oa (g**oa**t), ay (l**ay**),** and **ey (hon**ey**).** For the most part, **ai (s**ai**l), ea (cr**ea**m),** and **oa (b**oa**t)** require that readers pay attention to the middle of words. The vowel combinations **ey (hon**ey**)** and **ay (pl**ay**)** frequently require that readers pay attention to the ending letters in words. The pattern **ee** can occur at the end (s**ee**) and in the middle of words (s**ee**d). The **VV** neighborhood usually represents the long vowel sound, with exceptions, of course (see Appendix B). Teach children to try the long vowel sound and then to try the short vowel sound as a back up, if necessary.

Consonant-Vowel (CV) Long Vowel Letter-Sound Neighborhood

The **CV** neighborhood represents a long vowel sound, as in **me** and **sp**i**der** (refer to Appendix B). When this letter-sound neighborhood comes at the beginning of words, it gives readers lots of excellent information to combine with context cues. The **CV** long vowel neighborhood has some exceptions (particularly in unaccented syllables) and hence takes more experiences with print than neighborhoods in the less challenging category (look for a detailed explanation of syllables in Chapter 6).

Double oo Letter-Sound Neighborhood

The **oo** neighborhood does not represent a long sound as do other **VV** long vowel neighborhoods and, in fact, stands for two sounds, as heard in **school** and **book.** Since children have only two choices, tell them to try one sound first, and, if that does not make a sensible word, to try the other sound. Look in Appendix B for examples of words with the **oo** letter-sound neighborhood and a way to help readers manage the two options for its pronunciation.

Diphthong Letter-Sound Neighborhoods

Diphthong neighborhoods are formed when the letters **ow, ou, oi,** and **oy** are next-door neighbors. The neighborhood **ow** represents the sounds heard in <u>c**ow**</u>, **ou** the sounds heard in <u>**ou**t</u>, **oi** the sounds heard in <u>**oi**l</u>, **oy** the sounds heard in **b<u>oy.</u>** Since the sounds represented by diphthong neighborhoods are different from the sounds that letters represent in other letter-sound neighborhoods, readers must learn totally new letter-sound associations. And, added to this, **ow** sometimes represents the long **"o"** sound, as heard in **cr<u>ow</u>.** For these reasons, letters in diphthong neighborhoods take more attention and more experiences with print than letters in less challenging letter-sound neighborhoods.

Most Challenging Letter-Sound Neighborhoods

C or G Plus Vowel Letter-Sound Neighborhoods

As for the most challenging letter-sound neighborhoods, I find that neighborhoods made up of a **c** or a **g** plus a vowel, as in <u>**c**ircu**s**</u> and **gem,** are quite challenging for the children whom I teach. Both consonants represent two sounds—**c** the **"s"** heard in **city** or the **"k"** in **candy; g** the **"j"** heard in **gem** or the **"g"** in **golf.** Not only do readers have to think very carefully about the left-to-right letter sequence, but there are, of course, exceptions. I suggest that you help children develop the habit of trying more than one sound, should the first fail to produce a real, meaningful word. Look in Appendix B for a more detailed explanation of the **c** and **g** plus vowel letter-sound neighborhoods and examples of words with these neighborhoods.

Au, aw, ue, and ew Letter-Sound Neighborhoods

These four neighborhoods, as in the words **fraud, claw, due,** and **blew** are quite challenging. They take a good bit of practice and, not surprisingly, emerge later in both reading and writing. Give children lots of practice reading and writing words with these neighbors.

Vr R-Controlled Vowel Letter-Sound Neighborhood

The r-controlled neighborhood (**Vr**) is challenging to learn and use because the **r** changes the sound represented by the vowel letter. This is so regardless of which vowel precedes the letter **r.** This combination, **Vr,** appears at first glance to be a **VC** short vowel neighborhood because, after all, **r** is a consonant letter. Children must learn to pay attention to the **r** and to anticipate its affect on the vowels it follows, as in **bar, her, sir, nor,** and **fur.** Do not be surprised if you have end-of-year second graders who need practice to efficiently and effectively use the **Vr** letter-sound neighborhood.

VCCe Letter-Sound Neighborhood

I also find it takes the readers whom I teach a while to develop competence reading and spelling words with the vowel-consonant-consonant-e (**VCCe**) neighborhood, as in **tense** and **chance.** Perhaps this is so because the **VCCe** short vowel neighborhood resembles the **VCe** long vowel neighborhood and is large, consisting of four or more letters. Unlike the **VCe** long vowel neighborhood, however, the first vowel in the **VCCe** neighborhood represents a short vowel sound. This, of course, means that readers have to be especially careful when reading and writing to differentiate long vowel **VCe** words (**lane**) from short vowel **VCCe** words (**lance**).

CLe Letter-Sound Neighborhood

The **CLe** neighborhood is also quite challenging for the readers whom I teach. This letter-sound neighborhood consists of sequences like the **ble** in **marble** and the **ple** in **staple.** It typically comes at the end of words and represents a separate syllable. The final **e** is the result of the evolution of English spelling, and so the sounds that **CLe** represent are not completely apparent from the letter sequence. For example, the **ble** is pronounced as **"bul"** in **marble** and the **ple** as **"pul"** in **staple** (see Appendix B). This is slightly different from the sounds represented by the **bl** consonant blend neighborhood in **black,** and the **pl** consonant blend neighborhood in **place.**

In the final analysis, the most challenging letter-sound neighborhoods typically require that children have much more practice reading all sorts of books, poems, articles, and stories, and many more opportunities to spell and write. So, if the children whom you teach take longer to figure out how to strategically use the most challenging neighborhoods, this is perfectly natural.

LESSONS TO HELP READERS LEARN AND USE LETTER-SOUND NEIGHBORHOODS

The six lessons that follow are blueprints for teaching the letter-sound neighborhoods. They help readers to think analytically about letter-sound neighborhoods and to apply strategically this information when reading and writing. It is up to you to decide which letter-sound neighborhoods to teach and when to do so. These lessons are in the explanation, guided practice, and transfer sequence described in Chapter 1. When using these lessons, change features so as to adapt them to your own teaching style and to the specific and special needs of the children in your classroom.

Building Words with Letter Tiles

This lesson is similar to the word building activity in Chapter 4, only here children use tiles with letters written on them instead of tiles with onsets and rimes. Word building has definitely withstood the test of time, for it has been around for decades in one form or another (Reed & Klopp, 1957). This lesson is appropriate for large, small, and flexible groups, and for children in any grade.

Things You'll Need: Letter cards (index cards with single, lower case letters on them); a pocket chart; as many sets of letter tiles as there are individual children or learning partners in the group; old magazines, newspapers, and advertising flyers for making scrapbooks. Letter tiles (Figure 5–4) are one-inch tiles with letters written on them.

Exploration: Begin by comparing and contrasting the letter neighborhoods in familiar words. For example, you might write words on the chalkboard that include the **VC** short vowel and the **VCe** long vowel letter-sound neighborhoods. Explain and dis-

Figure 5–4 Letter tiles are easy to make, are inexpensive, and give children opportunities to think about the way that the letters in a word's spelling form neighborhoods that represent pronunciation.

cuss the sounds the letters in these neighborhoods represent, and ask children to find examples of words with these letter-sound neighborhoods on the wall charts and bulletin boards in your classroom. Write these words on the chalkboard. Now explain that children are to build words that have these same letter-sound neighborhoods. Put letter cards one after the other in a pocket chart. For example, you might put cards with the letters **p, f, i, n,** and **e** in the top row of the pocket chart. Then say **"pin."** Say **"pin"** a second time, "rubber banding" it so that children distinctly hear each of the sounds. Ask children to think of letters on the top row of the pocket chart that represent the sounds they hear in **"pin."** Demonstrate how to line up the **p,** the **i,** and the **n** one after the other to build the word **pin.** Leave the word in its pocket and put new letter cards for **p, i,** and **n** on the top row of the pocket chart, thereby reproducing the original five letters. Following this same procedure, build the words **pine, fin,** and **fine.** Invite children to come up to the pocket chart and participate in word building. Talk about words, letter-sound neighborhoods, and the sounds the letters in neighborhoods represent. When children understand how to build many different words from the same set of letters, it is time for guided practice.

Guided Practice: Pass out tiles to individual children or learning partners, and ask them to build a word. For example, if children have letter tiles with **c, p, m, n, h, t, o, a,** and **e** they might build the word **can.** Talk about the **VC** short vowel letter neighborhood in this word, and then ask children to change **can** to **cane.** Now talk about the **CVe** long vowel neighborhood and its affect on the vowel sound. Continue building, asking children to spell one word and then to change it into another—**man** to **mane; hope** to **hop; cape** to **cap; not** to **note.**

Transfer: Have the children work in small groups to make letter-sound neighborhood scrapbooks. To do this, children look through magazines to find words with the same letter-sound neighborhoods, and then cut them out and paste them onto large pieces of paper that have the letter-sound neighborhood written at the top. Children then write sentences on the pages, using as many of the words on each page as possible. Last, fasten pages together to construct a scrapbook. Make the scrapbook available for everyone to read and enjoy; send it home overnight with children to share with their families; share it with other classrooms in your school.

Venn Diagrams

Venn diagrams are overlapping circles with shared characteristics inside the overlapping portion and unique characteristics inside each separate circle (Figure 5–5). Making diagrams creates in your classroom rich opportunities for discussion, analytical thinking, and group interaction. So, move the furniture, clear work spaces, and give the children who are working in cooperative groups plenty of support as they delve into letter-sound neighborhoods. With its focus on comparing and contrasting the letter-sound neighborhoods, this lesson is suitable for children in the second grade and above.

Things You'll Need: One piece of chart paper for each cooperative group in your class, markers, and poems or books written in verse that have a good selection of words that include the letter neighborhoods readers are to explore.

Exploration: Write on the chalkboard several words in which the same letters represent more than one sound, as the **ow** in **cow** and **snow**. Use a Venn diagram to illustrate the point that some letter sequences routinely stand for different sounds. Begin by drawing two overlapping circles on the board and then writing a letter-sound neighborhood that represents more than one sound (**ow,** for instance) in the overlapping portion. Next write a word that represents one pronunciation (**snow,** perhaps) in one circle; a word that represents another pronunciation (**cow,** for example) in the other circle. Challenge readers to think of words in which **ow** represents the sounds heard in **snow** and in **cow.** Support children as they draw conclusions about the way that **ow** signals pronunciation.

Guided Practice: Invite children to work collaboratively and cooperatively to make their own Venn diagrams. Challenge readers to find words written on the wall charts and bulletin boards in your classroom and in the books they are reading that include the letter-sound neighborhood featured in the Venn diagram. When they have finished, invite groups to share their diagrams with the entire class, to explain letter-sound neighborhoods, to talk about the words they found and to discuss spelling. Display diagrams in your classroom and encourage children to use diagrams as resources.

Figure 5–5   Venn diagrams give children opportunities to explore letter neighborhoods that represent more than one sound in words.

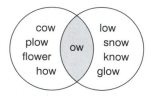

Transfer: Use modified cloze sentences to give children opportunities to use syntactic, semantic, and letter-sound associations to figure out word identity. To construct modified cloze sentences, delete portions of words so as to focus readers' attention on certain letter neighborhoods. For example, a modified cloze sentence from *Day of the Dragon King* (Osborne, 1998) might look like:

> "R__lly? Worms? That's n__t," said Jack. "Let me write that down." He r__ched into his sack. (p. 18)

In this example, readers use their knowledge of the **VV** long vowel neighborhood represented by **ea** (<u>**really**</u>, **n<u>eat</u>,** and <u>**reached**</u>) along with information gleaned from the sentence context. I suggest you begin with one letter-sound neighborhood that children would benefit from using in context. Then, when readers are familiar with the modified cloze procedure, focus on more than one neighborhood at a time. As for cloze sentences, you may want to use ones from familiar books and poems. This way children bring plenty of prior knowledge and reading experiences to this application portion of the lesson.

Word Puzzles

This lesson challenges advanced first graders, second graders, and older children to solve puzzles that have a clue word (like **steam**) and a set of instructions **(– ea + or =)** that transform the clue into a solution word (**storm**), as shown in Figure 5–6. Puzzle solvers delete letter-sound neighborhoods, add neighborhoods, and cross-check to verify solutions by finding words in content subject textbooks, storybooks, or poems. (The solution words in Figure 5–6 are from the zany rhyming book *Father Fox's Pennyrhymes* [Watson, 1971].)

Things You'll Need: A good imagination to create puzzles; colored chalk; words from familiar reading material; multiple copies of content subject textbooks, storybooks, novels, or poems.

Exploration: Discuss the letter-sound neighborhoods in words, focusing attention on one or two neighborhoods that recur frequently. Then write three or four puzzles on the chalkboard. Use colored chalk to highlight the transformations children are to perform. Demonstrate how to solve the puzzle **steam – ea + or =** by first reading the clue word. Then show children how to take away the **ea** (**VV**) long vowel

coin	–	oi	+	or	=	_____		steam	–	ea	+	or	=	_____
sheet	–	ee	+	ir	=	_____		house	–	ou	+	or	=	_____
coat	–	oa	=	ar	=	_____		dealing	–	ea	+	ar	=	_____

Figure 5–6   Finding solutions to word puzzles creates opportunities to think analytically about the sounds that the letters in neighborhoods represent in words.

letter neighborhood and add the **or** (**Vr**) neighborhood in its place to make **storm.** Model how to solve several puzzles and then turn to Guided Practice.

Guided Practice: Ask children to work individually or with a learning partner to solve puzzles. (Make sure the puzzles you construct use words with a letter neighborhood(s) that has been explained and discussed previously.) The examples in Figure 5–6 ask children to use the **Vr** letter-sound neighborhood to solve puzzles. I have found that puzzles work best when readers begin solving them by changing only one type of letter-sound neighborhood and when the neighborhood is among those that are less challenging. As readers become better at solving puzzles, construct puzzles with more challenging neighborhoods and use a variety of letter-sound neighborhoods in the same puzzle. Write several puzzles on sheets of paper and encourage puzzle solvers to explain in their own words how and why transformed words create solution words.

Transfer: Invite readers to work collaboratively and cooperatively to create their own word puzzles. Tell them to get the solution words from the books they are reading in class—content subject textbooks, storybooks, novels, and poems. As children make puzzles, ask them to (1) underline the puzzle words that are from books and (2) write the page numbers where words appear. When the puzzles are complete, groups trade puzzles, as well as the books with solution words. Groups then solve one another's puzzles and verify their solutions by finding the underlined words in books.

Letter-Sound Neighborhood Togetherness Charts

In this lesson, readers in the second grade and up work with a learning partner to make large charts that show how three- or four-letter-sound neighborhoods represent the same sounds. Charts are terrific to hang on the walls of your classroom and a great source for lively discussions about how and why letters represent sounds in many different, but predictable, ways.

Things You'll Need: As many large sheets of chart paper as there are learning partners or cooperative groups in your classroom, colored markers, a cardboard box, two dowels, a knife, tape, and butcher paper. The transfer portion of this lesson involves making mock movies. To make a movie projector, cut a rectangle in the bottom of a cardboard box to serve as a viewing screen. Cut two sets of holes on either side of the box: Cut one set toward the top of the box (one above the "screen"), the other toward the bottom (one below the "screen"). Make the holes large enough for a dowel to fit through. Slide each dowel through one set of holes. Now, working through the back of the box, tape the movie (which is written on the butcher paper) to the dowels. Wind the entire movie around one dowel; wind only the lead (the blank butcher paper that precedes the movie frames) around the other dowel. Turn the dowels to simulate a movie as the paper film moves from one dowel to another (Figure 5–7). Adjust the tension by turning either the top or bottom dowel. Advise children to make the pictures and text a little smaller than the actual frame. This way there is some leeway just in case the frames drawn on butcher paper are not positioned quite right on the movie screen.

Figure 5–7
Making letter-sound neighborhood charts creates opportunities to compare and contrast different letter neighborhoods that represent the same sounds in words.

Exploration: Challenge children to think of words that have a certain sound, the long **o** sound, for instance. Make a long list; cover the entire board with words! Explain that there are several ways to represent the long **o** sound. In the example of long **o,** you might focus on the **VV** long vowel neighborhood of **oa** (as in **boat**), the **VCe** long vowel neighborhood (as in **home**), the **ow** dipthong neighborhood (as in **snowman**), and the **old** rime (as in **gold**). Ask children to look for the words on the chalkboard list that use the same letter-sound neighborhood to represent the sound. Then use colored chalk to draw a lacy cloud around each word. For example, you might use pink chalk to draw clouds around all the words on the list in which **oa** represents long **o,** such as **coat, boat,** and **foam.** Then ask readers to find all the words in which a different letter-sound neighborhood represents the same sound, such as the **VCe** long vowel neighborhood that represents the long **o** sound. Use a different color of chalk, blue possibly, to make lacy clouds around the words that include this neighborhood. Continue until all the words with the **VV** (**oa**), **VCe, ow** and **old** sequences have been found.

Guided Practice: Explain that children are going to make a Letter-Sound Neighborhood Togetherness Chart of words in which the same sound (in this case long **o**) is represented by the **VV** (**oa**), **VCe,** and **ow** neighborhoods and the **old** rime. Give pairs of learning partners chart paper that is divided into equal parts. In each section, children are to write a word with a long **o** and to draw a picture of that word, as shown in Figure 5–7. Then partners are to add words to each section that use the same letter neighborhood to represent the sound of long **o.** Remind partners

Figure 5–8 Movie projectors made of a cardboard box, dowels, and butcher paper are inexpensive, sturdy, and reusable.

to look for words on wall charts and in dictionaries, storybooks, and textbooks. Share finished charts with the class; ask readers to compare and contrast words and to explain how different letter-sound neighborhoods signal pronunciation.

Transfer: Now it is time for children to write and produce "homemade" movies. Children do this by writing and illustrating movies on butcher paper and showing them on a projector made out of a cardboard box (Figure 5–8). To begin, ask groups to write a short story and to divide the story into brief episodes. Then give groups opportunities to revise and edit their stories. And, while writing, stress the importance of spelling and attention to the letter-sound neighborhoods in words. Next, ask groups to partition a long piece of butcher paper into movie frames by drawing horizontal lines at equal distances. In every frame, children write text and draw a picture for one episode in the story. (Leave one or two blank frames at each end of the butcher paper.) Fasten the butcher paper to dowels and insert it in the homemade movie projector. Now it's movie time. Put the spotlight on each group as they simultaneously turn the dowels to display one illustration after the other and read the accompanying text. After the presentations, invite the movie makers to talk about the movies and their meaning, some interesting words, and some of the letter-sound neighborhoods in the words in the movie scripts.

Neighborhood Mail

This lesson, which combines letter-sound neighborhood learning with sending mock postcards and real letters, is beneficial for first grade readers (and older children) who need to develop greater insight into long and short vowel letter-sound neighborhoods. It is suitable for small or large groups.

Things You'll Need: Two shoe boxes with tightly fitting lids to represent mailboxes, mock postcards, as many envelopes and real stamps as there are children in your classroom. To make mailboxes from shoe boxes, cover the lids with construction paper, stand each box on end, cut a single slit toward the top of each box and write

Figure 5–9 Mailing
postcards by deciding
whether the vowel
neighborhood represents a
long or short vowel sound
gives children practice
identifying important vowel
neighborhoods and sets the
stage for writing and sending
real postcards.

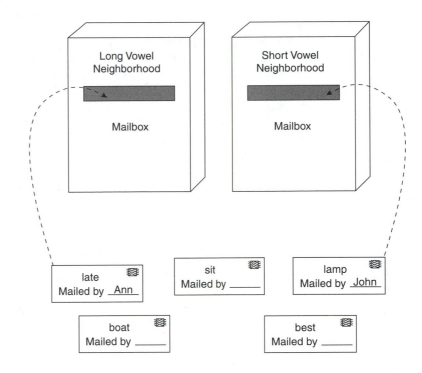

Short Vowel Neighborhood above one slit, and Long Vowel Neighborhood just above the other, as shown in Figure 5–9. To make mock postcards, cut paper into rectangles, draw a rendition of a stamp in the upper right corner and write **Mailed by:**_____ (the blank is for a child's name) on the bottom (see Figure 5–9). Now write a one-syllable word on each mock postcard, making sure you use a variety of long and short vowel neighborhood words.

Exploration: Begin by writing long and short vowel letter-sound neighborhoods on the chalkboard; call attention to the vowel sounds the neighborhoods represent; compare and contrast neighborhoods. Then show children the mock postcards with words on them and the two mailboxes. Explain that children are going to mail postcards by deciding whether the vowel neighborhoods in the words on the postcards represent a long or short vowel sound, and then putting the postcards in the long or short vowel neighborhood mailbox. Demonstrate further by giving a few postcards to volunteers to mail and discussing why certain postcards are mailed in long and short vowel boxes.

Guided Practice: Give each child several postcards. Remind children to sign their names on each postcard before putting it in the mail. Check the mailboxes daily. Should a child mistakenly mail a postcard in the wrong mailbox, return the postcard, writing on the back something like: **Returned to Sender (write the child's name): Mailed to the Wrong Address.** Once all the postcards are correctly mailed, take them out, review with children long and short vowel neighborhood words, compare and contrast neighborhoods, and conclude by giving children their own postcards to take home.

Transfer: Now it is time to write and send real letters. Discuss with children the reasons we write friendly letters and their basic form—salutation, body, and closing. I have had the most success when children write letters inviting their parents (or grandparents or caregivers) to school. Letters might announce special events like Open House or a celebration in your classroom. Write the important facts on the chalkboard—the event, time, and place. Ask each child to add a personal touch by including a special message, such as telling parents to bring brothers and sisters or describing how much fun the upcoming event is going to be. Emphasize the letter-sound neighborhoods in words and how this knowledge helps children spell. Last, put the letters in envelopes, add addresses and stamps, and drop them in the mail. Children now have something special to look forward to when the mail is delivered to their homes in a day or so.

Word Group Discovery

The Word Group Discovery lesson provides opportunities for first graders and older children to sort words according to the sounds of the letters in neighborhoods. Suitable for any letter neighborhood, this lesson is most successful when readers work with a partner or in cooperative groups.

Things You'll Need: As many sets of word cards (3×5) as there are cooperative groups in your class, a few large word cards (5×8) with tape on the back, lunch-size paper sacks, storybooks, gallon-size plastic bags that lock at the top, a hole punch, and ribbon. The gallon-size plastic bags, hole punch, and ribbon are for making bag books, which are stories with the pages inside sealable plastic bags and used in the transfer portion of the lesson.

Exploration: Select interesting words from familiar storybooks, poems and content area books, and write these words on large (5×8) cards. Randomly tape large word cards to the bulletin board (perhaps cards with an assortment of words like **snake, grain, snail, grape, rain, lake, tile, home,** and **gain** on them) and challenge readers to think of ways these words are alike. Children might, for example, point out that some words belong in the same group because they share the same letter-sound neighborhoods, such as **CVe, consonant blend,** or **ai (VV).** Talk about how and why words are grouped and regrouped in many different ways.

Guided Practice: Give each cooperative group several small paper sacks and a set of small (3×5) word cards. Ask children to sort words by putting words that have the same letter-sound neighborhoods and, therefore, belong in the same group in the same paper sack. (The words children sort should be words they know how to read.) For first graders, write the letter-sound neighborhoods on sacks so that children know beforehand the groups to which words belong, as in Figure 5–10. Second graders may decide for themselves which letter-sound neighborhoods to use for sorting or you may write something like **CVe** neighborhood, **consonant blend,** or **VV,** on the sacks. When finished sorting, children empty each sack, cross-check to make sure all the words inside are group members and then write each word on the sack in which it belongs. Tell children to write their names on the

Figure 5–10
Sorting helps readers discover letters neighborhoods that occur in many different words.

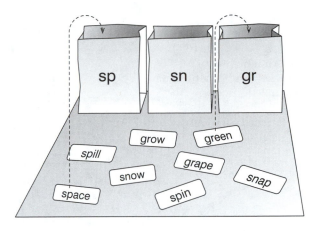

sacks, too, so you know how cooperative groups sorted words. Last, bring the whole class together: Invite children to compare and contrast letter neighborhoods; talk about how and why words are sorted by their letter neighborhoods.

Transfer: To transfer letter-sound neighborhood knowledge to spelling, ask children to make bag books; they are fun to make, lend themselves to group interaction, and are great to share (Figure 5–11). To make a bag book, ask children to write, revise, and edit stories; slip each page into a gallon-size plastic bag and seal the bag. When all the pages are inside bags, use a paper punch to make three holes on the far left of the bags. Thread colorful ribbon through holes and tie the ribbon in a bow. This fastens the pages of the book together and adds a cheerful splash of color, too. Share bag books with the class, and, when you do this, talk about story sequence, meaning, and the letter-sound neighborhoods.

EXTRA PRACTICE ACTIVITIES

If some of the children in your classroom stumble when they use the letter-sound strategy, cannot explain in their own words how the letters in neighborhoods represent sounds, and frequently connect the wrong letter neighborhoods with sounds, then the sixteen activities in this section will be helpful.

Easy-to-Do Extra Practice Activities

These eight activities are easy ways for children to get extra practice with letter-sound neighborhoods.

   1. *Personal Word Boxes:* This is especially helpful for first graders and struggling second graders; it works best when everyone in the classroom participates. Give each child a box with a lid, a handful of blank 3×5 cards, colorful ABC tabs to stick on the cards, and a moderate list of often-used words. Children write one

Figure 5–11 Writing stories that are then made into bag books gives children opportunities to use their knowledge of the alphabetic cues in letter-sound neighborhoods to communicate through written language.

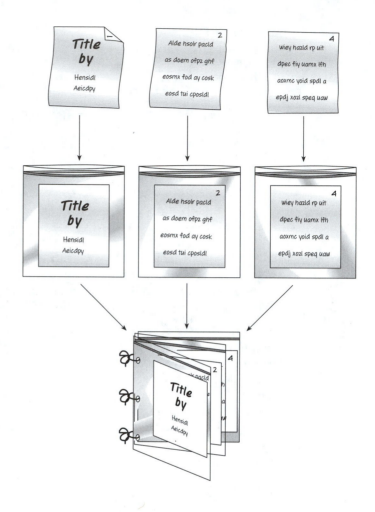

word on each card and file cards alphabetically in the box. The benefit of beginning with a common group of words is that you, the teacher, know which basic words readers have at their fingertips in boxes. As children need new words for writing, have them put the words on new cards and file the cards alphabetically in their own word box. Eventually children will have a different and very personal group of words in their boxes. The word cards in boxes are excellent references, and cards can also be used in games and other classroom activities. My experience with personal word boxes is that they are quick, easy, and give children a great deal of independence, not to mention lots of practice using alphabetical order.

2. *Dictionary Search:* Challenge large or small groups of second, third, and fourth graders to spot words in the dictionary that have specific letter-sound neighborhoods in their spellings. Ask children to write the words and page numbers on a sheet of paper, and to count the number of words they find.

3. *Wall Chart Lists:* This activity is appropriate for first and second graders, and is a large or small group activity. Begin by writing a word on a blank wall chart and discussing a letter-sound neighborhood in the word. Invite readers to think of other words that have the same letter-sound neighborhood and add those to the wall chart. Encourage children to be on the lookout for words with the same neighborhood and, when found, to add words to the wall chart list. Review the words, discuss the letter-sound neighborhood, and count the words to see how many children found. Leave the wall chart up for a while so that children can refer to the words when reading and writing.

4. *Chalkboard Compare and Contrast:* Make two columns on the chalkboard to represent different letter-sound neighborhoods. For example, to compare and contrast the **VC** short vowel and **Vr** neighborhoods, you would write a word like **cat** at the top of one column (along with **VC,** if helpful to children) and the word **car** at the top of the other (along with **Vr,** if helpful). Explain how the letter-sound neighborhoods are alike and different. Then ask children to suggest (or find) words with these two neighborhoods. Write words in the columns, thereby making two lists. Compare and contrast lists, and discuss the sounds neighborhoods represent in words.

5. *Write Neighborhood Advertisements:* Invite children who are second graders (or older) to write and illustrate an advertisement for a letter-sound neighborhood they are exploring. Ads should include examples of words with the letter-sound neighborhood and an imaginative illustration. If your classroom publishes a newspaper chronicling important events, place the advertisements in the paper. And, if you have readers in your classroom who have moved beyond the letter-sound strategy (see Chapter 6), ask them to write advertisements for the large multiletter chunks described in the next chapter.

6. *Illustrate Words:* This short activity adds variety to the daily routine. Select several words that share the same letter-sound neighborhood and are relatively easy to draw—**car, star,** and **bar,** or **seed, feet,** and **creek.** Tell children you are going to spell a word letter-by-letter. Children are to listen to the letters, write them down, figure out the word and sketch a quick picture of it. For instance, if you spell **c-a-r,** children would write **car** and draw a quick sketch, thus showing they recognize this word. Finally, write the words on the chalkboard and talk about the letter-sound neighborhood (in this case the **Vr** neighborhood).

7. *Silent Consonants:* Use this activity to call attention to the "silent" consonants in words. I find this particularly helpful for double consonants, one of which is typically silent, as in **rabbit** and **mitten.** Write several words with silent consonants on the chalkboard. Ask a volunteer to pronounce a word and then to come to the chalkboard and draw a line through the "silent" consonant. For example, the second **b** in **rabbit** and the second **t** in **mitten** would be crossed off.

8. *Red and Green Vowels:* This activity is beneficial for readers who need more practice with long and short vowel neighborhoods. It works equally well for large, small, or flexible skill groups, though I usually use it with flexible skill groups because of its intense focus on specific long and short vowel neighborhoods. Give each child a piece of paper, a pencil, and two crayons, one green and one red. Spell a word, **home** for instance, but do not pronounce it. Ask children to decide if the vowels are long, short, or silent. Children then spell the words, writing long vowels in red and short vowels in green and putting a slash through silent vowels (like the final **e** at the end of the **VCe** long vowel neighborhood).

🦋 *What's in a Name?*

This is a variation of the party game where players make as many words as they can from one large word, usually the name of a famous person, place, thing, or event. It is easy to integrate with social studies, science, math, and health by using words from these content subjects. This activity is best used with second graders and up, and lends itself to a large or small group format.

Things You'll Need: Paper and pencils; the names of famous people, places, things, or events from the content subjects children are studying or from the books they are reading.

Practice: On the chalkboard, write a long word from a content subject textbook that is the name of an important person, place, thing, or event on the chalkboard. Talk about why the person, place, thing, or event is important and write the things children know about it. Then challenge children to use the letters in the long word to spell as many short words as they can and to write words on a sheet of paper. I often put children together with a partner and tell them there are at least _____ (a figure that will challenge readers but not frustrate them) words that can be made from the letters in the large word. This gives partners a target and helps motivate children to get the most out of this paper and pencil form of word building.

🦋 *Letter-Sound Neighborhood Circle*

This practice activity focuses on the letter-sound neighborhoods in the familiar words written on a classroom wall chart. It is suitable for large, small, or flexible skill groups of first and second graders.

Things You'll Need: A wall chart with lots of words and colorful markers. (This activity calls for drawing colorful circles around the words on a wall chart, so make sure that the wall chart you use is ready to be replaced or that you have, or are willing to make, a duplicate.)

Practice: Write a few words with the same letter-sound neighborhood on the chalkboard. Talk about how the letters represent sounds in neighborhoods. Then ask readers to use a colored marker to circle words on the wall chart that have the same letter-sound neighborhood as those on the chalkboard. Should you choose to focus on more than one neighborhood, use a different color marker for each.

🦋 *Word Worms*

A Word Worm is formed when children with letter neighborhoods pinned to their shirts attach themselves to a child wearing a beginning letter-sound (an onset). As children form Word Worms, they practice blending and think analytically about the letter-sound associations in letter neighborhoods. With its emphasis on fanciful creatures, this activity is most appealing and most appropriate for large groups of first and second graders.

Things You'll Need: Word Worms made of colored construction paper, string, scissors, crayons, markers, and masking tape. Make Word Worms by cutting out heads and bodies, decorating heads, and writing an onset on each head (such as **spr**) and a vowel letter-sound neighborhood on each section that, when combined with the onset, makes a real word (such as **ay** or **inkle**).

Practice: Write an onset on the chalkboard, **spr** for example. Then write a word underneath it, **spray** perhaps, explaining that **spray** is formed by combining the **spr** blend neighborhood and the **ay** (**VV**) long vowel neighborhood. Encourage readers to think of other words that begin with the **spr** blend neighborhood. Write the words underneath **spr.** Make lists for two (or three) other consonant blend (or consonant digraph) neighborhoods that serve as onsets, such as **spr, st,** and **sl.** Now tape heads with onsets to the shirts of some children (**spr, st,** or **sl,** for example). On others, tape a body section, such as **ain, ang, awl, age, amp, and, ide, eep,** and **ice.** Children with body sections line up behind children wearing onsets to make meaningful words. In this example, **spr** (the head) combines with **ain, ang,** and **awl** (body sections) to build **sprain, sprang,** and **sprawl.** Children with **age, amp,** and body sections line up behind **st** to from **stage, stamp,** and **stand.** The **sl** head is followed by **ide, eep,** and **ice** to form **slide, sleep,** and **slice.** After word worms are created, children read the words formed by the consonant blend neighborhood at the head and the vowel letter neighborhood pinned to their shirts (the body section).

Clothespin Words

This large-group activity for first graders gets everyone involved, requires minimal preparation, and gives children lots of solid practice using letter-sound neighborhoods.

Things You'll Need: One rope for a clothesline, an assortment of clothespins, word cards (or construction paper in the shape of clothes with words written on each clothing article), blank cards (or pieces of construction paper in the shape of clothes), and markers.

Practice: String a clothesline (rope) across a corner of the room and give each child several cards (or pieces of construction paper cut in the shape of clothes). Some cards should have words spelled with a letter-sound neighborhood you want children to pay attention to, such as the **CVe** long vowel neighborhood in **came, bone,** and **time;** other cards should have words that are not spelled with the target neighborhood, such as **boy** and **jump.** Discuss the **CVe** long vowel neighborhood; point out the letter-sound associations. Then ask each child to read the words on their cards, to look for the **CVe** long vowel neighborhood, and to pin **CVe** words to the clothesline, as shown in Figure 5–12. When finished, everyone reads the words in chorus. Extend this activity by making a clothesline bulletin board. Do this by zigzagging a rope (clothesline) from top to bottom, pinning a word on the top of the clothesline (**home,** for example), underlining the **CVe** long vowel letter neighborhood, and writing **CVe** Neighborhood under the word. Invite children to find words in which the first vowel in the **CVe** neighborhood represents the long sound,

Figure 5–12 Pinning words that are spelled with the same neighborhood to a clothesline gives readers opportunities to analyze the letter neighborhoods inside words and to draw conclusions about how the alphabetic cues in neighborhoods represent sound.

to write the words on cards (or piece of colored paper cut in the shape of clothes), and to pin them to the clothesline with a clothespin.

Letter-Sound Neighborhood Bingo

An oldie but goodie for children of any age, bingo is a favorite because it has so many variations, gets everyone involved, and effectively targets letter neighborhoods. This is, of course, a great large or small group activity. The version I describe is appropriate for readers who have knowledge of long vowel letter neighborhoods, though you could easily make this practice activity easier by targeting less challenging letter-sound neighborhoods, such as the consonant blend neighborhood.

Things You'll Need: Bingo cards and pencils. When making bingo cards, begin by designing a model that has five rows with five boxes each. Duplicate the model and write partial words by omitting letter-sound neighborhoods as needed for the focus of instruction (shown in Figure 5–13). Words in this example feature the **VV** long vowel neighborhood of **oa** (fl__t to make **float**), **ee** (tr__ to make **tree**), and **ai** (tr__n to make **train**). Be sure to use a variety of words with letter-sound neighborhoods and place them in different boxes on cards.

Practice: Play bingo by first saying a word. Ask players to listen for the sounds that the **VV** long vowel neighborhood represents, to find the partial word, and then to write in the missing neighborhood. A completed word "covers" the square. Traditional rules hold: any five consecutively covered squares lined up diagonally, horizontal, or vertically wins. Four corners or postage stamps (four squares in any corner) are fun to play, too. Coveralls are always challenging, but they take more time, so save them for days when there is plenty of flexibility in the schedule.

Figure 5–13
When children play Letter-Sound Neighborhood Bingo, they use their knowledge of the sounds represented by letter-sound neighborhoods to fill in missing letters in words their teacher reads, in this example the **VV** neighborhood.

str__t	ch__n	fl__t	sl__p	tr__
sn__l	qu__n	t__st	ch__k	s__m
sh__t	p__n	Free	r__st	p__d
tr__l	g__t	br__n	thr__t	c__ch
sp__ch	s__p	l__f	cl__m	p__nt

Use ee, ai, and oa to make the words on this card.

Vowel-Sound Neighborhood Sort

This sorting activity is beneficial for any age reader who needs more practice identifying long, short, and r-controlled vowel neighborhoods. It works best as a small group or flexible skill group activity.

Things You'll Need: Sheets of paper with a grid showing spaces for long, short, and r-controlled vowel neighborhood words, as shown in Figure 5–14; pencils; cards with a variety of long, short, and r-controlled vowel neighborhood words.

Practice: Pair children with a learning partner. Give partners a sheet of paper with a grid showing different letter-sound neighborhoods, and a stack of word cards. Partners sort the words on the cards by their letter-sound neighborhood—long vowel, short vowel, or r-controlled—and then fill out the grid by writing each word in the appropriate square. To make this activity easier, use only two neighborhoods, perhaps the long and short vowel neighborhoods.

Long and Short Vowel Fly Away Words

In this activity, first and second graders read words on make-believe flies, bees, or mosquitoes and, as quickly as possible, smack the flies, bees, or mosquitoes with a swatter. This is a team game that takes a relatively short time to play, so plan on using it in the 20 minutes or so before special classes, on days when children finish projects early, or whenever an amusing bit of practice is a welcome addition to the

Figure 5–14 Sorting words by their vowel neighborhood gives children opportunities to compare and contrast the sounds the letters in neighborhoods represent.

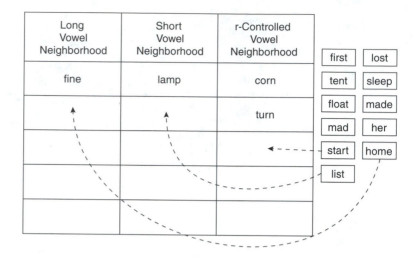

school day. Books like *The Giant Jam Sandwich* (Lord, 1972) and *Why Mosquitoes Buzz in People's Ears* (Aardema, 1975) are examples of stories that feature insects. Should your class be sharing these books or others like them, this game is a good way to reinforce letter neighborhood knowledge and to do so in keeping with the theme of familiar books.

Things You'll Need: Two fly swatters, tape, and construction paper cut into flies, bees, or mosquitoes, with one short or long vowel word written on each.

Practice: Tape the Fly Away Words (written on the insect forms) to the chalkboard, spacing them fairly far apart. Divide players into two teams. Call one player from each team up to the chalkboard; give each a swatter. Then say a word, **"tape"** for example, and tell players to swat a word that has the same vowel sound (a long sound). In the example, words like **came** or **made** would be swatted. If the player is correct, the swatted word is taken off the board—it "flies away"—and the team gets a point. The team with the most Fly Away Words wins. At game's end, hold up Fly Away Words and ask children to read them in chorus.

Letter-Sound Neighborhood Wheels

Wheels are made of two circles, one with letter-sound neighborhoods that come at the beginning of words (act as onsets) and one with vowel letter-sound neighborhoods that follow onsets (Figure 5–15). Though this kind of practice is strictly rote and individual, it pays off when readers have plenty of other opportunities to strategically use letter neighborhoods.

Things You'll Need: Colorful tagboard, a black marker, scissors, and one brad for each wheel. To make Letter Neighborhood Wheels, cut two wheels (circles) out of brightly colored tagboard. One wheel should be about nine inches in diameter, the other about six inches. Sizes may vary, however, depending on your personal

Figure 5–15
Children think about
the sounds the letters in
neighborhoods
represent and then turn
the wheels to form real
words.

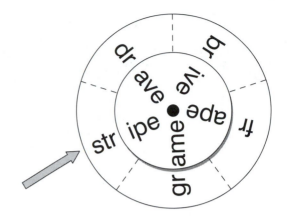

preference, as long as one is larger than the other. On the outermost portion of the
large wheel, write letter neighborhoods that come at the beginning of words. On
the outermost portion of the small wheel, write vowel neighborhoods that come
at the end of words. Poke a hole in the center of each and fasten them together
with a brad. Now spin the wheels to align letter-sound neighborhoods. Voila!
Words are formed (Figure 5–15).

Practice: Show children how to spin the wheels so that the letter neighborhoods on
the inner wheel line up with those on the outer wheel, thus forming words. To check
on children's success, ask them to write down all the words they form with each
wheel. Letter-sound Neighborhood Wheels are fine additions to learning centers
and the word lists children make are a permanent record of this practice activity.

MOVING TOWARD WORD IDENTIFICATION WITH MULTILETTER CHUNKS

Though the letter-sound strategy is an especially useful tool, it is also especially
challenging because it requires that readers put a lot of energy into word identification. Learning to use the letter-sound strategy is well worth the effort, however,
for this strategy taps into the basic feature of alphabetic writing—the sounds represented by the letters in neighborhoods. In addition, the letter-sound strategy
paves the way for the multiletter chunk strategy, which is the streamlined strategy
where readers use multiletter groups to identify words, as explained in the next
chapter. While the use of multiletter chunks develops early, it typically matures
only after children have lots of experience using the letter-sound associations in letter neighborhoods to identify and spell words. Not only does the use of multiletter chunks make word identification quicker, but knowing the meaning of one or
more of the large multiletter chunks in a word gives readers insight into that
word's definition, as you will learn in Chapter 6.

REFERENCES

Aardema, V. (1975). *Why mosquitoes buzz in people's ears.* New York: Dial Books for Young Readers.

Adams, M. J. (1990). *Beginning to read: Thinking and learning about print.* Cambridge, MA: MIT Press.

Bailey, M. H. (1967). The utility of phonic generalizations in grades one through six. *The Reading Teacher, 20,* 413–418.

Clymer, T. (1963). The utility of phonic generalizations in the primary grades. *The Reading Teacher, 16,* 252–258.

Ehri, L. C. (1998). Grampheme-phoneme knowledge is essential for learning to read words in English. In J. L. Metsala & L. C. Ehri (Eds.), *Word recognition in beginning literacy* (pp. 3–40). Mahwah, NJ: Lawrence Erlbaum.

Emans, R. (1967). The usefulness of phonic generalizations above the primary grades. *The Reading Teacher, 20,* 419–425.

Fowler, C. A., Shankweiler, D., & Liberman, I. Y. (1979). Apprehending spelling patterns for vowels: A developmental study. *Language and Speech, 22,* 243–252.

Gentry, J. R. (1987). *Spel . . . is a four-letter word.* New York: Scholastic.

Howe, D., & Howe, J. (1979). *Bunnicula.* New York: Avon Books.

Juel, C. (1983). The development and use of mediated word identification. *Reading Research Quarterly, 18,* 306–327.

Lord, J. V. (1972). *The giant jam sandwich.* Boston: Houghton Mifflin.

Massaro, D. W., & Hestand, J. (1983). Developmental relations between reading ability and knowledge of orthographic structure. *Contemporary Educational Psychology, 8,* 174–180.

Nation, K., & Hulme, C. (1997). Phonemic segmentation, not onset-rime segmentation, predicts early reading and spelling skills. *Reading Research Quarterly, 32,* 154–167.

Osborne, M. P. (1998). *Day of the dragon king.* New York: Random House.

Reed, L. C., & Klopp, D. S. (1957). *Phonics for thought.* New York: Comet Press Books.

Rupley, W. H., & Wilson, V. L. (1997). Relationship between comprehension and components of word recognition: Support for developmental shifts. *Journal of Research and Development in Education, 30,* 255–260.

Scanlon, D. M., & Vellutino, F. R. (1997). A comparison of the instructional backgrounds and cognitive profiles of poor, average, and good readers who were initially identified as at risk for reading failure. *Scientific Studies of Reading, 1,* 191–215.

Snow, C. E., Burns, M. S., & Griffin, P. (Eds.) (1998). *Preventing reading difficulties in young children.* Washington, DC: National Academy Press.

Stuart, M. (1995). Through printed words to meaning: Issues of transparency. *Journal of Research in Reading, 18,* 126–131.

Watson, C. (1971). *Father Fox's pennyrhymes.* New York: Harper & Row.

Zinna, D. R., Liberman, I. Y., & Shankweiler, D. (1986). Children's sensitivity to factors influencing vowel reading. *Reading Research Quarterly, 21,* 465–479.

CHAPTER
6

The Multiletter Chunk Strategy

Using Groups of Letters to Identify Words

This chapter describes how readers use multiletter chunks to identify long, complex words. You will find out about the different types of multiletter chunks, how readers use them to identify unfamiliar words, and ways to support readers as they use this streamlined word identification strategy.

KEY IDEAS

➤ Chunks are the multiletter chunks in words that readers recognize and automatically pronounce.

➤ Meaningful multiletter chunks contribute to pronunciation and meaning, for example, the root word **sign** in **signature** and **signal;** the prefix **re-** in **replay;** the suffix **-ly** in **friendly.** Nonmeaningful chunks contribute to pronunciation only, as the **tion** in **transportation.**

➤ Structural analysis is the use of meaningful and nonmeaningful multiletter chunks to identify and learn long and complex new words.

➤ Readers who use the chunk strategy streamline word identification by pronouncing and blending multiletter groups as intact units.

At a mere glance, you know how to pronounce **astroport** (Figure 6–1), recognize that it is most likely an interstellar station for the space traveling public, know it is a noun, and, if asked, could use **astroport** in a sentence. All this is quite interesting since **astroport** is not a real word, at least not yet.

The way to unlock this word's pronunciation and at the same time to get insight into its meaning is to divide **astroport** into the two large, meaningful multiletter chunks—**astro** and **port.** Each multiletter chunk is spelled the way it sounds and contributes to the word's definition, provided you know that **ast(er)** means "star" and **port** means "to carry." With this knowledge, you might logically infer that an **astroport** is a site to which space travelers are transported, just as an airport is a site to which airline passengers are transported.

After reading and writing the same letter groups time and time again, readers perceive these groups as large, intact units (Stuart & Coltheart, 1988). In so doing, readers chunk, or join together, groups of letters in their minds. The use of multiletter chunks significantly reduces the energy readers put into word identification and, when readers know the meaning of chunks, provides them with insight into the definition of words as well. Readers who use multiletter chunks do not recall analogous onsets and rimes in known words to identify unknown words as do users of the analogy with onsets and rimes strategy, nor do they sound out and blend the sounds of letters in neighborhoods as do users of the letter-sound strategy. Instead, readers recognize and pronounce all at once entire groups of letters in words.

Multiletter chunks may indicate both meaning and sound, as the **un-** in **unhappy,** or sound only, as the **tion** in **nation.** Meaningful and nonmeaningful chunks together are called **structural cues.** Meaningful multiletter chunks consist of prefixes (the **re-** in **repay**), suffixes (the **able** in **payable**), contractions (**is + not = isn't**),

Figure 6–1   Meaningful chunks give insight into pronunciation and word meaning. The student who drew this picture used knowledge of **astro** and **port** to show what they might mean if put together.

astroport

compound words (**cow** + **boy** = **cowboy**) and root words (**pay**). Syllables are the predominant nonmeaningful multiletter chunks (the **sta** and **ble** in **stable**). When you, the teacher, help readers use multiletter chunks to identify unfamiliar words, you are teaching **structural analysis.**[1] Rather than focus on the sound level, which is the scope of phonics instruction and the letter-sound strategy, structural analysis focuses on the large structural units that make up words—prefixes and suffixes, compound words, contractions, root words, and syllables and accents.

When you demonstrate how the meaning of **effort** is changed by adding **-less** to make **effortless,** you are teaching structural analysis by helping readers use the meaningful multiletter groups in words. When you point out that the **g** in **sign** is there to show the meaningful relationship between **sign, signal,** and **signature,** you are also teaching structural analysis. And when you help a fifth grader use a hyphen to divide the word **government** into syllables so as to write part of the word on one line (**govern-**) and part on another (**ment**), you are teaching word

---

[1]Analysis of meaningful units in words is part of morphology, a specialized study in linguistics which concentrates on word forms and their connections to meaning. Prefixes and suffixes, contractions, compound words, and root words, including Greek and Latin roots, are more accurately described as morphemic analysis because each deals with meaning. Syllables, accents, and other pronunciation units, such as rimes, represent sound and therefore are associated with phonic analysis. Combining meaningful and nonmeaningful chunks under the umbrella of structural analysis makes sense for the purpose of teaching inasmuch as readers recognize these letter groups as single, intact units.

structure. Interestingly, the use of chunks is not unique to reading, for you chunk all sorts of information, and you do this for good reason.

WHY CHUNKS?

You form chunks whenever you bundle several small bits of information together into one unit. For example, when you combine the letters **p + r + e** in **precook** into one whole unit **pre-,** you create a multiletter chunk in your mind. You use chunks to prevent a bottleneck in short-term memory. All information goes through short-term memory on its way to long-term memory. Your short-term memory holds all the information about whatever you happen to be paying attention to at the moment. Long-term memory, in turn, is the storehouse for all the information, words, ideas, and memories you accumulate throughout your life. Consequently, you want to get as much information as possible out of short-term memory and into long-term memory.

While there is a great deal of space to store information in long-term memory, the storage space in short-term memory is extremely limited. In fact, only five to seven thought units are held in short-term memory at once (Miller, 1956), and this information lasts only a few seconds before it is either forgotten or moved into long-term memory. A thought unit can be small (one letter, such as **p**) or large (a group of letters, as **pre-**). A bottleneck occurs when there are so many thought units in short-term memory that some are forgotten before information is sent to long-term memory.

When you combine small bits of information (a single letter, **p**) together into a large chunk (a group of letters, **pre-**), you pack more information into a single thought unit. This prevents overcrowding and makes it easier to keep more information in short-term memory. It also makes it possible to get more information into long-term memory because a number of small bits of information are grouped together in each thought unit.

Take **astroport** as an example. If you consider the nine letters separately **(a + s + t + r + o + p + o + r + t)**, you are sure to overburden short-term memory. However, if you consider multiletter chunks, you reduce information to just two thought units: **astro** and **port.** With only two thought units in short-term memory, you are less likely to forget information, and there is room left over to make a little sense of **astroport** before it goes to long-term memory. Added to this, the use of multiletter chunks decreases the number of spoken language segments to be blended. Blending a few large chunks—**"astro" + "port"**—makes it less likely that individual sounds will be forgotten or reversed.

Given the advantages of multiletter chunks, it is not at all surprising that as readers increase the number of chunks they recognize, their efficiency in word identification improves (Invernizzi, 1992). All in all, readers who use chunks put less mental attention and less mental energy into word identification than is the case with other forms of word identification. This means that readers who use large letter groups return to textual reading more quickly and hence the disruption to comprehension created by unfamiliar words is reduced.

What Readers Know about Phonemic Awareness and Multiletter Chunks

Readers who use multiletter chunks know that spoken words can be divided into a variety of sound units, some small and some large. They also know that the same multisound units are part of many different words, as the **"ter"** in **"butter"** and **"terrific."** And, of course, users of the multiletter chunk strategy can separate spoken words into individual sounds and multisound units, and they can blend individual sounds and multisound units together to form recognizable words. Readers who look for and use multiletter chunks know that some of the multisound units in words are associated with pronunciation only (the **"ter"** in **"after"**), while others are associated with meaning as well as pronunciation (the **"astro"** in **"astroport"**).

Readers recognize many different size multiletter chunks in words, some meaningful and some nonmeaningful. Multiletter chunks are like large envelopes that contain all the information needed to identify and pronounce whole groups of letters. Unlike users of the letter-sound strategy, who associate sounds with the individual letters that reside in letter-sound neighborhoods, readers who use the multiletter chunk strategy instantly recognize and know how to pronounce multiletter groups in words. The more reading and writing experiences children have in school, the more they learn about the multiletter chunks in language, and the more accomplished they become at using the multiletter chunk strategy. When children use multiletter chunks, it takes less mental attention to identify words and, by extension, requires less time away from understanding authors' messages.

What Readers Do with Their Knowledge

The multiletter chunk strategy hinges on recognizing and using the multiletter chunks in words, as you will see when Peter comes across the word **antiseptic** in this sentence from his science book (Hackett, Moyer, & Adams, 1989): "Perhaps you recall getting a cut on your knee. Someone may have disinfected the cut with an **antiseptic**" (page 27).

Peter's science class has already discussed antiseptics and their function, so this word is in his speaking and listening vocabularies. Added to this, Peter knows that **anti** means "against" or "preventing" when it is in common words like **antismoking** and **antitheft.** All things considered, Peter brings a good deal of knowledge to word identification. He knows (1) what the word **antiseptic** means, (2) how **anti** contributes to a word's definition, (3) how letters form neighborhoods in words, and (4) how to recognize many different types of multiletter chunks in the words he reads. Here is how Peter goes about using the multiletter chunk strategy:

1. Peter recognizes **anti** as a part of other words he knows and, in so doing, instantly recalls its pronunciation and meaning.
2. He identifies two additional multiletter chunks—**sep** and **tic.** Peter now has divided **antiseptic** into three pronounceable chunks: **"anti" + "sep" + "tic."**
3. Peter blends **"anti" + "sep" + "tic"** into **"antiseptic."**
4. Last, he cross-checks to make sure that he pronounces and understands the word in the context in which it is used in his science book. He asks himself: Does **antiseptic** sound and look right? Does **antiseptic** make sense in the passage? If **antiseptic** makes sense, Peter continues reading the passage.

In the way he separated them, the first group of letters is a meaningful chunk with two syllables (**anti**) and the last two chunks correspond to individual syllables (**sep** and **tic**). But there are other chunks Peter might have chosen. Though the **septic** in **antiseptic** is a meaningful multiletter chunk, it is not in Peter's speaking or listening vocabulary. Had he known the meaning of **septic,** Peter might have divided **antiseptic** into the two meaningful multiletter chunks—**anti + septic.** Or he could have divided **antiseptic** into **an + ti + sep + tic** or into **an + ti + septic.** Though the specific multiletter groups individual readers use will vary depending on each reader's background knowledge, all multiletter chunk strategists are sensitive to which letter chunks are chunks and which are not, and which multiletter groups are meaningful and which are not.

Take the multiletter chunk **ing** as an example. Readers know that **ing** represents meaning and sound in **playing,** and a nonmeaningful rime in **swing.** They also know that **ing** is not a viable multiletter chunk in **derringer.** When identifying chunks, readers consider the letter neighborhoods in a word. This explains why Peter did not identify the **ise** as a multiletter chunk in **antiseptic.** Though **ise** is a pronounceable multiletter chunk in **advise** and **demise,** it is not a viable chunk in **antiseptic** because it is not consistent with the surrounding letter neighborhoods. Peter, and readers like him, use their knowledge of letter neighborhoods to determine the groups of letters in unfamiliar words that are most likely to be chunks. This type of in-depth knowledge of is not an overnight phenomenon. Rather, it develops gradually over time as readers strategically use structural cues to read and write.

Correcting Misidentifications

Readers who do not successfully identify pronounceable words on the first try choose from among the following alternatives:

1. Rechunk (divide words into different multiletter groups and then reblend).
2. Fall back on either the letter-sound or analogy strategy.
3. Look up words in the dictionary.
4. Ask expert readers for help.

Rechunking or falling back on the letter-sound or analogy with onsets and rimes strategies are, of course, less efficient ways to identify never-seen-before words.

With its dependence on an in-depth knowledge of structural cues, the multiletter chunk strategy does not come into its own until after readers have had experience using the analogy and letter-sound strategies, which brings us to the next section.

ROOTS OF THE MULTILETTER CHUNK STRATEGY

The multiletter chunk strategy is rooted in both the analogy and the letter-sound strategies. In fact, there is reason to believe that the very origin of multiletter chunks in readers' minds comes from using rimes and letter neighborhoods to identify words (Ehri, 1991). When readers use the analogy with onsets and rimes strategy, they learn how to capitalize on large, regular letter groups in spelling. This helps them develop a predisposition to look for and to use "rime" chunks. So, the use of analogous rimes presents early opportunities for readers to strategically use multiletter chunks and, in this sense, constitutes a step toward the more sophisticated chunk strategy.

When readers use the letter-sound strategy, they think analytically about the letter-sound neighborhoods in words. In so doing, they have opportunities to form hypotheses about recurring multiletter chunks within and across neighborhoods. As a consequence of reading and writing the same multiletter groups, readers eventually fuse letters together to recognize common chunks (Stuart & Coltheart, 1988). Children then refine their knowledge of multiletter chunks through even more reading and writing experiences and, as reading maturity increases, so too does the ability to take advantage of multiletter chunks (Santa, 1976–1977).

Once the chunk strategy develops, it coexists with the analogy and letter-sound strategies. And as readers become sensitive to more and more multiletter chunks, they remember more words with the same multiletter chunks and hence become much better at word learning (Ehri, 1998). As is to be expected with such a streamlined route to word identification, understanding nonmeaningful and meaningful multiletter chunks is crucial, which brings us to the use of multiletter chunks and movement toward word fluency.

THE CONSOLIDATED PHASE OF MOVEMENT TOWARD WORD FLUENCY AND THE TRANSITIONAL PHASE OF SPELLING

Readers who use large multiletter chunks to identify words are at the consolidated phase of movement toward word fluency. These readers are not neophytes just cutting their teeth on our alphabetic writing system. They have insight into the letter-sound associations in neighborhoods and have consolidated, or chunked, letter sequences in memory (Ehri, 1998). Readers at the consolidated phase recognize meaningful chunks (the **ing** in **fishing**), syllables (the **bac** in **bacteria**), and parts of syllables (the **est** in **digest**). While the transition into the use of multiletter chunks comes toward the end of second grade for most children, some will move into this phase during the third grade.

Readers at the consolidated phase use the reading context to help them identify words and use cross-checking to determine if words make sense in the passages they read. These readers know when to self-correct and, because their focus is on meaning, know when it is necessary to fix a word identification miscue and when it is not profitable to do so. They do not sound out words letter-sound by letter-sound, nor do they think about analogous portions of known words to identify unknown words. Instead, these readers automatically recognize large intact letter groups in words. Readers recognize nonmeaningful letter chunks, such as the **tion** in **portion** and the **ture** in **picture.** They also automatically recognize meaningful prefixes (the **post-** in **postgame**); **suffixes** (the **-er** in **smaller**); **syllables** (the **por** and **tion** in **portion**); and **root words** (the **clean** in **cleaning,** for example). Using large, multiletter chunks is the last strategy to mature before readers reach the point where they automatically recognize all the words in text.

Readers at the consolidated phase of word fluency are transitional spellers who have insight into the structure of words and hence use this understanding when spelling (Gentry, 1987). When you look at the writing of transitional spellers, you will notice that they: (1) conventionally spell common word endings (such as **-s, -ed, -ing,** and **-ly**); (2) include a vowel in every syllable; (3) put a vowel before **r** (though not necessarily the correct vowel, **buttur** instead of **butter**); and (4) use the **CVe** long vowel pattern and the **VV** long vowel neighborhood. You will also notice that the transitional spellers in your classroom sometimes substitute alternative spellings for the same sound, **naym** or **naim** for **name,** is an example.

By late spring of second grade, Shania (Figure 6–2), a transitional speller, is sensitive to some of the meaningful multiletter chunks that make up the structure of words. She spells common word endings correctly (**lives, fishing,** and **lunches,** for instance), uses the **VV** long vowel neighborhood (**street** and **each**) and puts a vowel in every syllable. She writes a vowel before **r** (**together** and **over**), though she sometimes writes letters in the wrong sequence (**evrey**). And, of course, she conventionally spells most of the words in her fluent reading vocabulary. When Shania misspells, she writes words the way she believes they sound (**comin** for **common**). From her misspelling of **snaping** for **snapping,** we can infer that Shania is still learning how to add endings to words that require doubling the last consonant. The more literacy experiences she has the more sensitive she will become to the multiletter chunks in words and the more effectively she will use this knowledge when she reads and spells.

Fifth-grade Kristen (Figure 6–3) spells all words conventionally, with the exception of **restaurant,** which she spells as **restarant.** She has a large fluent reading vocabulary and, therefore, identifies many words automatically. When she does not automatically recognize a word, she is most likely to look for pronounceable multiletter chunks. Kristen's knowledge of multiletter chunks will continue to grow in middle and high school. This is important because she will rely on this

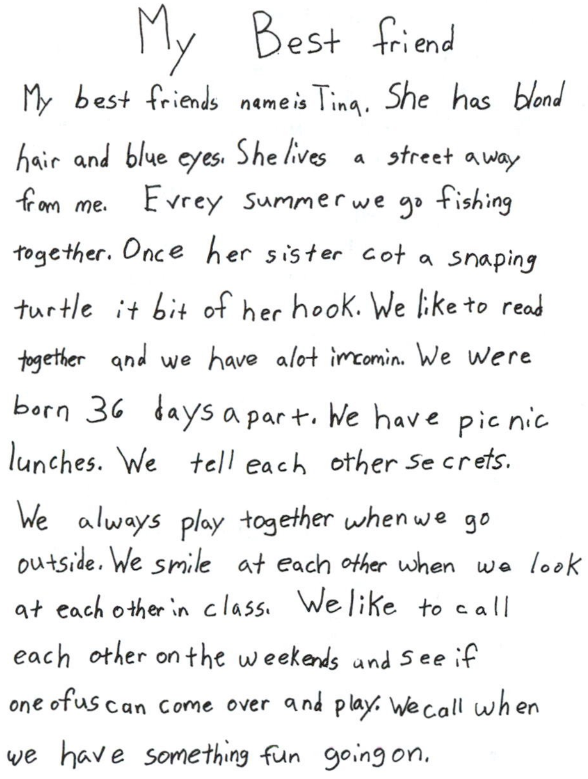

Figure 6–2 Having internalized alphabetic cues, Shania now recognizes multiletter chunks in words, and uses this knowledge when she reads and spells.

My Best friend

My best friends name is Tina. She has blond hair and blue eyes. She lives a street away from me. Evrey summer we go fishing together. Once her sister cot a snaping turtle it bit of her hook. We like to read together and we have alot in comin. We were born 36 days apart. We have picnic lunches. We tell each other secrets.

We always play together when we go outside. We smile at each other when wa look at each other in class. We like to call each other on the weekends and see if one of us can come over and play. We call when we have something fun going on.

strategy when she is challenged to learn the many long and complex technical terms in high school textbooks.

In due time, children's reading vocabulary becomes so enormous that it includes all the words they typically see in text. Children who automatically recognize all the words they read are at the fifth and final phase—**fluent recognition**—of movement toward word fluency. Now word recognition is completely automatic, with the exception, of course, of unusual words and some content subject words (Ehri, 1998). Readers who automatically recognize all the ordinary words authors use also spell conventionally (Gentry, 1987). Not only do children spell known words correctly, including irregular words, but they know when words are not spelled right and fix their own misspellings. Accomplished high school readers use many effective comprehension strategies and, because they automatically recognize words, they concentrate on comprehending and learning from their textbooks. When these readers encounter new words, they use the multiletter chunk strategy, calling upon their extensive knowledge of meaningful multiletter groups to learn words in subjects like geometry, physics, geography, and American literature.

Figure 6–3
Kristen, a fifth grader, conventionally spells the words in her fluent reading vocabulary. When reading, she looks for pronounceable multiletter chunks in the words she does not automatically recognize.

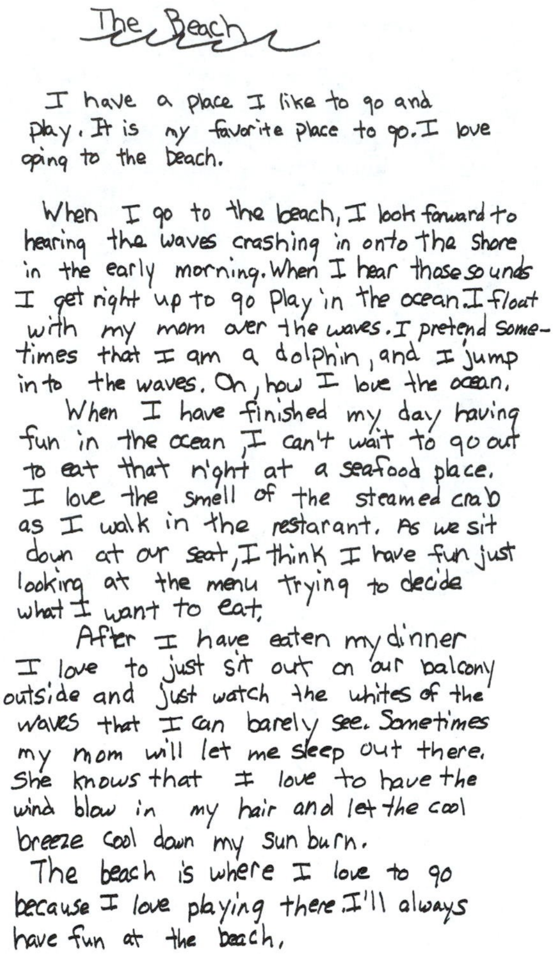

The Beach

I have a place I like to go and play. It is my favorite place to go. I love going to the beach.

When I go to the beach, I look forward to hearing the waves crashing in onto the shore in the early morning. When I hear those sounds I get right up to go play in the ocean. I float with my mom over the waves. I pretend sometimes that I am a dolphin, and I jump into the waves. Oh, how I love the ocean.

When I have finished my day having fun in the ocean, I can't wait to go out to eat that night at a seafood place. I love the smell of the steamed crab as I walk in the restarant. As we sit down at our seat, I think I have fun just looking at the menu trying to decide what I want to eat.

After I have eaten my dinner I love to just sit out on our balcony outside and just watch the whites of the waves that I can barely see. Sometimes my mom will let me sleep out there. She knows that I love to have the wind blow in my hair and let the cool breeze cool down my sunburn.

The beach is where I love to go because I love playing there. I'll always have fun at the beach.

MEANINGFUL MULTILETTER CHUNKS

Meaningful multiletter chunks give readers insight into the definition of words, which explains why meaningful chunks are so important for word recognition (Nagy, Anderson, Schommer, Scott, & Stallman, 1989). Insight into meaning is particularly important for older readers who meet a good many long and complex words in content subject and leisure reading books. Many of these words are not in readers' speaking and listening vocabularies. However, when readers combine multiletter chunks with syntactic and semantic context cues, growth in reading vocabulary extends and expands the number of words in children's speaking and listening vocabularies. Now, at last, vocabulary learning by reading surpasses learning by speaking and listening. The meaningful multiletter groups—prefixes and suffixes, root words, compound words, and contractions—are described next.

Prefixes and Suffixes

Prefixes are separate syllables attached to the beginning of words and hence are usually quite easy to recognize. Prefixes either change the meaning of the root word completely, as in **non + fatal = nonfatal** (which results in an opposite), or make meaning more specific, as in **pre + pay = prepay** (which means to pay "before"). In Appendix C, you will find a list of common prefixes and their meanings.

Suffixes, on the other hand, are the multiletter chunks attached to the end of words. Like prefixes, suffixes are separate syllables (with the exception of plurals like the **-s** in **dogs**). Some suffixes change grammatical function. For example, adding **-ly** to **bright** changes an adjective (**the bright sun**) to an adverb (**the sun shone brightly**). Other suffixes clarify meaning or add information, as in **cat + s = cats** (**s** marks the plural); **cup + ful = cupful; friend + ship = friendship; sea + ward = seaward.** Readers who know how suffixes affect meaning understand that **prepares, prepared,** and **preparing** are variations of a single word, **prepare,** not three brand new words. Look in Appendix D for a list of common suffixes and their meanings.

Using these two structural cues is important because the number of words with prefixes and suffixes doubles from fourth to fifth grade, and doubles again by the seventh grade (White, Power, & White, 1989). It is estimated that fifth graders may meet an average of about 1,325 words a year that include the prefixes **in-, im-, ir-,** and **il-** (meaning "not"), and **un-, re-,** and **dis-.** Seventh graders may well identify 3,000 words, and perhaps as many as 9,000 words, with these prefixes as well as a variety of suffixes. As readers move into higher and higher grades, their knowledge of suffixes increases (Nagy, Diakidoy, & Anderson, 1993), quite possibly as a consequence of earlier experiences with phonetic spelling and increased grammatical awareness (Nunes, Bryant, & Bindman, 1997). So, it is not surprising that fourth, sixth and eighth graders use their knowledge of suffixes to read new words in context, and that sixth and eighth graders are better at this than fourth graders (Wysocki & Jenkins, 1987).

Though older readers meet a great many prefixes and suffixes, words with prefixes or suffixes do not make up the major portion of text in the storybooks younger children read (Ives, Bursuk, & Ives, 1979). Nevertheless, it is wise to begin to explore meaningful multiletter chunks early, and suffixes are a better investment in learning than are prefixes (Durkin, 1993). This is because authors who write for young readers frequently use words that end with **-s/es, -ing,** and **-ed,** which makes these suffixes extremely important (Templeton, 1991). These three word endings make up to 65 percent of the suffixes children in grades three through nine are likely to read (White, Sowell, & Yanagihara, 1989), and they are marked by an asterisk in Appendix D. The majority of readers become aware of **-s(es), -ing,** and **-ed** by the end of the first grade, and **-er, -est,** and **-ly** by the end of the second grade. In Appendix F, you will find generalizations for adding the five most frequently used suffixes—**s(es), -ed, -ing, -ly,** and **-er**—to words (White, Sowell, & Yanagihara, 1989).

Ross's story (Figure 6–4) illustrates how a precocious first grader uses common suffixes. Ross conventionally spells words with **-ed, -ing,** and **-s/es,** and correctly forms contractions. Ross has internalized—cemented in memory—these multiletter groups so well that they are second nature when he reads and writes.

Figure 6–4
Through his writing
Ross demonstrates that
he knows how to
correctly use and
conventionally spell
common suffixes, and
how to form
contractions.

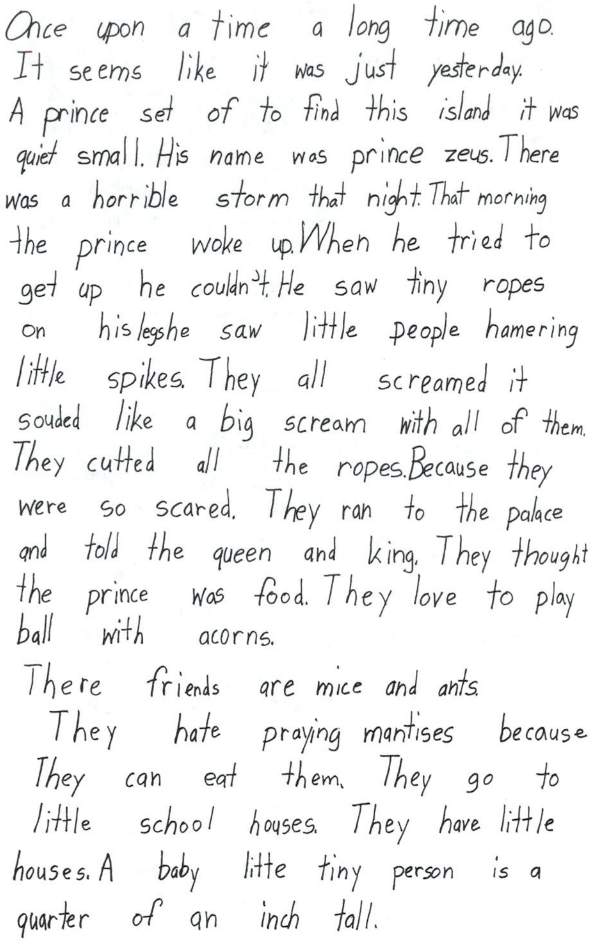

Once upon a time a long time ago.
It seems like it was just yesterday.
A prince set of to find this island it was
quiet small. His name was prince zeus. There
was a horrible storm that night. That morning
the prince woke up. When he tried to
get up he couldn't. He saw tiny ropes
on his legs he saw little people hamering
little spikes. They all screamed it
souded like a big scream with all of them.
They cutted all the ropes. Because they
were so scared. They ran to the palace
and told the queen and king. They thought
the prince was food. They love to play
ball with acorns.

There friends are mice and ants.
They hate praying mantises because
They can eat them. They go to
little school houses. They have little
houses. A baby litte tiny person is a
quarter of an inch tall.

For example, he drops the final **y** in **try** and writes an **i** before adding **-ed** to spell
tried. Notice the word **cutted,** which does not need an **-ed** to signal past tense.
Ross writes the way he talks, and he sometimes says **"cutted"** when he means
"cut." Though Ross does not use **cut** conventionally, he shows us that he understands the convention of doubling the last consonant, the letter **t,** before adding
the **-ed.** Ross's teacher thinks he will benefit from learning more about writing in
complete sentences, and using periods and capitals, so she has formed a small,
flexible skill group to give Ross and a handful of his classmates extra help with
punctuation. Ross reminds us that streamlined word identification and a large fluent reading vocabulary are not tied to children's grade in school but are instead a
consequence of in-depth knowledge of our alphabetic writing system coupled
with a plethora of reading and writing experiences.

By the third grade, children have had enough reading and writing experience to begin to understand and use suffixes like **-able** and **-ous** (Henderson, 1990). Generally speaking, those suffixes that have a significant affect on word meaning—the **-less** in **faithless**—present greater learning challenges than more frequent endings that are part of the grammatical structure of English (the plural **-s** attached to **cats** or the past tense **-ed** in **played**). For this reason, endings like the **-or** in **actor** and the **-logy** in **biology** are more easily learned when readers are in the upper grades.

By and large, readers learn the meaning of prefixes after they have learned easy-to-recognize suffixes. Prior to second grade, children are likely to recognize and use the prefix **un-,** but not necessarily other prefixes. In general, third grade is the time when readers add important prefixes to their knowledge of structural cues, such as **super-** (**superman**), **dis-** (**disagree**), **re-** (**redo**), and **pre-** (**pretest**).

White, Sowell, and Yanagihara (1989) identified the twenty most important prefixes and suffixes for children in grades three through nine. You can find them marked by an asterisk in Appendixes C (Prefixes) and D (Suffixes). According to White et al. (1989), a mere smattering, four to be exact, account for 58 percent of the words with prefixes that third through ninth graders are likely to read. Among this group, **un-, re-, in-** (meaning "not"), and **dis-** are the four that occur most frequently. **Un-** accounts for the lion's share: A full 26 percent of words with prefixes were found to begin with **un-**. While **un-, re-, in-,** and **dis-** are certainly useful, older readers benefit from knowledge of more difficult prefixes because these prefixes offer considerable insight into word meaning (Harris & Sipay, 1990).

My advice is to begin by exploring prefixes and suffixes that occur frequently or that have only a moderate affect on the meaning of words in the books and poems that children read, such as **-(es), -ing, -ed, un-, re-, in-,** and **dis-**. Then, as children's knowledge expands, introduce prefixes and suffixes that occur less frequently or that have a significant affect on meaning. Rest assured that as children gain knowledge of prefixes and suffixes, they also gain the ability to dramatically expand their reading vocabularies, which in turn makes it feasible to read increasingly more complex and conceptually demanding text.

Root Words

Root words are complete, recognizable words and therefore different from syllables, which are units of pronunciation. A root word can have one syllable (**play**) or several syllables (**elephant,** which is three syllables: **el-e-phant**). Though the number of syllables may vary, root words themselves are the smallest real English words to which prefixes and suffixes are added. Suppose readers come across the word **disinfected** for the first time. To identify this word, advise them to:

1. Look for a prefix. Ask, "Do I see a prefix I know?"
   If found, peel it off:
   disinfected = dis + infected

2. Look for a suffix. Ask, "Do I see a suffix I know?"
   If found, peel it off, too:
   dis + infect + ed
3. Look at the root word. Ask, "Do I see a root word I can read?" What does it mean?

Analyzing words into prefixes, suffixes, and roots gives readers a way to infer meaning (Alverman & Phelps, 1998). And, should the prefixes and suffixes confuse readers, peeling them off reveals a root word that is already part of readers' fluent reading vocabulary.

When root words are not in readers' speaking and listening vocabularies, readers might look for clues to meaning in the chunks that have a Greek or Latin origin. When the scholars, philosophers, and authors of the Renaissance became interested in writing in their own language, English, they borrowed liberally from ancient Greek and Latin (Ayers, 1980). Just as the great thinkers and writers of the Renaissance used Greek and Latin words to coin lots of new words, so too do we continue this tradition today. When we ventured into space in the middle of the twentieth century, a new word was needed for space explorers. Rather than devising a whole new word from scratch, the term **astronaut** was coined by combining the Greek root **aster,** meaning "star," with **naut,** meaning "sailor." Considering the Greek origin, modern-day **astronauts** are **star sailors,** a term that suggests all sorts of engaging images.

Words that share the same Greek or Latin roots, such as **infirm, firmament,** and **confirm,** form meaning families (Henderson, 1990; Templeton, 1991). Content subjects in the upper grades are peppered with words built from Greek and Latin roots—**carnivorous, democracy, multiple, polygon, document, epidermis, corpuscle,** and **dogmatic,** to mention but a few. By organizing words into meaning families, readers have a platform for figuring out the meaning of unfamiliar words with the same root. For example, **aqua** (a Latin root) means "water," and therefore words with this root also have something to do with water, as in **aquarium, aquatic, aqueduct,** and **aquaplane.** Likewise, **poly** (a Greek root) means "many;" and so, **polynomial, polygon, polysyllabic,** and **polygamy** all pertain to conditions in which there are many different facets, sides, conditions, or individuals. From a practical standpoint, you can expect readers who recognize and appreciate the chunks made up of Greek and Latin roots to learn a great many technical terms with relative ease and to do so with less guidance from you than their classmates who do not understand the contribution Greek and Latin roots make to English words.

Though Greek and Latin roots are powerful tools for word identification, readers are not likely to figure out the meaning of roots from normal reading experiences. In part, this is because roots are semihidden in words and in part because each word that includes a root has a slightly different meaning (**aquarium** and **aquaplane** both pertain to water but the meaning of individual words is quite different). Consequently, to develop the ability to strategically use Greek and Latin roots, readers need explicit explanations of them and modeling of how to use them to unlock word meaning, as well as many opportunities to read and write words with them.

In Appendix E, you will find lists of common Greek and Latin roots, their meanings, and examples of words that contain roots. As with all appendixes in this book, there are many items from which to choose, so select those roots you believe will be beneficial for the children whom you teach. Use Greek and Latin roots in meaningful reading contexts, relate the roots to everyday life experiences, discuss and explore roots, and support readers as they use roots to expand and refine their reading, writing, speaking, and listening vocabularies.

Compound Words

Compound words are formed when two words—for example, **finger** and **print**—are glued together to create a third word—in this case, **fingerprint.** Compounds differ depending on how far afield meaning wanders from the definitions of the individual words that are put together (Miller & McKenna, 1989). In the case of **fingerprint,** the general definition of each word is unchanged. A second sort of compound is made of words whose meanings are somewhat different than that of the combined form, such as **basketball, driveway, skyscraper,** and **spotlight.** In a third category of compounds, the meaning of the compound has practically nothing to do with the meaning of the individual words. Examples include **butterfly, fireworks, dragonfly, hardware, turtleneck,** and **peppermint.** Knowing the words that make up this sort of compound provides precious little insight into the meaning of the compounds themselves.

The readers whom I teach find compound words to be the easiest meaningful multiletter chunks to learn. Perhaps this is because compounds are made of two whole words and hence are not overly challenging to identify. And when the words that make up compounds are already in children's fluent reading vocabularies, pronunciation is merely a question of saying the words together. As for the meaning of compounds, I find that readers are intrigued by the changes in meaning that occur when words are glued together. First graders enjoy finding words that are glued together in compounds. Older learners, on the other hand, have had so many rich experiences with print that the compounds they see in everyday reading usually pose no challenge whatsoever.

Contractions

Contractions are formed when one or more letters (and sounds) are deleted from words. Missing letters are replaced in writing by an apostrophe, which is a visual clue telling readers that a word is abbreviated, as in **hasn't, he's, she'll,** and **let's.** Words mean exactly the same thing whether they are written as a contraction or individually. First graders meet contractions in everyday reading material, so it is important that these readers learn to recognize the contractions they see in storybooks.

All children encounter contractions in reading and use them in writing, so working with contractions is a good large group activity. I use a set of magnetic letters with a magnetic apostrophe to illustrate how contractions are formed. I ask first and second graders to use magnetic letters to change words like **she** and **will** into **she'll,** as well as to reverse the process by changing contractions (**she'll**) into two words (**she** and **will**). Another way to explore contractions is to write two sentences on the chalkboard. In the first sentence, underline two words that can be combined to form a contraction. In the second sentence, leave a blank where the contraction should be. For example, you might write the following:

1. The dog <u>did not</u> find the bone.
2. The dog _____ find the bone.

Children read the first sentence, form a contraction from the two underlined words (**did** and **not**), and write the contraction (**didn't**) in the blank in the second sentence. Everyone then reads both sentences together in chorus while you sweep your hand under the words as they are read. When you do this, you might want to use sentences from storybooks the students have read so as to make sure that written language is familiar and a part of readers' background knowledge.

NONMEANINGFUL MULTILETTER CHUNKS

Accurately speaking, the frequently occurring rimes in Appendix A are non-meaningful chunks. This is true even for rimes like **at** and **it,** because these rimes do not have meaning when combined with onsets in words like **rat** and **fit.** We learned about rimes in Chapter 4 because readers notice and use them far earlier than more complicated multiletter chunks (Invernizzi, 1992). When readers meet long, complex words, they look for rimes, to be sure, but they also consider syllables. Most syllables, such as the **sep** in **antiseptic,** are nonmeaningful multiletter chunks that signal pronunciation, yet give no clue as to a word's meaning.

The way to figure out the pronunciation of long words is to break them into manageable, pronounceable multiletter chunks. Readers do this by first identifying meaningful letter chunks—prefixes, suffixes, and root words—and then looking for other pronounceable, though nonmeaningful, chunks. The nonmeaningful, pronounceable multiletter chunks are typically syllables. My recommendation is use whole, intact words to teach readers about syllables, to relate syllables to pronunciation, and to expect readers to apply knowledge when reading and writing. As with phonics rules, I see no value in teaching rules in isolation or expecting readers to memorize them by rote. I have, however, included syllable rules here so that you, the teacher, bring to children's instruction a knowledge of syllable conventions that informs your own classroom teaching.

We shall use as an example the words **tympanic membrane,** the scientific term for eardrum in a ninth-grade biology book. Suppose for purposes of illustration that **tympanic** is the troublesome word. By dividing **tympanic** into syllables, readers break it into three pronounceable chunks: **tym-pan-ic.** It is then relatively simple to associate sounds with the letters in neighborhoods. Deciding on the stress pattern is more challenging, but you will learn guidelines to help make this determination. Blending results in **"tym-PAN-ic,"** with **PAN** the accented, or stressed, syllable.

When we say words aloud, it is sometimes hard to decide where one syllable ends and another begins. And when consulting the dictionary, we find occasionally that syllable division does not reflect pronunciation. As the teacher, you do not want readers to memorize dictionary style syllabification. Rather, your goal is to help readers divide words into syllables so that complex words can be identified, pronounced, and learned. This brings us to the syllable and accent patterns themselves.

Syllable Patterns

The syllable is the basic unit of pronunciation. Each syllable has one vowel sound, so the number of syllables in a word equals the number of vowels heard. Try saying **metabolic.** How many vowels do you hear? **"Met"-"a"-"bol"-"ic"** has four vowel sounds and hence four syllables. Now try **trample.** When you pronounce the last syllable, **ple,** you do not notice a distinct vowel. You hear instead a vowel-like sound—**"pul."** So when we divide words into syllables, we listen for vowel and vowel-like sounds. One vowel or vowel-like sound equals one syllable.

Readers can identify the syllables in unfamiliar words by counting vowel letter neighborhoods. Just as a spoken word has as many syllables as vowel sounds, so too does a written word have as many spoken syllables as the number of vowel neighborhoods. Words with one vowel neighborhood have one syllable—the **VC** neighborhood in **got; CV** in **go; VV** in **goat; VCe** in **gave.** Words with two vowel neighborhoods have two syllables—**ba-con** and **bea-con,** for example. Those with three vowel neighborhoods have three syllables (**in-ter-nal**), four neighborhoods have four syllables (**in-ter-nal-ize**) and so on.

Mysterious Thelonious (Raschka, 1997), written entirely in syllables, graphically demonstrates how the syllable is the unit of pronunciation within the word. In this short, captivating book, Raschka cleverly plays with language, music, and color by moving syllables and color around on the pages. This tribute to the jazz artist Thelonious Monk is especially captivating, for it uses words and color to paint a visual picture of Monk's music. The author shows how words, like music, are made of individual syllable-length sounds. He shows his readers that the syllable is the unit of pronunciation in words just as the note is the unit of sound in music. One after the other, syllables rise and fall on the pages making words as they imitate the music of the great jazz pianist and composer. Because of its abstract and sophisticated subject, *Mysterious Thelonious* (Raschka, 1997) is wonderfully appealing to readers and writers in the middle grades and high school. Encourage them to analyze the way words are built of syllables just as music is built of notes. And encourage them to write their own short books in words divided into syllables, just as Raschka has so artfully done.

And, when you and the children in your classroom write books like Raschka's that play with the syllables in English words, consider the following five syllable patterns. These syllable patterns are guidelines for dividing words into pronounceable multiletter chunks, though with exceptions, of course.

1. **Open syllable.** An open syllable ends in a vowel that generally represents a long sound. You can easily recognize the open syllable because it is the **CV** long vowel neighborhood. For example, the one-syllable word **go** is a single **CV** long vowel neighborhood. **Modem,** a two-syllable word (**mo-dem**), begins with a **CV** long vowel neighborhood, **mo,** and ends with a **(C)VC** short vowel neighborhood, **dem.** When there is a single consonant between two vowels, as in **modem,** that consonant frequently begins the second syllable, as in **mo-dem, be-gan,** and **si-lent.** Notice that the letters in these words form a **CV-CVC** pattern. Other examples of a single consonant between two vowels are **a-corn, lo-cal, o-ver,** and **si-lo.** The **Vr** neighborhood is a logical exception to this syllable division pattern because this neighborhood is not divided (**for-um,** not **fo-rum; mer-it,** not **me-rit;** and **chor-us,** not **cho-rus**). There are other exceptions, so advise readers to try the long vowel first and, if that does not work, to try the short sound.

2. **Closed syllable.** A closed syllable ends in a consonant, and the vowel typically represents a short sound. The closed syllable includes the **VC** short vowel neighborhood, as in the one-syllable words **at** and **in.** Most words will have one or more consonants that precede the vowel, as in the one-syllable words **chat** and **skin.** Examples of words that have closed syllables with the **VC** short vowel neighborhood include **static** (**stat-ic, CCVC-VC**), **ticket** (**tick-et, CVCC-VC**), and **transmit** (**trans-mit, CCVCC-CVC**). If there are two consonants between two vowels, as in the words **mental** and **napkin,** the syllable usually divides between the consonants (**men-tal** and **pub-lic**). Look for a **CVC-CVC** pattern as in **men-tal** and **nap-kin.** When words have double or twin consonants, the syllable divides between the two like consonants (**pup-pet** and **rab-bit**). Generally speaking, advise readers to avoid dividing between the letters of a digraph (**fash-ion**) and a blend (**se-cret**).

3. **Prefixes** and **suffixes.** Prefixes and suffixes are usually separate syllables, with the exception of **-s,** which does not have a vowel sound and hence cannot be a syllable. Examples include **dis-avow-ing, re-bill-ed,** and **non-work-er.**

4. **Le syllable.** When a word ends in **-le** preceded by a consonant—**ble, cle, dle, fle, gle, kle, ple, sle,** and **zle**—the consonant usually begins the syllable. Examples include: **fum-ble, mir-a-cle, can-dle, ri-fle, bea-gle, wrin-kle, dim-ple, has-sle, ti-tle,** and **driz-zle.** As explained in Appendix B, **bul** is pronounced as "bul," **cle** as "cul," **dle** as "dul," **fle** as "ful," **gle** as "gul," **kle** as "kul," **ple** as "pul," **sle** as "sul," **tle** as "tul," and **zle** as "zul."

5. **Compound words.** Compounds are divided between the two words, for instance **pop-corn, snow-man,** and **cow-boy.**

Looking at the five syllable patterns, we see that the closed syllable explains why we double the last consonant when adding suffixes to words ending with a **VC** short vowel neighborhood like **hop** and **sit.** By doubling the last consonant in a **VC** short vowel neighborhood, we spell **hopped** and **sitting,** thereby keeping the vowel in its proper neighborhood. It takes a lot of reading and writing experiences for children to learn when to double (or not to double) the last consonant. I have read many stories, poems, and reports by fourth and fifth graders who spell **hopped** as **hoped** and **sitting** as **siting.** Anticipate spending extra time helping children edit their writing and, perhaps, form a flexible skill group to give special practice to those who need it.

Accent Patterns

The syllables in complex words are given different stress. Accent, the stress given to syllables, is very important, for it affects vowel pronunciation. There are three levels of stress: primary, secondary, and reduced (or unaccented). For simplicity, we will call the syllable with the most stress the primary accent. The vowels in accented syllables tend to follow the pronunciation we would expect from their placement in letter neighborhoods. Most vowels in unaccented syllables have a soft, or short, sound. We will therefore focus on accented syllable and will put a (') after the syllable to indicate primary stress.

When we shift the primary accent, we also shift pronunciation. Try saying these words by placing the primary accent on the first or second syllable, as indicated: **con' tent** and **con tent'**; **ob' ject** and **ob ject'**; **con' vict** and **con vict'**. In these examples, shifting the primary accent from the first to the last syllable changes word meaning. Reread **con' tent, ob' ject,** and **con' vict.** What do you notice about these words? If you conclude that they are nouns, you are right. The primary accent tends to fall on the first syllable of a noun. Here are five guidelines to indicate where to place the primary accent:

1. All one-syllable words are accented syllables.
2. The primary accent most often falls on the first syllable of a two-syllable word (**ma' ple** and **gen' try**), unless the last syllable includes two vowels (**con ceal'** and **ap proach'**) and then that syllable is stressed.
3. Prefixes and suffixes are ordinarily not accented. The root word receives the primary accent, as in **name' less** and **ex chang' ing.**
4. The primary accent usually falls on the first word of compounds, such as **snow' man** and **base' ball.**
5. When a word has twin consonants, the primary accent generally falls on the syllable that closes with the first twin letter, as in **be gin' ning** and **ham' mer.**

Two additional tips help with certain spellings: First, **le** syllables are generally not accented, as in **tram' ple** and **tur' tle.** And second, syllables ending in **ck** are often accented, such as **buck' et** and **nick' el.**

After children have had a great deal of practice reading and writing complex words, syllable and accent patterns are learned so well that they are applied automatically. In fact, as an expert reader you can read, with the proper accent, nonsense words that conform to English spelling, even though you may not be able to "say" the rules. To prove this, read and divide into syllables these two nonsense words: **quimlar** and **plygus.** Did you divide them into the syllables of **quim-lar** and **ply-gus?** And did you pronounce them with the accent on the first syllable— **quim' lar** and **ply' gus?** If so, you are doing what other good readers do, using your in-depth knowledge of our writing system, including syllable and accent patterns, to identify and pronounce words.

LESSONS TO HELP READERS LEARN AND USE MEANINGFUL MULTILETTER CHUNKS

As children's reading ability increases, you can expect their knowledge of multiletter chunks to expand as well (Gibson & Guinet, 1971; Invernizzi, 1992; Santa, 1976–1977). Whereas sixth graders, ninth graders, and college students identify the correct vowel and consonant multiletter patterns in one and two syllable nonsense words, the choices of kindergartners through third graders are not above chance (Cassar & Treiman, 1997). My advice is to teach common often-used prefixes and suffixes to children in the primary grades, and then, as children move into the upper grades and beyond, teach the less common prefixes and suffixes, as well as meaningful Greek and Latin roots. Emphasize the common origin of words (like **aquarium, aquatic,** and **aqualung**) and help children use this knowledge to continually expand their reading vocabularies. Allocate plenty of time for writing and, when children spell, call their attention to the multiletter chunks in words.

Asking readers to memorize the lists of multiletter chunks like those in Appendixes C, D, and E is pointless because readers are unlikely to use the multiletter chunks in memorized lists. This is just as true for prefixes and suffixes (Lapp & Flood, 1992), as it is for Greek and Latin roots, compounds, and contractions. Instead of rote memorization, use the lessons that follow to help readers learn and use multiletter chunks. These lessons give children opportunities to recognize, remember, and use the multiletter chunks in words. Differentiate instruction by creating a large group if many readers would benefit from the same lessons, and a small group if lessons meet the needs of only a few readers. Use those lessons you believe will be most beneficial and adapt them to suit your own special classroom environment and teaching style. The more readers know about the multiletter chunks in English words, the more effective and efficient they are at word identification and spelling, and the closer they move toward the last phase of word fluency—the fluent recognition of all the words they read.

 ## *Coin-a-Word*

New words are added to our language all the time and here is a chance for the readers in your classroom to have a hand in the process. The goal is to increase readers' insight into meaningful Greek and Latin roots, prefixes, and suffixes. To accomplish this, readers and writers coin their own words, which means that they must have some familiarity with meaningful multiletter chunks before you use this lesson. Coin-a-Word is especially suited to social studies and science, and best used with readers who are in the fifth grade and up. (**Astroport,** the word at the beginning of this chapter, is an invention of a fifth grader.)

Things You'll Need: Wall charts of the prefixes, suffixes, and Greek roots and Latin roots from content area textbooks and the books written by readers' favorite authors, a wall chart of common nouns, a good imagination!

Exploration: Invite readers to make a list of the prefixes, suffixes, and Greek and Latin roots they find in their science, mathematics, and social studies texts. Then demonstrate, with children's help, how to combine these meaningful multiletter chunks together to create new words. (Creative Compounds, described later in this chapter in the Extra Practice Activities section, is similar and suitable for first or second graders.)

Guided Practice: Challenge readers to work individually or in small groups to combine chunks to form totally new words, to write a definition of each new word, and to illustrate each coined word. Put the coined words and illustrations on bulletin boards, along the chalk tray, or anywhere else where they are in plain view so that readers can use them in the transfer activity that follows.

Transfer: Invite cooperative groups of three or four readers to make crossword puzzles with the words they find in content area textbooks and with the words they have coined. Each crossword puzzle should include (1) a brief definition of each word and (2) either the page where the word is written in a content area textbook or a note that the word is an invention on display in the classroom. Last, invite groups to trade puzzles and to solve the puzzles their classmates have created.

🦋 *Complimenting Classmates*

This lesson gives children opportunities to read and discuss literature, learn about adjectives and suffixes, and compliment their classmates all at the same time. The book used as an illustration in this lesson, *The Best School Year Ever* (Robinson, 1996), is appropriate for end-of-year third graders and from easy to just right for fourth graders. You can make this lesson more challenging by selecting a book that is harder to read, less challenging by selecting an easier book.

Things You'll Need: Multiple copies of *The Best School Year Ever* (Robinson, 1996), one piece of colored tagboard cut in the shape of a shield for every child in your class, pens, a list of everyone in the class (one list per child), and several thesauruses.

Exploration: In the *Best School Year Ever* (Robinson, 1996), fourth graders are assigned a year-long project called "Compliments for Classmates" in which they must identify one positive character trait for each class member. Begin by having the class read and discuss the book. Talk about feelings, character traits, and the way children and adults treat one another. Define compliments as positive character traits, such as friendly, imaginative, or inventive.

Guided Practice: Challenge children to make a list of adjectives, and talk about how adjectives like the compliment **cheerful** describe nouns and about the suffixes attached to adjectives (the **-ful** added to **cheer** to make **cheerful,** a positive character trait). Point out that many of the adjectives in the list have suffixes, such as the **-ive** in **inventive.** Discuss how suffixes change a noun (**friend**) or a verb (**imagine**) into an adjective (**friendly** or **imaginative**). Talk, too, about how some suffixes, such as **-er** and

-est, show the relationship among adjectives, such as a **big box, bigger box, biggest box.** Then give the readers in your class a list of adjectives and a list of suffixes, and ask them to add the suffixes to as many adjectives as they can. Count the number of words built with suffixes and save the list for the transfer portion that follows.

Transfer: Give a class list to each child. Ask children to think of one compliment—a positive character trait—for each of their classmates, just like the assignment in *The Best School Year Ever* (Robinson, 1996). When writing compliments, children cannot use worn out adjectives and cannot use the same compliment twice. For example, if a child uses **imaginative** to describe one classmate, the child cannot use that same word to compliment another classmate. Tell children to use the thesaurus to find synonyms. After each child has written one compliment next to the name of each of their class-mates on the class list you have given them, pass out a colored tagboard shield (called an Honor Shield) to each child. Ask each child to write his/her name on the shield. Then, using the list of classmates and compliments, children write a compliment on each child's shield. When finished, a shield has as many compliments as there are chil-dren in your class. To avoid messy mistakes, ask children to write compliments in pen-cil, not pen. Then, when everyone has contributed, have the person to whom the shield belongs trace over the penciled compliments in ink. Laminate shields and put them on the bulletin board. The shield in Figure 6–5 was done by fourth graders. Talk about the nice things classmates say about one another on the shields; use the adjec-tives and the suffixes as examples and resources for other classroom activities.

Figure 6–5 Making shields to compliment classmates gives readers opportunities to better understand adjectives and to consider how suffixes affect meaning, all centered around an engaging book for young readers.

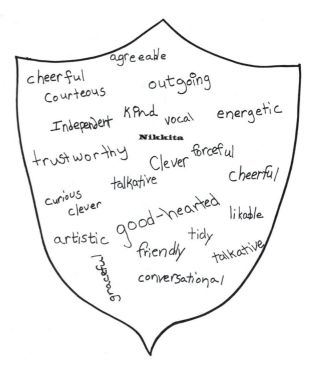

 *Explosion*

Best suited for fifth graders and above, this lesson highlights multiletter chunks from words in middle school content area subjects and can be used over and over with different words throughout the school year.

Things You'll Need: Tagboard sentence strips cut in half, markers, masking tape, dictionaries, scissors, colored construction paper, glue, and tape.

Exploration: Select a content area word that has an easy-to-spot root, plus a prefix or a suffix (or both). Write the word on the chalkboard and then read the sentence(s) in the textbook that includes the word. Talk about the word's meaning in the sentence(s). Ask readers to identify the prefix, root, and suffix. Explain that the word is made up of several different multiletter chunks (prefixes, suffixes, or Greek and Latin roots) and that the multiletter chunks contribute to the word's definition. Invite readers to use their background knowledge, the dictionary, or explanations in the textbook to help them understand the meaning of each multiletter chunk.

Guided Practice: To give readers practice identifying words that have the same prefixes, suffixes, or roots, divide the word into meaningful chunks and write the chunks about twelve to fifteen inches apart. Ask readers to think of words that include one of the chunks. As children think of words, write them under the chunks, thereby forming lists of words that include some of the same chunks.

Transfer: Divide a different word from a content area subject into meaningful chunks, and write each chunk on a separate piece of tagboard. Tape the three tagboards—one each with a prefix, suffix, and root—fairly far apart on the chalkboard. Pass out dictionaries, content area textbooks, blank tagboard strips, markers, and tape to groups of learners. Assign (or ask groups to choose) one meaningful chunk from the tagboard pieces taped to the chalkboard. Each group then finds words in dictionaries and context area textbooks that include the meaningful chunk for which the group is responsible. Groups are to write each word with a chunk on a blank tagboard strip and then tape the tagboard strip under the designated chunk on the chalkboard. Conclude by inviting volunteers from each group to discuss word meaning and explain how the chunks contribute to the definition of the words on the tagboard strips.

 Word Webs

In my experience, the most intriguing webs are those that begin with a single prefix or root and then spin off into many different mini-webs, as shown in Figure 6–6. This is a challenging activity best suited for children who are fifth graders or older, and most successful when children work cooperatively in groups.

Things You'll Need: Dictionaries, paper and pencils, one large piece of chart paper for each cooperative group, colored construction paper, colorful markers, scissors, glue, and a large piece of tagboard for each cooperative group to make games.

Figure 6–6
Creating word webs
helps readers draw the
conclusion that there is
a common thread of
meaning among words
that share the same
meaningful chunk.

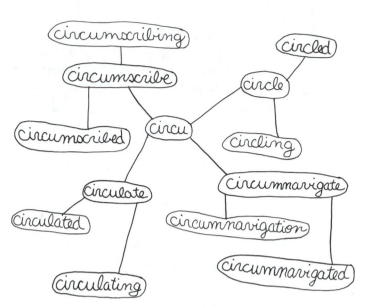

Exploration: Select a meaningful chunk from a word in a novel, play, or textbook that children are currently reading. On the chalkboard, write a sentence from the familiar book that includes a word with the meaningful chunk. Underline the word. Talk about the word's meaning in the sentence and about the way that the meaningful chunk contributes to the word's definition. Then write the chunk in the center of the chalkboard and draw a bubble around it. Now write the word from the sentence to the upper right of the chunk; make sure that the chunk and the word are at least 12 inches apart. Draw a line from the chunk to the word. Put a bubble around the word.

Challenge readers to think of words that include the meaningful chunk. Then, for each word readers think of, draw a line (called a web strand) that extends from the center chunk. At the end of the web strand, write a word that includes the meaningful chunk and put a bubble around that word, too. Next, create mini-webs around each word by adding prefixes or suffixes, as shown in Figure 6–6. When finished, talk about the words and support readers as they draw the conclusion that there is a common meaningful thread that ties the words together.

Guided Practice: Ask readers to work together collaboratively and cooperatively to create their own word webs, using words found in materials they study throughout the day, as well as words they find in dictionaries, wall charts, signs, and posters. After webs are perfected to the satisfaction of group members, invite the groups to share their webs with the entire class and explain the connections among words, telling why and how each word is a member of the meaning family.

Transfer: Discuss various learning games readers have played in school and at home. Talk about how games are constructed and played, the importance of clear directions, good examples, and meaningful activities. Explain the types of meaningful multiletter chunks children in the lower grades find in reading materials and write these chunks on the chalkboard (or put multiletter groups on a handout). Challenge groups to work collaboratively and cooperatively to make an easy-to-play game that includes frequently used meaningful multiletter groups and that can be shared with children in a lower grade. Try games out in your classroom and then arrange to go to a classroom of younger children to share the games. It takes more than one day to plan, create, and share games, so budget adequate time in your daily schedule. You and the children in your classroom will not be disappointed.

Moving Words (Prefixes)

The goal of this activity is to increase children's insight into the use of prefixes and to give them opportunities to think analytically about the meaningful multiletter chunks. With its emphasis on easy prefixes and a lot of body movement, this activity is appropriate for second and third graders.

Things You'll Need: Large cards with prefixes written on them, word cards, masking tape, colored construction paper, markers, and scissors.

Exploration: Select several words with prefixes from the books that children read, and write sentences with them on the chalkboard. Underline the words that have prefixes attached to them, and talk about the effect that prefixes have on word meaning. Then make two lists on the chalkboard: one of the prefixes and one of the words. Discuss the meaning of words and the meaning of prefixes. Ask children which prefixes can be combined with which words. Make a wall chart for each prefix by writing the prefix at the top and words with the prefix underneath. Support readers as they draw the conclusion that some of the words, the word **paid** for example, may be combined with more than one prefix, **unpaid** and **repaid** for instance. Leave the lists in your classroom to serve as references for the guided practice and transfer activities that follow.

Guided Practice: Tape large cards with prefixes to the chalkboard. Next, give each child a word card with a piece of tape on it. Ask children to read the word and to find a prefix on the chalkboard to which their word might be meaningfully attached and tape their word underneath the prefix. When finished, the chalkboard looks like a giant chart with columns of prefixes and words. Now challenge children to think carefully about the prefixes and words. Are there any mistakes? Does every combination make sense? If children are unsure, ask them to check the dictionary. How about other combinations? Can some prefixes be attached to several different words? If so, which ones? Leave the chalkboard display up so that it can serve as a reference for the transfer activity that comes next.

Transfer: Invite children to find words with prefixes in the books they read every day, and on signs and posters in the hallways of your school. Make a whole wall of words with the prefixes children find. Now count the number of times the same prefix occurs. Make a bar graph showing the frequency of occurrence and talk about how prefixes help authors share ideas with readers.

Roots and Branches

Roots and branches is appropriate for third grades and above. It is suitable for children working individually, in centers, or with a learning partner. The purpose is to help readers develop insight into the meaningful relationships among words that share the same root, and to learn more about the many prefixes and suffixes that are added to root words.

Things You'll Need: Pencils, dictionaries, frequently read books, copies of a Roots and Branches paper with several drawings of different trees showing roots and branches, such as a pine tree, cedar tree, or palo verde tree (see Figure 6–7).

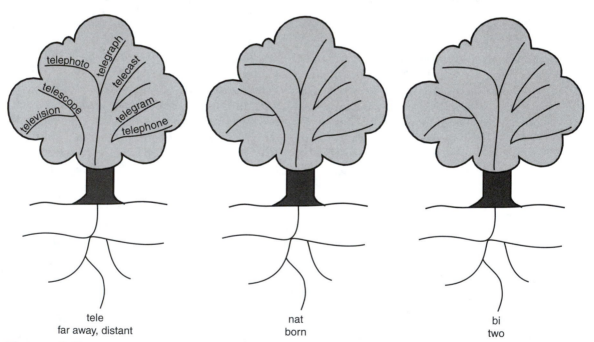

Figure 6–7   Writing words on branches that grow from the same root helps readers develop more in-depth knowledge of the relationship among prefixes, suffixes, and root words.

Exploration: Review root words, prefixes, and suffixes. Use an overhead projector to demonstrate how to create new words by adding prefixes and suffixes to different root words. For example, you might write **act** and then ask readers to add prefixes and suffixes to make **acting, enact, acted, action,** and **active.** Once readers have reviewed many different prefixes and suffixes and how they affect root words, it is time to move to Guided Practice.

Guided Practice: Give children the Roots and Branches paper with a tree showing its roots and branches (Figure 6–7). Explain that each tree shows how a root word can be changed into many different "branches" by adding prefixes and suffixes. Readers are to think about the root word of each tree and then decide which prefixes and suffixes can be added to the root and then write those words on the branches. Readers may consult dictionaries and books they are currently reading. Make Roots and Branches easier by writing a list of prefixes and suffixes above the trees, more challenging by giving readers a Roots and Branches sheet with root words only. Ask readers to share the root words and the words grown from them on the branches.

Transfer: Ask children to look in content subject textbooks and to write down all the words they see that have prefixes or suffixes. As children make lists, ask them to draw a line under the root word they write. Give children several days to do this part of the lesson. When the time is up, make a huge list of the prefixed and suffixed words that is organized so that all the words that share the same root are grouped together. Leave the list up in your classroom as a reference for readers and spellers.

✾ Suffix Construction Project

This lesson is a good way for cooperative groups of readers in the fifth grade and up to review suffixes, not to mention a terrific vehicle to promote discussion, collaboration, and dictionary use.

Things You'll Need: Each cooperative group needs the following: a large piece of tagboard, a ruler, a dictionary, a pencil, a set of directions, a large piece of plain paper, and colorful markers.

Exploration: After readers have had a great deal of experience reading and writing words with suffixes, write several suffixes on the chalkboard. Focus on only one suffix at a time, and ask readers to think of words to which the suffix may be attached. Make a list of words for each suffix. Talk about the meaning of the suffixes, and discuss their affect on the definition of words. Next, explain that groups are to make a chart that shows how suffixes and words are combined. Demonstrate by drawing a large rectangle on the chalkboard and then dividing it into four columns and four rows. Write a word beside each row and a different suffix at the top of each column. For each permissible combination of a word and a suffix, write the new word in the appropriate space in a row. Ask readers to double-check words in their dictionaries.

Guided Practice: Pass out a set of directions, a large piece of tagboard, a ruler, a colored marker, and dictionaries to each group. Directions consist of two pages: One page is a list of twenty words and ten suffixes. The other page explains how to complete the construction project containing these steps:

1. Use a ruler to make a chart that has twenty-one rows and eleven columns.
2. Write the ten suffixes, one at the top of each column. Leave the first column blank.
3. Write the twenty words in alphabetical order at the far left of rows. Begin in the second row.
4. Use the dictionary to check that each word and suffix combination makes a "real" word before writing it on the chart.
5. Color each empty space. These are ones for which you cannot combine the prefix and word to make a "real" word.
6. Sign the names of group members on the back of the chart when it is finished. Share charts with the class and discuss words.

Transfer: Challenge readers to create their own cartoons with the use of dramatic illustrations, dialogue balloons, and some of the words from the Suffix Construction Project. Cartoon writing is a natural way to use suffixes and can be an individual or a small-group activity, whichever suits the organization in your classroom. Tell each writer (or group of collaborative writers) to divide a large piece of tagboard into boxes and then to use one box for each scene. Challenge writers to create fictional characters, to write dialogue using a smattering of suffixes from the charts completed in class, and to illustrate their work, as in the cartoon in Figure 6–8. Cartoons become a part of social studies learning when writers create fictional characters and events from social studies topics; the same is true of science, only in this case writers describe scientific events, real or imagined. Give writers opportunities to share cartoons with their classmates. Discuss the characters, events, and the dialogue. Challenge writers to identify words with suffixes and talk about how words with suffixes contribute to meaning.

EXTRA PRACTICE ACTIVITIES

These thirteen extra practice activities are for readers who (1) cannot identify words when prefixes or suffixes are added, even though children identify the same words without prefixes and suffixes, (2) cannot identify words when written as contractions, and (3) do not use Greek and Latin roots to gain insight into the meaning of the words in content area textbooks and other reading material. As with all practice and reinforcement activities, include these activities as part of the ongoing learning in your classroom and give readers lots of in-depth experiences with print.

Figure 6–8 Writing cartoons is a natural opportunity to use suffixes and to explore the contribution that suffixes make to word and passage meaning.

Easy-to-Do Extra Practice Activities

1. *Find Prefixes, Suffixes, and Root Words in Magazines and Newspapers:* Make a variety of old magazines and recent newspapers available in your classroom, and then challenge readers to circle words that have prefixes, suffixes, or roots they are learning about in class. Ask readers to write words on a sheet of paper and then use them for the next activity.

2. *Make and Categorize Lists of Words with Prefixes and Suffixes:* Use the words with prefixes, suffixes, or roots that readers find in magazines and newspapers to make lists of words used in everyday reading materials. Categorize lists according to the prefixes and suffixes that appear in words. Encourage the readers in your class to add to the lists on their own, thus making the lists an ongoing part of learning.

3. *Add Many Different Prefixes and Suffixes to a Single Root Word:* Write a word on the chalkboard, such as **final.** Then challenge children to add prefixes and/or suffixes to it, for example, **semifinal, finally, finalist.** Count how many different prefixes and suffixes are added to the word and discuss how prefixes and suffixes affect word meaning. Do this with several different words.

4. *Prefix Row Races:* In this easy-to-do activity, rows of children compete against one another. Children line up in rows, and then, one at a time, a child from each row goes to the chalkboard. The teacher then says a word with a prefix, and each child writes the word on the chalkboard. Then each child writes a brief definition, such as **not happy** for **unhappy** or **play again** for **replay.** Every correct answer earns one point for the row. Speed up the game by awarding a point only to the row that writes the answers first. And, if writing is not legible or if row members are not paying attention, then that row does not earn a point.

5. *Modified Cloze Sentences:* Use modified cloze sentences where readers must consider prefixes or suffixes to complete a meaningful sentence. When completing cloze sentences, readers write on the line the word that looks right, sounds right, and makes sense in sentences, such as the following:

The man_____his house dark brown.
                    (painted, painting, painter)

The boy shouted_____than all the rest of the
                    (loud, louder, loudly)
fans at the baseball game.

Sheila's blue satin dress looks_____on her.
                    (lovely, lover, loving)

A second version is to write the word in the sentence but without its prefix or suffix. Children then read the cloze sentences and write the prefix or suffix to complete the word. For example:

Mr. Johnson was work_____ in his garden.

Ms. Smith was_____happy that his favorite team lost.

Johnny thought the blue car was the fast_____.

6. *Connect Prefixes and Suffixes with Their Definitions:* Make cards with prefixes, suffixes, and their definitions. Randomly tape the prefixes and suffixes to the bulletin board or chalkboard. Move over about 3 feet and randomly tape the definition cards to the bulletin board or chalkboard. Now, readers match the definitions to the prefixes and suffixes by moving the cards so as to line up each definition with the correct prefix or suffix. Discuss how prefixes and suffixes affect meaning.

7. *Suffix Connections:* Begin by putting several cards with suffixes in a shoe box, such as **ed, ing, ly, es/s.** Now write several verbs on the chalkboard, like **pay,**

talk, hop, jump, paint, sip, and **try.** Divide the class (or group) into two teams. Alternating from team to team, a child selects a suffix card from the shoe box, goes to the chalkboard, selects one of the verbs (**hop**), writes the word, and adds the suffix (**hopping**). If the suffix and verb make a meaningful word that is spelled conventionally, the team gets a point and that verb is erased, in this example leaving **pay, talk, jump, paint, sip,** and **try** to choose from. Continue playing until all the words are erased. Take this opportunity to discuss when and when not to double the final consonant or change the **y** to **i** before adding a suffix.

Fold-Over Contractions

Fold-Over contractions are words on paper strips that fold together to make contractions. This hands-on activity is beneficial for children who find contractions bewildering. It provides quick and easy practice, can be used with any contraction, and is appropriate for large and small groups of children from first through third grade.

Things You'll Need: Construction paper cut into strips, markers, and masking tape.

Practice: Begin by writing on the chalkboard words that can form contractions. Discuss contractions and invite volunteers to change each word pair on the chalkboard into a contraction. Now demonstrate how to make Fold-Over Contractions, which look like accordions with deleted letters simply folded out of sight and replaced by a piece of masking tape with an apostrophe on it. The tape holds the Fold-Over Contraction in place, as shown in Figure 6–9. Give each child a paper strip about 2 inches wide and 6 inches long, and a small piece of masking tape. Then select one example from the chalkboard, say **are** and **not.** Ask children to count the letters in **are not** and to fold their paper strips accordion style to make as many boxes as there are letters in these two words (six). Second, children write the two words one after the other, putting one letter in each box. In this example, children write six letters: **a-r-e-n-o-t.** Third, children write an apostrophe on the small piece of masking tape. Fourth

Figure 6–9 Fold-Over Contractions is a hands-on activity in which children fold deleted letters in contractions out of sight and replace them with an apostrophe.

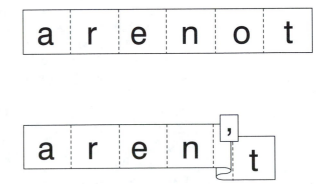

and last, children turn the accordion into a contraction by (1) folding the square with the letter to be deleted (**o**) under the square with the preceding letter on it (**n**) and (2) putting the masking tape apostrophe at the top to hold the contraction together, thus forming **aren't.** Encourage children to describe in their own words the idea behind missing letters, as well as the purpose and placement of the apostrophe.

Flip-up Suffixes (or Prefixes)

This is another version of the memory game in which players remember which two facedown cards of twenty (or less) match. The objective is to flip up cards that are a match between a word on one card with a root word (**swim,** for example) and another card that has the same word only with a suffix added (**swimming**). This game becomes Flip-up Prefixes by using prefix cards, such as **happy** (root word) and **unhappy** (the root with a prefix added). It is appropriate for readers of any age and, of course, two or three readers play at a time.

Things You'll Need: Playing cards with pairs of words that do and do not have suffixes.

Practice: Nearly all children will be familiar with this old standby, so little explanation is needed. This activity is easiest when all suffixes are the same, more difficult when suffixes are different. Turn Flip-up Suffixes into Flip-up Prefixes by writing words with prefixes instead of suffixes, such as **play** and **replay.**

Creative Compounds

In this activity, small or large groups of first- through third-grade readers put two everyday words together to create their own unique compounds.

Things You'll Need: Large pieces of white construction paper, pencils, and crayons or colored markers.

Practice: Explain that children are to think of two words they use every day and then put those words together to make a brand-new compound word. Demonstrate how to coin new compounds by writing a few nouns on the chalkboard and then putting them together to form new, imaginative compounds. When children understand what they are to do, pass out construction paper and crayons or markers. Invite children to coin their own compounds, to define, and to illustrate the newly coined compounds, as in Figure 6–10.

Greek and Latin Prefix/Suffix Posters

This practice activity involves groups in cooperatively planning and designing posters and calls for thinking analytically about prefixes or suffixes borrowed from Greek and Latin. It is most successful with readers in the fifth grade and up.

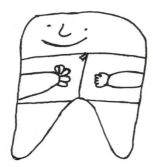

A tooth coat is a coat for your teeth

Figure 6–10 Coining new compounds gives children opportunities to creatively use their knowledge of word meaning and to write definitions for the unusual compounds they create.

Things You'll Need: Small slips of paper with either a prefix or suffix written on each, tagboard, colorful markers, glue, colored construction paper, scissors, and dictionaries for each cooperative group in your classroom.

Practice: Explain that each poster must include (1) a definition of a prefix or suffix, (2) four special words (found in the dictionary or content area textbooks) that are spelled with the prefix or suffix, (3) at least one illustration, and (4) a brief sentence or two telling why this prefix or suffix is especially helpful. Allocate more than one work period for groups to make their posters. Then, when posters are complete, hold a poster-sharing session and invite groups to explain their posters to their classmates.

Pin-Up Suffixes

Pin-Up Suffixes is appropriate for large and small groups of first and second graders. It is designed to give children practice adding suffixes to words. This activity can be used for practice with just one suffix or with many different suffixes, depending on children's needs.

Things You'll Need: One lightweight rope several yards long; 5 × 8 cards or similar size cutouts of seasonal objects (leaves for fall, pumpkins for Halloween, hearts for Valentine's Day, and so on); colored paper, pens, pencils or chalk, and clothespins. Write a root word on the top half of a 5 × 8 card or seasonal shape. Put all the words in a shoe box.

Practice: Write **-ed** and a few root words, perhaps **jump, hop, help,** and **hope,** on the chalkboard. Demonstrate how to add **-ed** to the root words to make **jumped, hopped, helped,** and **hoped.** Discuss how the **-ed** affects meaning by showing that something happened in the past. Then explain that there are lots of words in a shoe box, but that **-ed** cannot be added to every one of them. Children are to pick out a word and decide if **-ed** can be added to it. If so, children write the word with the **-ed** suffix on the bottom half of the 5 × 8 card (or seasonal shape) and use a clothespin to put the word on the line, as shown in Figure 6–11. Words that cannot have an **-ed** at the end stay in the shoe box. After all the words with **-ed** are pinned up, read them in chorus. Then, to reinforce the idea of doubling the final consonant (as in a one-syllable word or stressed syllable with a short vowel + consonant), ask children to write words like **hopped** and **hoped** on the chalkboard. Talk about why the consonant (**p**) in **hop** is doubled when adding **-ed** and why the last consonant (the **p**) is not doubled when adding **-ed** to **hope.** When finished, focus on another suffix, such as **-ing** or **-ly.**

Root Roundup

This extra practice activity encourages readers to look for meaningful multiletter chunks in words, to use dictionaries, and to work together in a spirit of competition among teams. It is suitable for readers in the fifth grade and up.

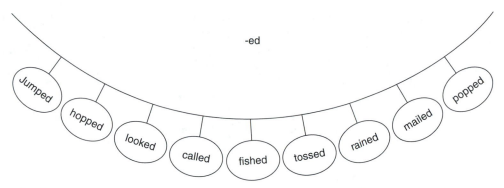

Figure 6–11   In this example, children pin up words to which the suffix **-ed** can be added. Later, words are taken down and children write them on the board with the suffix.

Things You'll Need: A sheet of instructions for each team that explains Root Roundup rules.

Practice: In this activity, cooperative groups find as many different Greek and Latin roots as possible over a five-day period. The rules are as follows:

1. Each team is to find as many different words as possible that include Greek or Latin roots.
2. Teams are to write words with roots on a sheet of paper and to indicate where words were found. (This can be done by including a sample of the document in which the word is used or by explaining where the word appears, such as on a cafeteria menu.)
3. A dictionary definition must accompany each word.
4. Each Greek and Latin root must be defined. Teams are given one point for each different word they find that includes a Greek or Latin root. At week's end, the whole class works together to verify words with Greek and Latin roots. Each team shares the words it has found during the week, discusses the roots inside words, and explains the contribution roots make to word meaning.

The team that finds the most roots by the end of the fifth day receives an appropriate prize.

WHEN EXTRA PRACTICE IS NOT ENOUGH

Readers learn to use a variety of word identification strategies through the in-depth literacy instruction, activities, reading, and writing that are part of today's classrooms. Though most children develop word identification strategies as they advance in school, some have difficulty strategically using our alphabetic writing system.

These children are frustrated by the words they see on the pages of storybooks and novels because their fluent reading vocabularies are underdeveloped. When this happens, younger children lack reading fluency and cannot read age-appropriate library books on their own; older children are vexed by the ideas and concepts in content area textbooks because the technical vocabulary is out of reach. Children who have had a great many reading and writing opportunities and who still cannot use word identification strategies to figure out unknown words while reading need extra help to do so. This is the topic of the chapter that follows.

REFERENCES

Alverman, D. E., & Phelps, S. F. (1998). *Content reading and literacy* (2nd ed.). Boston, MA: Allyn and Bacon.

Ayers, D. M. (1980). *English words from Greek and Latin elements.* Tucson, AZ: University of Arizona Press.

Cassar, M., & Treiman, R. (1997). The beginnings of orthographic knowledge: Children's knowledge of double letters in words. *Journal of Educational Psychology, 89*, 631–644.

Durkin, D. (1993). *Teaching them to read* (6th ed.). Boston: Allyn & Bacon.

Ehri, L. C. (1991). Development of the ability to read words. In R. Barr, M. L. Kamil, P. Mosenthal, & P. D. Pearson (Eds.), *Handbook of reading research* (Vol. II, pp. 383–417). New York: Longman.

Ehri, L. C. (1997). Sight word learning in normal readers and dyslexics. In B. Blachman (Ed.), *Foundations of reading acquisition and dyslexia* (pp. 163–189). Mahwah, NJ: Lawrence Erlbaum.

Ehri, L. C. (1998). Grapheme-phoneme knowledge is essential for learning to read words in English. In J. L. Metsala & L. C. Ehri (Eds.), *Word recognition in beginning literacy* (pp. 3–40). Mahwah, NJ: Lawrence Erlbaum.

Gentry, R. J. (1987). *Spel . . . is a four-letter word.* New York: Scholastic.

Gibson, E. J., & Guinet, L. (1971). Perception of inflections in brief visual presentations of words. *Journal of Verbal Learning and Verbal Behavior, 10*, 182–189.

Hackett, J. K., Moyer, R. H., & Adams, D. K. (1989). *Merrill Science.* Englewood Cliffs, NJ: Merrill/Prentice Hall.

Harris, A. J., & Sipay, E. R. (1990). *How to increase reading ability* (9th ed.). New York: Longman.

Henderson, E. H. (1990). *Teaching spelling* (2nd ed.). Boston: Houghton Mifflin.

Invernizzi, M. A. (1992). The vowel and what follows: A phonological frame of orthographic analysis. In S. Templeton & D. R. Bear (Eds.), *Development of orthographic knowledge and the foundations of literacy* (pp. 105–136). Hillsdale, NJ: Lawrence Erlbaum.

Ives, J. P., Bursuk, L. Z., & Ives, S. A. (1979). *Word identification techniques.* Chicago: Rand McNally.

Lapp, D., & Flood, J. (1992). *Teaching reading to every child* (3rd ed.). New York: Macmillan.

Miller, G. A. (1956). The magical number seven, plus or minus two: Some limits on our capacity for processing information. *Psychological Review, 63,* 81–97.

Miller, J. W., & McKenna, M. (1989). *Teaching reading in the elementary grades.* Scottsdale, AZ: Gorsuch Scarisbrick.

Nagy, W. E., Anderson, R. C., Schommer, M., Scott, J. A., & Stallman, A. C. (1989). Morphological families and word recognition. *Reading Research Quarterly, 24,* 262–282.

Nagy, W. E., Diakidoy, I. N., & Anderson, R. C. (1993). The acquisition of morphology: Learning the contribution of suffixes to the meaning of derivatives. *Journal of Reading Behavior, 25,* 155–170.

Nunes, T., Bryant, P., & Bindman, M. (1997). Morphological spelling strategies: Developmental stages and processes. *Developmental Psychology, 33,* 637–649.

Raschka, C. (1997). *Mysterious Thelonious.* New York: Orchard Books.

Robinson, B. (1996). *The best school year ever.* New York: Scholastic.

Santa, C. M. (1976–1977). Spelling patterns and the development of flexible word recognition strategies. *Reading Research Quarterly, 12,* 125–144.

Stuart, M., & Coltheart, M. (1988). Does reading develop in a sequence of stages? *Cognition, 30,* 139–181.

Templeton, S. (1991). *Teaching the integrated language arts.* Boston: Houghton Mifflin.

White, T. G., Power, M. A., & White, S. (1989). Morphological analysis: Implications for teaching and understanding vocabulary growth. *Reading Research Quarterly, 24,* 283–304.

White, T. G., Sowell, J., & Yanagihara, A. (1989). Teaching elementary students to use word-part clues. *The Reading Teacher, 42,* 302–308.

Wysocki, K., & Jenkins, J. R. (1987). Deriving word meanings through morphological generalization. *Reading Research Quarterly, 22,* 66–81.

CHAPTER
7

Children Who Need Extra Help

This chapter explains why some children struggle with word identification and what you can do to help them. In this chapter, you will learn how to give extra help to readers who over rely on picture and incidental cues, do not effectively use the analogy with onsets and rimes and the letter-sound strategies, or speak languages other than English at home.

KEY IDEAS

➤ Some children need extra help because they do not effectively use word identification strategies (1) to identify the unfamiliar words they meet in text or (2) to build a large fluent reading vocabulary.

➤ Some children whose families speak languages other than English need extra help because the language spoken at home is different from the language in which English-speaking authors write.

➤ When you give children extra help, it is important to strike a balance between (1) the knowledge and abilities children bring to reading and writing and (2) the challenges of reading interesting and age-appropriate literature and of writing for a variety of purposes.

Perhaps you are wondering why this chapter begins with a drawing of a seesaw (see Figure 7–1). As it turns out, a simple playground seesaw demonstrates a fundamental principle of physics that has a great deal of relevance to teaching and learning. Seesaws are simple levers. The purpose of levers is to make it easier to lift heavy loads, in this case the weight of playmates at either end of the seesaw. The seesaw board is the lever and the support on which the board is balanced is called the fulcrum.

The weight of the playmates in Rich's drawing (Figure 7–1) is about equal, so the effort needed to push each player into the air is exactly the same. Should a heavier playmate get on one end, the lighter playmate must push harder. And, if the heavier playmate weighs quite a bit more, the lighter playmate will not have the strength (or force) to lift the heavier one. The way to make the seesaw work is to balance the load at either end, to make the effort needed to lift each playmate equal to the weight of each child. Moving the fulcrum changes the balance point. With a new balance point, it takes less effort (force) to lift the heavier playmate (load).

Just as seesaw playmates differ in weight, so too do the children we teach differ in the strategies they bring to reading. While some children develop a full complement of word identification strategies through the normal reading and writing experiences in your classroom, others need extra help. Learning experiences, just like seesaws, can be adjusted so as to balance the load and the force, thereby making it possible for all children to succeed.

Whereas the success of a seesaw hinges on finding the right balance point between the force and the load, the success of learning and using word identification strategies hinges on finding the right balance point between the force (children's abilities) and the load (reading and writing activities). Sometimes regular classroom activities (the load) are too great for the knowledge and strategies children bring to activities (the force). Under this condition, children are in a similar position to that of a lightweight seesaw playmate who lacks the strength to lift a heavier playmate. When this happens, children need extra help.

Figure 7–1 A simple seesaw demonstrates a fundamental principle of physics that is relevant to supporting literacy in today's classrooms.

Children who need extra help succeed when reading and writing activities (the load) are roughly balanced with their ability to use word identification strategies (the force). In practical terms, this means finding activities with which children are successful and then using those activities to improve achievement. In this chapter we focus on children who do not understand the alphabetic principle, lack knowledge of print and speech relationships, or do not effectively use word identification strategies. If you teach children like this, balancing the load and the force means providing direct, systematic instruction in phonemic awareness and letter and sound.

While the focus of this book is on word identification, good comprehension is the goal of our classroom reading programs. We teach word identification strategies so as to build large fluent reading vocabularies. The idea is to reach such a high level of word fluency that children concentrate completely on understanding what they read, not on figuring out the words. We know from research that many children who struggle with reading in the later grades had difficulty using the alphabetic principle to identify unfamiliar words when they were in the early grades (Torgesen, 1998). As they moved through the early grades, struggling readers learned new words, but at a far slower pace than average readers. As a consequence, when struggling readers reach the upper grades, they have many fewer words in their fluent reading vocabularies than needed to comprehend grade appropriate novels and content subject textbooks.

Many struggling readers have underdeveloped phonemic awareness, and this impairs their ability to take full advantage of the alphabetic principle when identifying and learning words (Foorman et al., 1997; Metsala, Stanovich, & Brown, 1998). For children whose reading progress is limited by difficulty identifying and learning words, we will focus on teaching what they need to know about phonemic awareness and about print-to-speech relationships to become proficient at word learning. However, improving phonemic awareness and print-to-speech relationships is not enough. The children whom you teach must not only have good phonemic awareness and understand the relationships between spoken and written language, they must also know when and why to use different strategies while reading. And so, it is also important to provide direct, systematic instruction in when to strategically use word identification strategies while reading (Snow, Burns, & Griffin, 1998; Stahl, 1998). It is also important to give children opportunities to apply these strategies when reading and opportunities to spend enough time reading so as to maintain and extend their reading achievement (Torgesen, Wagner, Rashotte, Alexander, & Conway, 1997).

CHILDREN WHO OVER RELY ON PICTURE CUES AND INCIDENTAL CUES

When children over rely on picture cues and incidental cues, they take advantage of some, but not nearly enough, of the information available in written language. These children do not strategically use onsets, rimes, letter-sound neighborhoods, or multiletter chunks to identify the unfamiliar words authors write. Instead, children overlook the actual words written on pages, focusing instead on pictures and, when pictures fall short, on colored ink, word shape, letter shape, and visual reminders like smudges and dog-eared pages.

Shandra

First-grader Shandra, whose story is shown in Figure 7–2, over relies on pictures and incidental cues. If you were to listen to Shandra read easy books with which she is familiar, you would hear something akin to fluent reading. Shandra's fluency is misleading, however, because she memorizes the text in familiar books. After

Figure 7–2 Children who are glued to picture and incidental clues by the end of first grade may be trying to figure out exactly which written symbols—letters, numbers, or shapes—make up words.

reading the same short books time and time again, Shandra knows the pictures and written sentences by heart. As a consequence, the fluent reading you hear is in actuality the result of Shandra reciting sentences much like preschoolers (Chapter 3) imitate the reading of adults by retelling stories from memory.

Though Shandra thinks about print, she does not pay attention to the rimes and letter-sound neighborhoods in words. For this reason, Shandra recognizes a mere handful of words. What's more, the words she reads with ease in familiar stories are seldom recognized when she meets them in other reading materials. When the words Shandra recognizes in often-read books are written in sentences on the chalkboard, in stories on wall charts, or in unfamiliar library books, Shandra behaves as though she has never seen these words before. For example, having read the word **down** without a moment's hesitation in a short, familiar storybook, Shandra read **down** as **"come"** in a storybook she had never seen before and pointed to **happy** when asked to find **down** in a sentence on a wall chart. Shandra needs to learn a good deal about written language, which raises the question of how to find the right balance point between the load and the force.

As for phonemic awareness, Shandra is aware of spoken words and is developing insight into rhyme. However, Shandra cannot identify the individual sounds in words, separate words into sounds, or blend sounds together to pronounce words. From Shandra's writing, we might infer that she understands that written language is made up of letters and that writing goes from top to bottom on the page. Shandra also seems to be developing awareness of punctuation and is working out exactly which written symbols—letters, numbers, and shapes—make up words. Even with these understandings, toward year's end, Shandra has fallen far behind her classmates.

After a year of kindergarten and most of first grade, Shandra is still at the pre-alphabetic phase of movement toward word fluency and the precommunicative phase of spelling. She knows how to read and write her own name, the names of some, but not all, of the letters, and recognizes a few words. In these respects, Shandra's print knowledge does not resemble that of a typical pre-alphabetic kindergartner at the beginning of the school year because she has developed some understandings as a consequence of spending nearly two years in school. However, Shandra does not understand the alphabetic principle, which is a hallmark of children at the pre-alphabetic phase. To make up for this lack of insight, Shandra has become very good at interpreting pictures. When she reads short books that she has not memorized, she combines picture cues with her background knowledge to construct plausible stories. She is a cheerful, cooperative child who wants to learn to read and who is using the insight and knowledge at her disposal to bring meaning to print.

For Shandra, the load (the usual demands of end-of-year first grade) and the force she brings to reading (her rudimentary phonemic awareness, knowledge of only a few letter names, and lack of insight into the alphabetic principle) are misaligned. Shandra will succeed when the load (the demands of classroom reading) and the force (what Shandra knows and can do) are more closely aligned. To this, Shandra's reading and writing opportunities must build on what she knows and at the same time help her develop new insights and knowledge.

What Shandra Needs to Know to Move Toward Word Fluency
For starters, Shandra needs to become more print focused. She needs to know how the onsets, rimes, letter-sound neighborhoods, and multiletter chunks in our alphabetic writing system represent pronunciation. She must also increase phonemic awareness: Shandra needs to be able to identify the rhyme and individual sounds in words, and she needs to be able to blend individual sounds together. Shandra also needs to learn to cross-check so as to keep word identification meaning centered.

Though the ultimate goal is for Shandra to develop the analogy with onsets and rimes, letter-sound, and multiletter chunk strategies, the most immediate aim is to help her strategically use onsets and context cues together. Onsets (the beginning letters in words) are an excellent way to help children like Shandra increase attention to print, because onsets are quite predictable and, when used in conjunction with context cues, provide insight into a word's identity (as explained in Chapters 3 and 4). After onsets, the rimes in words are the next thing to teach. As large bundles of sound, rimes require less phonemic awareness than letter-sound neighborhoods (as mentioned in Chapters 2 and 5). Though Shandra needs to develop the letter-sound strategy, this strategy puts more demands on phonemic awareness than the analogy with onsets and rimes strategy. Hence, it is best to begin with a combination of onsets and context cues, progress to analogous onsets and rimes, and then to move to letter-sound neighborhoods. And, certainly Shandra needs to learn to cross-check, that is, to think about meaning and to use strategies to identify words that make sense in the messages authors write.

Teaching Phonemic Awareness
Children like Shandra who over rely on picture and incidental cues usually have very low phonemic awareness and hence benefit from activities that target rhyme and beginning sounds. Since spoken rhymes are easier to detect than individual sounds, the load is lighter when activities help children develop sensitivity to the rhyming sounds in words and heavier when activities focus on the middle and endings sounds in words. While it is important to develop awareness of both beginning sounds and rhyme, do not be surprised if children like Shandra initially find rhyme easier to detect (Layton, Deeny, Tall, & Upton, 1996). The lessons Hands Up for Rhyming Words and Rhyme Puppet (described in Chapter 2) are beneficial because they give Shandra opportunities to listen to and identify rhyming words. Rhyming Picture Bookmark Rhyming Picture Sack Sort, Picture-Rhyme Pages, and Rhyme Collage (also described in Chapter 2) are helpful because with them Shandra has experience using her knowledge of pictures names to identify and act on the rhyme in spoken language. I have found that making rhyming word lists and putting these lists on wall charts is very useful. But remember, when making rhyming lists, the rhyme in words must look and sound alike—**hat** and **cat,** not **paid** and **shade.** I also suggest that Shandra, her teacher, and her classmates share books with a lot of rhyming words, such as those written by Dr. Seuss. If you have children like Shandra in your class, make rhyming chants and poetry part of the ongoing experiences in your classroom, and provide lots of opportunities for children to read and write every day.

Of all the individual sounds—beginning, middle, ending—in words, beginning sounds are the easiest for children like Shandra to identify. Not only are the beginning sounds easiest to identify from a phonemic awareness standpoint, but beginning letter-sounds plus the reading context give children considerable insight into the identity of unfamiliar words. And so, I find it useful to focus on beginning sounds while simultaneously teaching children to detect rhyming language. There are a variety of activities to help Shandra become aware of beginning sounds, including the version of Puppet Talk (explained in Chapter 2) where children listen to a puppet say two words—**"mop"** and **"milk,"** or **"mop"** and **"bed"**—and tell whether the words begin alike. Shandra will also benefit from opportunities to sort pictures according to their shared beginning sounds (look in Chapter 2 for a description of Sound Sack Sort). Of the Easy-Extra-Practice Activities in Chapter 4, Celebrate Onsets, Alliterative Shopping Lists, Personalized Onset and Rime Lists, and Onset Houses are also beneficial. The children I teach enjoy the modification of Rime Pick-Up (described in Chapter 4) where children pick up sticks with onsets written on them. ABC books with lots of alliteration, collages, and alliterative sentences (such as tongue twisters) are examples of other effective ways to call attention to the beginning sounds in words.

Teaching Onsets and Rimes

Because of the mutually supportive relationship between phonemic awareness and letter-sound knowledge, you can expect Shandra's awareness of the beginning sounds in words to improve as she learns how to use onsets and context cues together to identify unfamiliar words when reading. Do the following to help children use onsets and the reading context to figure out the identity of unfamiliar words: (1) show Shandra how to read to the end of the sentence and then (2) show her how to think of a word that makes sense and begins with the sound the first letter represents. If you teach children like Shandra, point out words in your classroom that begin with the same sounds and letters; make lists of words that begin with the same sound; and challenge children to find examples of words in the storybooks they read. In this way, children stay focused on the meaning and at the same time have opportunities to become aware of the beginning letters and sounds in words.

Encourage children like Shandra to pay more attention to print by asking them to point to each word as it is read. This reinforces the concept that specific written words represent specific spoken words. As a consequence of pointing to words, children are encouraged to match the words they read with the words authors write. If you are not already sweeping your hand under words as you read them aloud, now is the time to do so. Talk about print; point out individual words in big books, poems, and familiar storybooks and make wall charts of often-used words.

Another activity I find highly beneficial is to ask children to arrange word cards into sentences. I use three different versions of this activity, depending on the abilities of the children whom I teach:

1. The easiest version is to write a short, familiar sentence on a tagboard strip and to ask children to arrange word cards so as to reconstruct the sentence. To do this, children need only match the words on cards with the words on the tagboard sentence.

2. The next easiest is to have children dictate a sentence while you write it on a tagboard strip. Read the sentence and ask children to point to each word. Then, with children watching, cut the sentence into words and ask children to arrange the words to form the original sentence.

3. The most challenging version is to ask children to use word cards to make sentences that they think of themselves or that you dictate. It is also challenging to change statements (The boy likes cake.) into questions (Does the boy like cake?).

Additionally, it is beneficial for children to make their own personal dictionaries that include words they have seen in books and in their everyday surroundings. Listed alphabetically, the words in personal dictionaries are perfect for calling attention to onsets and for increasing reading vocabulary. Another alternative is to use the Personal Word Boxes described in Chapter 5. Personal dictionaries and Personal Word Boxes are references that are used regularly, so think of them as an ongoing part of children's everyday reading and writing experiences and include words from all the subject areas explored in your classroom.

Predictable books offer immediate success and for this reason probably will be one of the reading experiences children enjoy. Predictable books are best used when children are just entering into reading, and, therefore, are appropriate for Shandra and children like her. With pictures highly supportive of the text and some text repeated over and over again, predictable books will help children develop many critical and preliminary concepts, such as: (1) reading is meaningful; (2) print is important; (3) writing goes from left-to-right and from top-to-bottom on pages; (4) white spaces separate words; and (5) there is a one-to-one match between spoken words and written words. However, children like Shandra frequently memorize predictable books, so make sure that the children you teach actually look at the words while reading. And when Shandra has basic print awareness and book handling skills, and understands that reading is meaningful and that spoken words match written words, it is time to move beyond predictable books and into easy text that gives Shandra lots of opportunities to use the reading context combined with onsets to identify and learn unfamiliar words, and ultimately to use rimes and letter and sound to support word identification and word learning.

CHILDREN WHO DO NOT EFFECTIVELY USE THE ANALOGY WITH ONSETS AND RIMES AND LETTER-SOUND STRATEGIES

Children who do not effectively use the analogy with onsets and rimes and letter-sound strategies misidentify rimes, get bogged down in the middle of words, blend sounds into the wrong words, and associate the wrong sounds with the letters in neighborhoods. These difficulties impair word identification and, of course, interfere with comprehension. You will notice that, while the fluent reading vocabularies of these children do increase, the pace of vocabulary growth is much slower than that of average readers. Because children's fluent reading vocabulary is limited and because children cannot effectively use the analogy and letter-sound strategies to identify unfamiliar words, they may bypass many of the words authors write, opting instead to reconstruct the meaning of stories from their own background knowledge, picture cues, and, perhaps, a few letter and sound cues.

Relying predominantly on background knowledge, picture cues, and a few letter and sound cues works fine when stories are familiar. In fact, material that closely parallels children's life experiences is understood remarkably well, given the fact that children do not identify many of the words authors write. These are the children about whom you hear teachers say, "He does not know many words in the story, but his comprehension is good." Or you hear, "Even though her reading vocabulary is weak, her comprehension is okay."

Bypassing a large number of words in favor of background knowledge, picture cues, and a handful of letter and sound cues does not work at all well when pictures do not tell the story and reading materials do not closely parallel children's own lives. This approach fails altogether when books and articles introduce new ideas, concepts, and information. Comprehension suffers because children (1) do not recognize enough words to reconstruct sensible messages based on what authors write and (2) do not have enough life experiences to fill in the gaps created by the many unfamiliar words. The difficulty is especially apparent when the topics of stories are outside children's own personal experiences, the books do not have a large number of highly descriptive illustrations, or the content subject textbooks introduce many new terms and concepts.

To take a closer look at children, consider the following descriptions of three children who do not effectively use the analogy with onsets and rimes or the letter-sound strategies. The first child, Raymond, brings less knowledge of letter and sound cues and less phonemic awareness to reading and writing than Melissa, the second child, and Mike, the third child. Raymond will benefit from extra help to develop the analogy with onsets and rimes strategy, Mike and Melissa from extra help to develop the letter-sound strategy.

Raymond

By the end of the second grade, Raymond's reading progress has come to a near standstill. His fluent reading vocabulary is growing very slowly which, in turn, has a negative affect on comprehension. When he meets an unfamiliar word while reading, Raymond looks for picture cues and letter and sound cues from the beginning (and sometimes ending) letters in words. He does not look inside words so as to consider all the letters (especially the vowels), and hence miscues frequently. You can infer from his story (Figure 7–3) that Raymond uses some knowledge of onsets and ending letters when he writes and that he is working out how vowel letter-sound neighborhoods represent sounds in words. He copies words from the print in his classroom, such as **was, Lisa,** and **bad,** and he conventionally spells a few

Figure 7–3 The writing of children who have underdeveloped phonemic awareness and who lack full knowledge of letter-sound neighborhoods may include words that are copied, high-frequency words spelled conventionally, words spelled phonetically, and words in which the sounds do not match the letters.

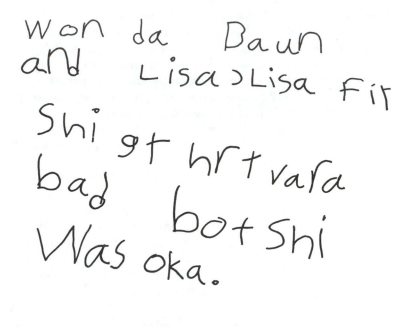

won da Baun and Lisa ꙩLisa fir shi gt hrt vara bad bot shi Was oka.

high-frequency words in his fluent vocabulary, such as **and** and **go.** And, though letters and sounds are not always completely on target, some of the letters Raymond chooses are similar to the sounds represented in words.

Raymond's spelling includes a few words that are spelled semiphonetically (spelling that includes some of the important sounds in words), as we see in his use of **gt** for **got** and **hrt** for **hurt.** Sometimes Raymond spells phonetically by writing letters that he thinks represent the sounds he hears in words, as in **bot** for **but,** **won** for **one,** and **vara** for **very.** The way he pronounces the **"ot"** in **"bot"** is not far from the sounds heard in **"but."** This is also true for the word **very,** spelled **vara.**

Though Raymond strategically uses some letter-sound neighborhoods when he spells, he is a long way from spelling conventionally and a long way from reading the kinds of books his second-grade classmates enjoy. Raymond has moved beyond the partial alphabetic phase of movement toward word fluency because he understands and can use the **VC** short vowel neighborhood, and he attempts to represent other vowel neighborhoods. From his writing we can infer that he has not developed a good working knowledge of the letter-sound cues in neighborhoods. His development as a reader is in serious jeopardy, for letter-sound he has not made the transition into the full use of alphabetic cues, as is expected of a first and second grader. Additionally, Raymond does not have the knowledge base to begin moving into the consolidated phase of word fluency, which generally happens toward the end of the second grade or the beginning of the third. To develop the foundation upon which the efficient and effective use of word identification strategies rests, the load and the force must be brought into balance so as to nurture Raymond's reading growth, the development of word identification strategies and, through effective use of word identification strategies, the expansion of his fluent reading vocabulary.

What Raymond Needs to Know to Move Toward Word Fluency

The most immediate aspects of phonemic awareness that children like Raymond need to further develop are the abilities to detect rhyming sounds, and to blend beginning sounds and rhymes together to form words. Becoming aware of all the individual sounds in words is also important and will develop through direct instruction (Chapter 2) combined with learning letter-sound neighborhoods (Chapter 5).

If children have difficulty with both the analogy with onsets and rimes and letter-sound strategies, as is the situation with Raymond, then analogous rimes are the place to begin. Teaching children like Raymond to use analogous rimes helps them become aware of relationships among written and spoken language and, additionally, helps them overcome their overreliance on the sounds represented by the first and last letters in words (Greaney, Tunmer, & Chapman, 1997). Hence, the most immediate things that children like Raymond need to know about our writing system are (1) how rimes represent sounds and (2) how to strategically use analogous rimes to identify unfamiliar words. As children begin to gain insight into the way that rimes signal pronunciation, then letter-sound neighborhoods can be profitably explored. And, as children understand how the letters in neighborhoods represent sounds, they have opportunities to strategically use their knowledge to identify and learn words.

Teaching Phonemic Awareness

Children like Raymond may have difficulty detecting rhymes and individual sounds in spoken words. Should this be the case, my advice is to concentrate first on developing sensitivity to rhyming sounds and then to introduce activities that support awareness of individuals sounds. Not only is this the normal sequence in which phonemic awareness develops, but identifying rhyming sounds is much easier than identifying the individual sounds in words.

Look in Chapter 2 for activities to develop the ability to detect rhyme. And when you share these activities with children like Raymond, be sure to include Arm Blending (which is also described in Chapter 2). Children like Raymond may find blending quite difficult, and Arm Blending is a highly successful technique. The description in Chapter 2 says to divide words into individual sounds, which places high demands on children who are not completely certain of the rhymes in words. To lighten the load, divide words into beginning sounds (onsets) and rimes. Hence, the word **"bat"** would be separated into **"b"** and **"at,"** which is well within Raymond's capability. Modify the directions in Chapter 2 by placing your hand in the crook of your elbow when you say **"b"** and then on your wrist when you say **"at."** Arm Blending is easy, gives children a visual and kinesthetic platform from which to blend, and transfers to many different reading situations. This, in turn, increases the force children like Raymond bring to reading, which means they are then capable of reading materials in which authors use more challenging words.

Combine phonemic awareness activities with reading and give children plenty of opportunities to write.

Teaching Rimes and in Letter-Sound Neighborhoods

If children like Raymond are to develop greater force, they must bring greater knowledge of rimes and letter-sound neighborhoods to reading, and they must use word identification strategies in support of comprehension. Since Raymond is not able to sound out words with the letter-sound strategy, the way to lighten the load is to concentrate first on developing the analogy with onsets and rimes strategy.

From his writing, we can infer that Raymond understands onsets, so rimes are a good focus for learning. Activities that highlight written rime are important because this knowledge paves the way for development of the analogy strategy. To help Raymond and children like him expand their knowledge of rimes, invite them to work collaboratively to make wall charts of words that share the same rimes. This activity is appropriate for many children, so include children who are glued to picture and incidental cues, as well as better readers who bring more in-depth letter-sound knowledge to reading. When the charts are complete, tape them to the chalkboard and challenge children to explain in their own words why words are included in lists and to think of other words that might be added. In so doing, children have opportunities to think critically about spelling and everyone has a chance to participate.

The lessons in Chapter 4 are helpful, especially Building Words with Onset-Rime Tiles, and Predicting and Writing Rime. Use, too, the Easy-to-Do Extra Practice Activities called Egg Words, Rime Pick-Up, Rime Tic-Tac-Toe, Onset-Rime Tachistoscope, and Muffin Tin Words. And, give children like Raymond ample opportunities to find rimes in the words they read in storybooks and poems.

When children know frequently occurring rimes, challenge them to look inside rimes to discover the letters in neighborhoods. The idea is to use what children know, in this case rimes, as a basis for teaching something they do not know. I suggest that you begin by teaching rimes with **VC** short vowel letter neighborhoods, such as in **mad, tap, dim,** and **fin.** Then help children look inside rimes to analyze the vowel sound. And, when children do this, help them understand that one vowel in a short word most likely represents a short sound. As children look for the vowel and consonant patterns the letter-sound neighborhoods in rimes represent, children's knowledge of letter-sound relationships increases and their ability to use this knowledge while reading also improves. In this way, children use their knowledge of common rimes to learn how a letter-sound neighborhood, in this example the **VC** short vowel neighborhood, represents the sounds of a whole host of different vowel and consonant (**VC**) combinations.

Next, compare and contrast the **VC** short vowel neighborhood in common rimes with the **VCe** long vowel neighborhood. An effective way to do this is to challenge children to think of words that include a **VC** or a **VCe** neighborhood in their spelling. Analyze the spelling of **VC** words—**mad, tap, dim,** and **fin**—and **VCe** words—**made, tape, dime,** and **fine.** Discuss the sounds that vowel letters represent in these two neighborhoods; talk about how and why children might use this information when they read. Then invite children to work with a partner or in small groups to make charts of words that are spelled with **VC** (short vowel) and **VCe** (long vowel) neighborhoods. Ask children who have less knowledge of letter-sound neighborhoods to work with those who have more knowledge. And encourage children to find words that include the **VC** and **VCe** letter-sound neighborhoods on the bulletin boards, wall charts, and chalkboards in your classroom. Support children as they work with one another to make charts; share finished charts with the whole class; display charts in your classroom; and use them as references. (Consult the letter-sound neighborhoods in Chapter 5 that are less, more, and most challenging, and look in Appendix B for an explanation of letter-sound neighborhoods.)

The effect of beginning with large segments of spoken and written language (rimes) and then moving to smaller segments (the letters that reside in letter-sound neighborhoods) is that activities progress from less demanding to more demanding. Hence, the load (the demands of identifying words while reading) is first brought into line with the force (children' abilities). Then the load can gradually increase as the force children bring to reading grows, that is, as children learn the sounds that the letters in neighborhoods represent and use this knowledge to identify words when reading.

Melissa

At the end of second grade, Melissa, whose story is shown in Figure 7–4, is far behind her classmates. An intelligent, well-behaved child, Melissa seldom causes trouble in class. Though Melissa seems to pay attention in school, by the mid-fall of second grade her fluent reading vocabulary is limited, and she can barely read easy first-grade books. When Melissa meets an unfamiliar word, she sometimes considers the beginning letter but not always. When the pictures are highly supportive of the text, Melissa's comprehension is good. When pictures do not help tell the story, Melissa creates in her mind a plausible story, filling in details from her background knowledge. Because Melissa's reading development lags far behind her peers, the load (the type of reading expected of end-of-year second graders) and the force (Melissa's underdeveloped phonemic awareness, rudimentary knowledge of letter-sound neighborhoods, and weak fluent reading vocabulary) are significantly out of

Figure 7–4   By fall of second grade, Melissa is far behind her classmates in reading. She spells known words conventionally and others she spells phonetically. When Melissa's teacher asked her to write about an experience Melissa had discussed with her teacher, Melissa wrote: She was looking at a house and she said it is pretty.

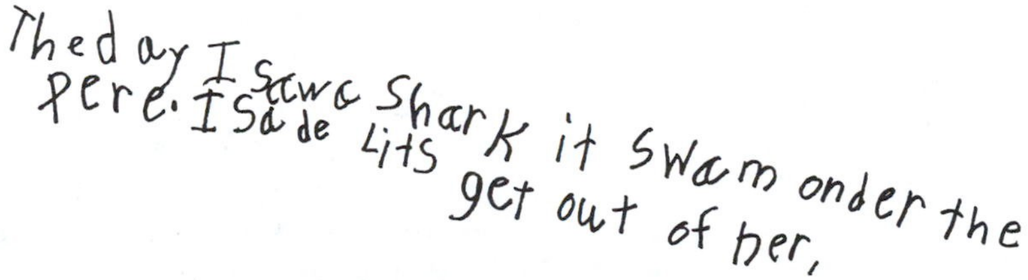

One day I was on my mommy's bed watching T.V. Then my mom said, "I am going to go check on the baby rabbits." When she got to the rabbit cage, she opened the back and she saw a black snake eating the baby bunnies. The mother rabbit was in the back corner. My mom saw her shivering and she thought she was scared. Then she ran to the house as fast as she could. She called my grandma and grandpa and they sent Matt and my grandma over to kill the snake. Then Matt got a shovel and opened the back door and mommy held the door. Then he tried to hit the snake with the shovel, but he missed the snake. Then the snake crawled out of the back of the pen and went under the barn. They put something on the ground that snakes don't like the smell of to keep the snake from ever coming back. Matt and grandma went home and mommy and I went back in the house.
The End

Figure 7–5   Melissa dictated this story about a snake in the rabbit hutch to her second-grade teacher. Melissa's story shows us that she effectively uses spoken language when telling about the events in her life.

balance. It is the load imposed by the reading difficulty of second-grade books, not the ideas in books, that creates the mismatch.

When someone else reads to her, Melissa easily understands stories written on or above her second-grade level. Melissa dictated the recounting of the snake in the rabbit hutch to her teacher (Figure 7–5). From this story we can infer that Melissa is not at a loss for words when talking and that she has a sense of the sequencing of events and cause and effect. She has a rich family background and has been read to since she was a very young child. And, as you would expect, Melissa uses language effectively when communicating with her friends and adults. Melissa's difficulty, then, is not a lack of background experiences, early print experiences, or spoken language.

At this point in her development as a reader, Melissa is hampered by her underdeveloped fluent reading vocabulary, lack of phonemic awareness, poor knowledge of letter-sound neighborhoods, and ineffective use of the letter-sound strategy. Melissa spells conventionally the words in her fluent reading vocabulary, other words she spells phonetically (Figure 7–4). She knows enough about letter-sound neighborhoods to be beyond the partial alphabetic phase. She has entered into the alphabetic phase of movement toward word fluency and the phonetic phase of spelling, yet her progress moving through these phases is slow. While many of her second-grade peers are entering into the consolidated phase of movement toward word fluency, Melissa is lingering at an immature state in the alphabetic phase.

Melissa's reading vocabulary is growing very slowly, her reading progress is minimal, and she does not like to write. If Melissa is to succeed, there must be a better balance between the load (reading demands) and the force (Melissa's abilities and knowledge). Because Melissa does not know how the consonants and vowels of English are sequenced in letter-sound neighborhoods, she frequently confuses words, cannot remember words, and ignores letters in words, most frequently the vowel letters. If her fluent reading vocabulary and her ability to comprehend grade level chapter books are to develop, Melissa must consider all the letters in words, including the trick vowels. She must forego overdependence on picture cues and guessing without enough letter-sound information, and she must learn to efficiently and effectively use the analogy with onsets and rimes and the letter-sound strategies.

What Melissa Needs to Know to Move Toward Word Fluency

Melissa, like Shandra and Raymond, needs to increase phonemic awareness. Melissa must improve her ability to separate words into sounds and to substitute sounds in words (exchange the **"p"** in **"pig"** for a **"d"** thereby making **"dig"**). Melissa also needs to improve her ability to blend more than two sounds together to pronounce words. While Melissa can blend **"b"** + **"e"** to say **"be,"** she is frequently unsuccessful when blending three or more sounds together. To succeed, Melissa must learn to blend three and four sounds together, such as blending **"d"** + **"i"** + **"sh"** to pronounce **"dish,"** and **"l"** + **"a"** + **"m"** + **"p"** to pronounce **"lamp."** Additionally, Melissa needs to expand her knowledge of the in letter-sound neighborhoods. And she absolutely must learn to use this knowledge when she reads and when she spells words during writing.

Teaching Phonemic Awareness

Melissa has no trouble whatsoever identifying beginning sounds (onsets) and rhyming words. And, she can separate short words (words of two phonemes, such as **me** and **so**) into individual sounds. However, it takes Melissa a long time to separate three- and four-sound words into phonemes. For example, when asked to separate a three-phoneme word—**mad,** for example—into sounds, Melissa is very slow to identify the sounds. Whereas Melissa's second-grade classmates separate **"mad"** into sounds almost effortlessly, Melissa has to think about her answer. As word length increases, Melissa has more and more trouble identifying and manipulating the individual sounds in words. Not surprisingly, Melissa is a very weak blender. Melissa, and children like her, blend two sounds together quite well, but they frequently have trouble blending three or four sounds together. When blending, Melissa omits, adds, and rearranges sounds, which interferes with use of the letter-sound strategy.

To further develop Melissa's phonemic awareness, combine the sound awareness and blending activities in Chapter 2 with the lessons and activities in Chapter 5 that teach letter-sound neighborhoods. As mentioned previously (Chapter 2), there is a mutually supportive relationship between phonemic awareness and letter-sound knowledge. Children like Melissa are in just the right position to take advantage of this two-way (phonemic awareness and letter-sound knowledge) relationship. Of the lessons in Chapter 2, I especially recommend Counting Sounds, Listening for Sounds, and Sound Boxes. When using Sound Boxes, write the letters in the boxes so as to re-inforce and extend Melissa's letter-sound knowledge, while at the same time devel-oping phonemic awareness. The Sound Sort activity (also described in Chapter 2) is helpful too, provided that Melissa sorts for the vowel letter-sound neighborhoods in words. As for blending sounds together, Melissa needs lots of direct instruction and practice blending three- and four-sound words. Arm Blending is remarkably benefi-cial for Melissa and children like her. Arm Blending not only helps Melissa remember the sounds to blend, but Arm Blending can be used anytime and anyplace. I recom-mend reinforcing Arm Blending with Sliding Sounds together (both explained in Chapter 2). And, when using blending activities, encourage children like Melissa to pay attention to the sounds in the middle of words, and to always pay special atten-tion to correct blending when using the letter-sound strategy.

Teaching the Letter-Sound Neighborhoods

Melissa already knows the sounds represented by the single consonant, consonant blend, and consonant digraph neighborhoods. Generally speaking, it is the vowel letter-sound neighborhoods that are the most troublesome for children like Melissa. Use the lesson Building Words with Letter Tiles (described in Chapter 5) to develop vowel letter-sound neighborhood knowledge. When building words, ask children like Melissa to make changes that affect the vowel neighborhoods, such as building **mad (VC)** and then changing it to **made (VCe),** or building **seat (VV)** and then building **set (VC).** (Consult Chapter 5 and Appendix B for other vowel neighbor-hoods to highlight when building words.) The Word Puzzles lesson combines phonemic awareness with knowledge of letter-sound neighborhoods and thus re-inforces and extends the foundations upon which the letter-sound strategy rest. The children whom I teach succeed when they first solve puzzles as a group activity, and then, when they are confident of their ability, I ask them to solve puzzles individu-ally. I find the Easy Extra Practice Activities of Chalkboard Compare and Contrast, and Red and Green Vowels (both described in Chapter 5) to be very beneficial as both call special attention to vowel neighborhoods. What's in a Name?, Letter Neighborhood Circle, Vowel Neighborhood Sort, and Long and Short Vowel Fly Away Words are also useful practice activities that target vowel letter-sound neigh-borhoods. After children apply basic vowel letter-sound neighborhoods when read-ing and spelling, teach other letter-sound neighborhoods and how to use them (neighborhoods are described in Chapter 5 and Appendix B).

    Children like Melissa benefit from reading decodeable books—books with words that are spelled like they sound and therefore can be pronounced using the letter-sound strategy. Decodeable books give children practice using the letter-sound strategy while reading. Using the letter-sound strategy in turn reinforces children's knowledge of the sounds the letters in neighborhoods represent. And, because so many words can be successfully identified using the letter-sound strat-egy, decodeable books help children like Melissa appreciate the benefits of apply-ing this strategy when reading. Melissa, and children like her, need many and var-ied opportunities to use phonemic awareness (particularly blending) along with letter-sound knowledge when identifying unfamiliar words in reading and spelling while writing. The more opportunities to apply knowledge (both phonemic awareness and letter-sound knowledge) the better.

Melissa's reading ability will improve as she develops more phonemic awareness, knowledge of letter-sound neighborhoods, and the ability to strategically use this information to identify and learn new words. As Melissa's fluent reading vocabulary expands, the difficulty of the material (chapter books, content subject books, poems, articles, and so forth) will rise and hence the load (the requirements of grade level reading materials) and the force (what Melissa knows and can do) will come into balance.

Mike

Mike, whose story is shown in Figure 7–6, has developed some knowledge of onsets, rimes, and letter-sound neighborhoods. Even so, Mike has not developed enough knowledge of letter-sound neighborhoods to support reading the normal fourth-grade materials in his classroom. Hence, the force that Mike brings to reading and writing is far less than the load imposed by everyday fourth-grade reading and writing activities.

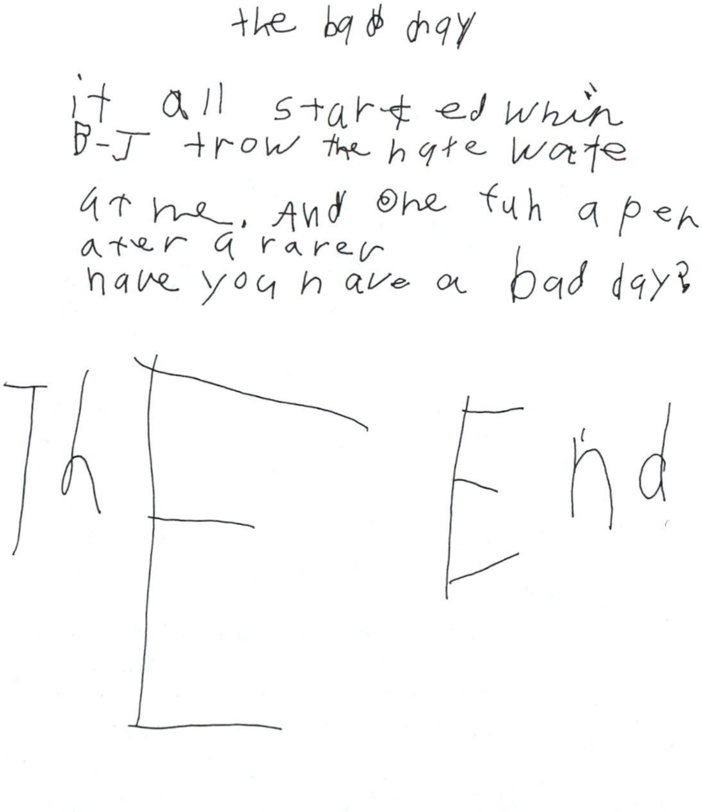

Figure 7–6 The reading and writing ability of children like Mike, who is midway through the fourth grade, will improve when they increase sound awareness and knowledge of letter-sound neighborhoods.

When Mike writes, he conventionally spells highly frequent words, such as **it, all, you, bad, day,** and **have.** He also spells phonetically, as we see in the word **weight,** written as **wate.** In so doing, Mike uses a **VCe** long vowel neighborhood (**ate**), which suggests that he has some knowledge of this more challenging vowel letter neighborhood (Chapter 5). Mike still has a good deal to learn about the letter-sound neighborhoods in words, for even with the support of story context, we cannot figure out words such as **fuh** (intended to be the word **thing**), **ararer** (meant to be **another**), and **hate** (supposed to be **heavy**). Like Melissa, Mike has moved beyond the semiphonetic phase of movement toward word fluency. Also like Melissa, Mike's development as a reader is encumbered by his inability to effectively use the letter-sound strategy (and the multiletter chunk strategy) to identify unfamiliar words and to increase the size of his fluent reading vocabulary. While Mike struggles with the letter-sound neighborhoods in English, his classmates are using the multiletter chunk strategy to add words to their fluent reading vocabularies. Other fourth graders in his class are at the consolidated phase of movement toward word fluency (explained in Chapter 6) and are transitional spellers. Nevertheless, the beginning sentence in Mike's story introduces readers to action and his thoughts flow logically. And, what's more, Mike is an enthusiastic learner when the load and the force are in balance.

What Mike Needs to Know to Move Toward Word Fluency

Mike needs to know more about the letter-sound neighborhoods in words and needs to be able to strategically use this knowledge when he reads and writes. As a fourth grader, Mike needs to develop the knowledge of, and ability to use, multiletter chunks to identify and learn words. Mike has to increase his awareness of the individual sounds in words and improve his ability to blend sounds together. Mike also needs to continue to be meaning focused, to use context cues along with letter and sound cues, and to cross-check for meaning when identifying unfamiliar words while reading.

Teaching Phonemic Awareness

Children like Mike benefit from activities that increase their awareness of the individual sounds in words and their ability to blend. It is critical that Mike's blending ability improve, for at present Mike typically adds, deletes, and rearranges sounds when he blends. Asked to blend **"l" + "a" + "m" + "p,"** Mike may say something like **"slamp," "lap,"** or "**plam.**" Arm Blending, which is a very effective technique, does not appeal to Mike because he does not want to use something so obvious in front of his fourth-grade friends. As an alternative, I suggest that he learn to tap the side of a table (or desk) with his pencil for each sound to be blended. Many of the older children I teach find that this is an effective and acceptable technique to use while reading in school. Finger blending is another beneficial way for children like Mike to blend short words. The Sliding Sounds activity is helpful, provided that it is modified to be appropriate for older children. Rather than drawing a slide on the chalkboard (as described in Chapter 2), give Mike and other children sheets of paper with slides on them. Mike then writes letters on the slide himself (beginning at the top and ending near the bottom), blends the sounds represented by letters, and then writes the whole word at the bottom of the slide. Writing letters individually down the slide and writing the whole word at the bottom helps children like Mike develop phonemic awareness as well as knowledge of alphabetic cues. As for increasing sound awareness, Tapping Sounds, Counting Sounds, and Sound Boxes are helpful for children who are as old as Mike. When using Sound Boxes, the letters should always be written in boxes so as to link phonemic awareness and letter neighborhood knowledge.

Teaching the Letter-Sound Neighborhoods and the MultiLetter Chunks in Words

If you have children like Mike in your classroom, teach phonemic awareness (Chapter 2) and the letter-sound neighborhoods (Chapter 5) concurrently. Both—phonemic awareness (especially blending) and letter neighborhoods—should be directly taught and both must be applied when identifying unfamiliar words during reading and spelling during writing.

You can expect the Building Words with Letter Tiles lesson (Chapter 5) to be effective and to shorten the time readers like Mike spend catching up with their classmates (Tunmer & Hoover, 1993). Word Group Discovery is an excellent small-group lesson that provides insight into the ways words are grouped based on letter-sound neighborhoods. The lessons that feature Word Puzzles and Venn Diagrams (explained in Chapter 5) are also appropriate because their focus on letter-sound neighborhood knowledge is sophisticated enough to appeal to older children like Mike. Mike, and children like him, benefit from lots of extra practice. Look in Chapter 5 for extra practice activities like What's in a Name? and Letter Neighborhood Bingo. Sorting is an effective activity, provided that Mike looks for letter-sound neighborhoods that he needs to learn. I recommend that you avoid writing words on sacks to designate the type of sort because children like Mike may very well bypass thinking about the sounds the letters in neighborhoods represent and simply sort based on a visual pattern. That is, rather than reading the words they are sorting, children may only look for a special sequence, such as vowel-consonant-e, and sort by visual pattern alone. (In this case, all **VCe** words would be put together without paying attention to the sounds the vowels in this neighborhood represent.) When this happens, sorting is a purely visual activity, not an activity that combines knowledge of letters and sounds.

I also recommend using mini-chalkboards to develop knowledge of letter-sound neighborhoods. Not only is spelling with mini-chalkboards a good way to extend children's knowledge of letter-sound neighborhoods, but it is a surefire way for you to find out who effectively uses letter-sound neighborhood knowledge to spell and who does not. Just give children mini-chalkboards and ask them to spell words with certain letter-sound neighborhoods. Put children in small groups, ask them to spell words with the letter-sound neighborhoods they are learning, and have children hold up mini-chalkboards when they are finished spelling. When children do this, you see right away who uses letter-sound neighborhoods correctly and who does not. Misspelled words are not penalized in any way, however. Children simply erase misspellings and fix words with minimal disruption to learning. As children spell, talk about letter-sound neighborhoods, compare and contrast words, and discuss word meaning.

We know it is important for children like Mike to develop greater phonemic awareness and letter-sound neighborhood knowledge. Yet we also know that the average fourth grader has moved well beyond letter-sound learning. So it is important to include children like Mike in the ongoing, grade-appropriate aspects of multiletter chunk learning that are within their ability to master successfully. Introduce Mike to fourth-grade prefixes and suffixes, as well as prefixes and suffixes from earlier grades that Mike has not learned. When teaching vowel letter-sound neighborhoods, talk about and explore how syllables affect the sounds represented by the vowel letters in words. The Coin-a-Word lesson (explained in Chapter 6) is beneficial because the word creation focus is well within the competence of a child like Mike, provided that he works with a learning partner. So, too, is the Complimenting Classmates lesson appropriate for Mike (described in detail in Chapter 6), if it is modified to reduce the load so as to be in balance with the force Mike brings to reading. While Mike cannot independently read the book *The Best School Year Ever* (Robinson, 1996), he can enjoy listening to the book, participating in shared reading, and taking part in choral reading. Children like Mike are quite capable of making the Honor Shield. An added benefit is that the Honor Shield may very well boost Mike's self-esteem when he reads the compliments of his classmates. The Explosion and Word Webs lessons (both explained in Chapter 6) are group activities children like Mike enjoy, contribute to, and profit from. Many of the extra practice activities in Chapter 6 can be adapted so that the load and force are balanced for Mike by having him participate in learning as part of a team or small group.

All things taken together, children benefit most when they have a great many experiences in reading and writing, and many opportunities to use the analogy with onsets and rimes, letter-sound, and multiletter chunk strategies when reading and spelling. As children use the analogy with onsets and rimes and letter-sound strategies, their phonemic awareness and knowledge of letter-sound relationships increases simultaneously. With greater phonemic awareness and greater knowledge of letter-sound neighborhoods, children's ability to use word identification strategies also improves. Children then are able to refine the analogy and letter-sound strategies, and to develop the ability to use multiletter chunks to help them identify words. As a consequence, the force that children like Shandra, Raymond, Melissa, and Mike bring to reading is greater and, by extension, the load children are capable of lifting is heavier. By carefully and systematically adjusting the balance, children succeed, gain self-confidence, develop greater capacity to express themselves in writing, enjoy reading increasingly more difficult books, and eventually become independent readers with a large fluent reading vocabulary.

CHILDREN WHO SPEAK LANGUAGES OTHER THAN ENGLISH AT HOME

Many children whose families speak languages other than English benefit from extra help because the language spoken at home is different from the language in which English-speaking authors write. These children bring to your classroom rich ethnic, cultural, and linguistic backgrounds. They also bring to reading a different complement of syntactic structures and vocabulary than children whose families speak English. As a consequence, children whose families speak languages other than English at home have three things to learn (the stucture of a new spoken language, a new vocabulary, and a new written language), while native English speakers need only learn written English (Thonis, 1989). The challenge is even greater for older children who must not only learn English but must also master the technical information taught in content subject classes (Freeman & Freeman, 1993).

Children whose families speak languages other than English are most successful when they have opportunities to observe, infer, and grasp connections between spoken and written language (Verhoeven, 1990). One way to balance the load and the force is to explore speech and print together (Crawford, 1993). When children understand how the English alphabet represents sounds, children also have opportunities to become aware of syntactic structure (Dogger, 1981). Similarly, instruction in vocabulary not only increases children's reading comprehension (Bartley, 1993), but also extends their use of spoken English, and this, in turn, enhances children's abilities to form thoughts in English when they write.

Native language literacy is important for balancing the load and the force, too. Children who are literate in their home languages find it easier to learn to read and write English than children who are not literate in their native languages (Royer & Carlo, 1991). One reason for this is that children who can read and write their home languages understand the purpose of reading and writing. Children whose home languages are written in an alphabet understand the alphabetic principle. They may bring to the English alphabetic code some, if not all, of the word identification strategies described in this book, albeit applied to word identification in their home languages.

Sometimes you will see the influence of their home languages as children read and write, as shown in Juana's story (Figure 7–7). When Juana writes, she combines her knowledge of English with a rich knowledge of Spanish, her home language. Notice that Juana replaces **of** with **de,** the Spanish word that would ordinarily be used in this syntactic structure. Notice, too, that Juana writes **ticher** for **teacher.** The letter **i** in Spanish represents the sound heard in **routine,** not **line,** so Juana's spelling is consistent with her first language heritage. Juana is also aware of the way that the English alphabet represents sound, as you can see in her spelling of **tois** for **toys.**

Chan, whose story is shown in Figure 7–8, has attended schools where English is spoken longer than Juana has. Hence, Chan brings greater knowledge of spoken and written English to reading and is therefore capable of lifting greater loads—he reads and understands more challenging materials than Juana. Even so, Chan's home language, Vietnamese, sometimes crosses over into written and spoken English. For instance, when Chan writes, he does not always include all function words such as prepositions and conjunctions. And when Chan reads aloud, he pronounces **mother** as **"muder"** and leaves out most plurals, possessives, and many other word endings, thus reading **wanted** as **"want."** This is so even though Chan's story is a retelling of a familiar book, *The Great Kapok Tree* (Cherry, 1990), which his teacher read several times in class, and the class discussed a good deal in relation to science.

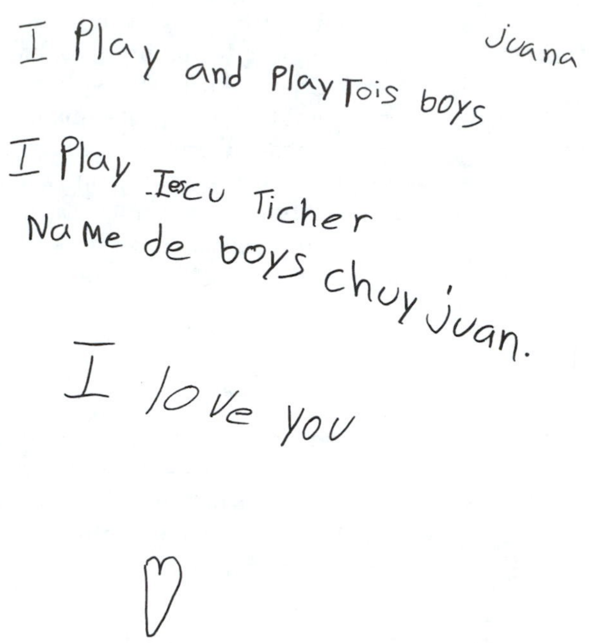

Figure 7–7 The written messages of children who speak languages other than English at home, such as Juana whose family speaks Spanish, may reflect a combination of children's home language and English.

I Play and Play Tois boys   Juana

I Play Iscu Ticher

Na Me de boys chuy Juan.

I love you

Chan is learning English syntax, semantics, and vocabulary, as we see from his writing (Figure 7–8). Children like Chan and Juana, like all readers of English, must automatically recognize the pronunciation and meaning of words, as explained in Chapter 1. Interestingly, languages may overlap with English up to 20% (Graves, Juel, & Graves, 1998). The greater the overlap, the closer the match between children's home language and English, and the more information children bring to learning to speak, read, and write English. Graves, Juel, and Graves (1998) point out that Juana's home language, Spanish, has a good deal of overlap with English, while Chan's home language, Vietnamese, has relatively little overlap. Hence, depending on her home background and previous literacy experience in Spanish, Juana may bring more prior knowledge to English vocabulary than Chan. This means that, for some children whose home languages have less overlap with English, you may need to concentrate more time and attention on building the background upon which a solid understanding of English vocabulary rests. And, of course, when children are gaining an understanding of English words, they need lots of support, including support from the reading context. So it is not surprising that children whose families do not speak English at home read words better in context than in lists (Wong & Underwood, 1996). According to Wong and Underwood's findings, you can expect children who do not speak English at home to benefit from the cues to words found in the reading context, while the native English speakers in your classroom may well show no difference in their ability to read words in lists or in context.

The great Kapot tree

The great kapot tree arse The raini forest.
The great kapot tree is larg.
The great kapot tree is where the
animales live. The butterfly and
The sasur live in The top
loge. The monkey, the sloth live
in The umbrella or canpy. The
tree frog and the snak live in the
uhderstory. The Last
is all the amimalscan live There.

Top
uhderstory
umbrella
Last

Figure 7–8   The transfer of home languages to spoken and written English suggests that children are interacting with English text in meaningful ways.

The crossover, or transfer, of home languages to spoken and written English (substituting **de** for **of,** spelling **teacher** as **ticher,** omitting word endings and conjunctions, and using verbs inappropriately) suggests that children are interacting with English text in meaningful ways. Transfer is, indeed, an important sign of progress toward English literacy. Though the home languages Juana and Chan speak result in different types of transfer, you can expect children like these to learn to speak and read English equally well (Piper, 1993).

Both Juana and Chan are moving toward accomplished use of written English, each at a different point on a continuum. Given that children bring a wealth of understandings and insights to written English, what types of materials are most likely to help balance the load and the force—to simultaneously support children's strategic use of our alphabetic writing system and enhance comprehension? For one thing, you can support children as they become literate in their home languages. For another thing, you can balance the load and the force so as to support the development of word identification strategies that are so important for literacy in written English. To this end, I suggest you consider achieving a point of balance by (1) using culturally familiar text, (2) using predictable books, (3) promoting leisure reading, (4) reading aloud to children, and (5) having children write for a variety of purposes.

Use of Culturally Familiar Materials

The children in your classroom who speak languages other than English at home will remember more information (Malik, 1990; Steffensen & Joag-dev, 1981) and make more elaborate connections when they read culturally familiar materials (Pritchard, 1990) than when they read materials that are far afield from their home cultures. Culturally unfamiliar materials require more background building and call for more explicit explanations than culturally familiar materials. Moreover, culturally unfamiliar text is not a good measure of reading ability and, in fact, is likely to underestimate children's actual reading achievement (Garcia, 1991).

From a practical point of view, you will find that children are better readers of the materials in your classroom—better at comprehending storybooks, novels, articles, and poems, and better at remembering information and concepts in content subject textbooks—when text is culturally relevant, worse readers when text is culturally unfamiliar. So, if you wish to get an informal assessment of children's reading abilities, use materials that correspond to children's background knowledge and experience and avoid materials that are detached from children's lives.

Establishing the right balance point depends to a considerable extent upon whether materials are culturally familiar to children. This means that books, poems, articles, and plays that are culturally familiar to children who speak English at home may not be suitable matches for children whose families do not speak English at home. Furthermore, materials that are a good fit for Hispanic children may not be such a good fit for Arabic, Asian, or Native American children. This, of course, underscores the importance of being sensitive to children's cultural heritage and personal life experiences.

The goal is to link children's life experiences with classroom learning (Weaver, 1994). To do this, take frequent field trips and invite guest speakers whose home language is that spoken by the children whom you teach (in this case, Spanish for Juana and Vietnamese for Chan). Encourage children to talk about their life experiences and incorporate those experiences into your everyday classroom routine. Cook children's traditional foods; write signs in children's home languages; and make bulletin boards, wall charts, and labels in both English and the children's home languages. Use pictures and real objects (an orange, a fork, a toy car) to support classroom discussions whenever possible. Read books and traditional tales that embrace children's cultures; role-play, retell, and illustrate stories, folk tales, and poems. Not only do such activities build a strong context for learning, but they provide ways to honor the cultures of children as well.

Predictable Books
While there are many types of books and ways to share them, predictable books hold a special promise because they bring English syntax and English words

within easy reach of young children who are beginning to read a language different from the one spoken at home. With pictures supporting comprehension and text that is patterned, predictable books open the door to literacy by presenting children with meaningful, enjoyable reading experiences that aid reading development (Heilman, Blair, & Rupley, 1998). Because the same English language patterns recur over and over again, predictable books encourage young, beginning readers to anticipate sentence structure. And, since the same words are read many times, children have many chances to remember them, thereby building their reading vocabularies. The same characteristics that make predictable books useful for younger children also make these books beneficial for older children who are novice readers of English (Arthur, 1991). So, do not hesitate to share predictable books with older children who are crossing the threshold of English literacy, provided, of course, that books are culturally and developmentally appropriate.

Leisure Reading

There is nothing so powerful as enjoying a good book just for the pure fun of it. As children read for pleasure, they use word identification strategies in context and have opportunities to develop a better understanding of English syntax and vocabulary. Intriguing storybooks, thrilling novels, touching poems, dramatic plays offer gateways to literacy. Take advantage, too, of the engaging magazines published for beginning and advanced readers: *Your Big Backyard* for young children interested in the world of nature; *Odyssey* for third graders and up who are intrigued by space travel and the science of the universe; *Ranger Rick* for second graders through fourth graders who like to read articles about nature; *Disney Adventures* for readers interested in a potpourri of articles, ideas, and activities; and *Ladybug* (ages two through six), *Spider* (ages six through nine), and *Cricket* (ages nine through fourteen) for children who are enchanted by stories, poems, and fantasy. This is just to mention a few. Look for books and magazines written in English and written in children's home languages, as well. Set aside time each day for children to read for pleasure and, while you make time for leisure reading, allow time for reading aloud to children.

Reading Aloud to Children

When you read storybooks, novels, plays, poems, and articles aloud, children have opportunities to develop a sense of the structure of stories, enjoy literature, and have experiences with English print that may not be available in their homes. Look, too, for ways to combine read-aloud stories with writing activities. After books have been read aloud, discussed, and enjoyed, invite children to write about a memorable event or a fascinating character. If you teach young children, cut out the stories children write, fasten the stories to construction paper, and staple construction paper sheets together to make a giant accordion-style book. Accordion books link reading and writing directly and are wonderful resources to share with younger children. Older children enjoy creating and publishing their own versions of favorite books and poems, not to mention rewriting the lyrics of songs, raps, and chants, which brings us to the use of writing to balance the load and the force.

Writing for a Variety of Purposes

Children whose families speak languages other than English at home express their thoughts in writing long before they speak English proficiently (Hudelson, 1984). Writing helps children reflect upon meaningful messages in print, creates opportunities to use English syntax and vocabulary in meaningful ways, and supports insight into our English alphabetic writing system. For these reasons, I suggest you use the language experience approach with the less accomplished children in your classroom and dialogue journals with the more accomplished children whom you teach.

Language experience is an approach whereby the stories that children read are stories written or dictated by them, are based on their life experiences, and reflect their spoken language. Language experience stories make a special contribution because the messages children write are the materials read, which directly links the text with the children's cultural background and daily experiences. Added to this, the words in language experience stories are a rich source of onsets, rimes, and letter-sound neighborhoods to include in activities described in earlier chapters.

Dialogue journals, which are two-way communications between children and their teachers, are particularly beneficial for children who read and write English with enough independence to put their thoughts on paper. When children like Chan write dialogue journals, they share their thoughts with their teachers. Their teachers, in turn, write reactions to children's messages, including personal comments and descriptions of relevant life experiences. This gives children opportunities to extend and refine their abilities to use the alphabet to write, as well as opportunities to learn how to form their thoughts in such a way as to communicate with English-speaking readers. Should you choose to use dialogue journals with the children whom you teach, you can expect children's confidence with written language to improve and their command of spoken English to increase, too (Nurss & Hough, 1992).

Language experience stories and dialogue journals are but two of the many ways to connect spoken and written English with children's cultural heritage. Children in the fourth grade and up enjoy writing cartoons (described in Chapter 6), especially when cartoons tap into children's everyday life experiences. Adding new endings for familiar poems, writing stories and scripts for homemade movies, writing humorous jokes and riddles, and creating entertaining alliterative sentences also add a great deal to children's overall understanding of spoken and written English.

Find lots of books, magazines, and newspapers written in children's home languages and put them in your classroom library. Then create a classroom newspaper or magazine featuring articles written by children. Articles can be in children's home language and in English, too. This way everyone has an opportunity to share in literacy experiences. Locate pen pals who can write in children's home languages. And locate, too, relatives of children who will be children's pen pals or who will visit your classroom to share their life experiences. Invite parents to volunteer in your classroom and celebrate holidays that are important to children's families. This type of classroom activity is a rich source for writing collaboratively in large and small groups. Emphasize meaning as children write, but also take the opportunity to discuss the onsets, rimes, letter-sound neighborhoods, and multiletter chunks in children's writing. In so doing, exploring the English alphabetic writing system will become an integral part of on-going classroom activities in which children read, write, speak, and listen to English.

All things considered, the greater the connection among everyday reading activities, writing, and the strategy-driven use of letter-sound cues, the more opportunities children have to transfer word identification to meaningful reading contexts. The challenge is to balance the load and the force so as to foster the development of word identification strategies, nurture literacy, and ensure that all children become competent, meaning-driven readers. Balancing the load and the force creates a supportive learning environment; honors children's individual differences, needs, and preferences; and provides the basis upon which children successfully read a wide variety of storybooks, novels, poems, articles, plays, and content subject textbooks.

REFERENCES

Arthur, B. (1991). Working with new ESL students in a junior high school reading class. *The Journal of Reading, 34,* 628–631.

Bartley, N. (1993). Literature-based integrated language instruction and the language-deficient student. *Reading Research and Instruction, 32,* 31–37.

Cherry, L. (1990). *The great kapok tree.* New York: Harcourt Brace.

Crawford, L. W. (1993). *Language and literacy learning in multicultural classrooms.* Boston: Allyn & Bacon.

Cricket. Mt. Morris, IL: The Cricket Magazine Group, Carus Publishing Company.

Disney adventures. Burbank, CA: Walt Disney Magazine Publishing Group.

Dogger, B. (1981). Language-based reading theories, English orthography, and ESL pedagogy. In C. W. Twyford, W. Diehl, & K. Feathers (Eds.), *Reading English as a second language: Moving from theory* (pp. 21–28). *Monographs in Teaching and Learning, 4* (March).

Foorman, B. R., Francis, D. J., Winikates, D., Mehta, P., Schatschneider, C., & Fletcher, J. M. (1997). *Scientific Studies of Reading, 1,* 255–276.

Freeman, D. E., & Freeman, Y. S. (1993). Strategies for promoting the primary languages of all students. *The Reading Teacher, 46,* 552–558.

Garcia, G. E. (1991). Factors influencing the English reading test performance of Spanish-speaking Hispanic children. *Reading Research Quarterly, 26,* 371–392.

Graves, M. F., Juel, C., & Graves, B. (1998). *Teaching reading in the 21st century.* Boston, MA: Allyn & Bacon.

Greaney, K. T., Tunmer, W. E., & Chapman, J. W. (1997). Effects of rime-based orthographic analogy training on the word recognition of children with reading disability. *Journal of Educational Psychology, 89,* 645–651.

Heilman, A. W., Blair, T. R., & Rupley, W. H. (1998). *Principles and practices of teaching reading* 9th ed. Columbus, OH: Merrill Publishing Company.

Hudelson, S. (1984). Kan yu ret an rayt en ingles: Children become literate in English as a second language. *TESOL Quarterly, 18,* 221–238.

Ladybug. Mt. Morris, IL: The Cricket Magazine Group, Carus Publishing Company.

Layton, L., Deeny, K., Tall, G., & Upton, G. (1996). Researching and promoting phonological awareness in the nursery class. *Journal of Research in Reading, 19,* 1–13.

Malik, A. A. (1990). A psycholinguistic analysis of the reading behavior of ESL-proficient readers using culturally familiar and unfamiliar expository text. *American Educational Research Journal, 27,* 205–223.

Metsala, J. L., Stanovich, K. E., & Brown, G. D. (1998). Regularity effects and the phonological deficit model of reading disabilities: A meta-analytic review. *Journal of Educational Psychology, 90,* 279–293.

Nurss, J. R., & Hough, R. A. (1992). Reading and the ESL student. In S. J. Samuels & A. E. Farstrup (Eds.), *What research has to say about reading instruction* (2nd ed.) (pp. 277–313). Newark, DE: International Reading Association.

Odyssey. Peterborough, NH: Cobblestone Publishing.

Piper, T. (1993). *And then there were two: Children and second language learning.* Markman, Ontario: Pippin Publishing.

Pritchard, R. (1990). The effects of cultural schemata on reading processing strategies. *Reading Research Quarterly, 25,* 273–295.

Ranger Rick. Vienna, VA: National Wildlife Federation.

Robinson, B. (1996). *The Best School Year Ever.* New York: Scholastic.

Royer, J. M., & Carlo, M. S. (1991). Transfer of comprehension skills from native to second language. *Journal of Reading, 34,* 450–455.

Snow, C. E., Burns, S., & Griffin, G. (1998). *Preventing reading difficulties in young children.* Washington, DC: National Academy Press.

Spider. Mt. Morris, IL: The Cricket Magazine Group, Carus Publishing Company.

Stahl, S. A. (1998). Teaching children with reading problems to decode: Phonics and "not-phonics" instruction. *Reading & Writing Quarterly, 14,* 165–188.

Steffensen, M. S., & Joag-dev, C. (1981). Cultural knowledge and reading: Interference of facilitation. In C. W. Twyford, W. Diehl, & K. Feathers (Eds.), *Reading English as a second language: Moving from theory* (pp. 29–46). *Monographs in Teaching and Learning, 4* (March).

Thonis, E. W. (1989). Language minority students and reading. *The Reading Instruction Journal, 32,* 58–62.

Torgesen, J. K. (1998). Catch them before they fail. *American Educator, 22,* 32–39.

Torgesen, J. K., Wagner, R. K., Rashotte, C. A., Alexander, A. W., & Conway, T. (1997). Preventive and remedial interventions for children with severe reading disabilities. *Learning Disabilities, 8,* 51–61.

Tunmer, W. E., & Hoover, W. A. (1993). Phonemic recoding skill and beginning reading. *Reading and Writing: An Interdisciplinary Journal, 5,* 161–179.

Verhoeven, L. T. (1990). Acquisition of reading in a second language. *Reading Research Quarterly, 15,* 90–114.

Weaver, C. (1994). *Reading process and practice: From socio-psycholinguistics to whole language* (2nd ed.). Portsmouth, NH: Heinemann.

Wong, M. Y., & Underwood, G. (1996). Do bilingual children read words better in lists or in context? *Journal of Research in Reading, 19,* 61–76.

APPENDIX A

Rimes

Rime	Words
ab*	cab, crab, drab, flab, grab, jab, lab, nab, scab, slab, stab, tab, prefab, taxicab
ace	face, brace, grace, lace, pace, place, race, space, trace, aerospace, anyplace, birthplace, boldface, carapace, commonplace, efface, embrace, fireplace, interlace, marketplace, outface, replace, shoelace
ack*	back, black, pack, quack, sack, track, attack, backpack, bushwhack, cossack, cutback, drawback, haystack, hijack, horseback, knapsack, piggyback, racetrack, ransack, rickrack, setback, skyjack, tamarack, thumbtack, tieback, wisecrack, zwieback
act	act, fact, abstract, artifact, attract, cataract, compact, contact, contract, detract, distract, extract, impact, intact, interact, protract, react, subtract, transact
ad	bad, clad, dad, fad, glad, had, lad, mad, pad, sad, dyad, ironclad, keypad, nomad, triad
ade	blade, fade, grade, made, shade, trade, wade, abrade, accolade, arcade, barricade, blockade, brigade, cascade, cavalcade, charade, crusade, decade, dissuade, escapade, evade, handmade, marinade, motorcade, parade, persuade, pervade, renegade, tirade
ag*	bag, brag, crag, drag, flag, gag, lag, nag, rag, sag, shag, slag, snag, stag, tag, wag, beanbag, carpetbag, handbag, mailbag, ragtag, saddlebag, scalawag, zigzag

ail*   bail, fail, grail, hail, jail, mail, nail, pail, rail, sail, snail, tail, trail, airmail, assail, bewail, bobtail, coattail, contrail, curtail, derail, detail, entail, fingernail, handrail, hangnail, hobnail, monorail, ponytail, prevail, retail, toenail, topsail, travail

ain*   brain, chain, drain, gain, grain, main, plain, sprain, stain, train, abstain, appertain, ascertain, attain, complain, constrain, contain, detain, disdain, domain, entertain, eyestrain, explain, ingrain, maintain, ordain, pertain, refrain, restrain, sustain, terrain

air   air, chair, fair, flair, hair, lair, pair, stair, affair, armchair, corsair, debonair, despair, eclair, horsehair, impair, mohair, wheelchair, wirehair

ake*   bake, brake, cake, fake, flake, lake, make, rake, shake, snake, stake, take, wake, awake, cheesecake, clambake, cupcake, forsake, fruitcake, grubstake, handshake, keepsake, mistake, muckrake, namesake, overtake, pancake, partake, snowflake

ale*   bale, dale, gale, hale, kale, male, pale, sale, tale, vale, wale, scale, shale, stale, whale, exhale, female, impale, inhale, regale, resale, baler, azalea, salesman

all*   ball, call, fall, hall, mall, small, squall, stall, tall, wall, appall, baseball, befall, carryall, catchall, coverall, downfall, enthrall, eyeball, fireball, football, forestall, install, meatball, nightfall, overall, pitfall, rainfall, seawall, snowball, snowfall, stonewall

am*   cam, clam, cram, dam, dram, gram, ham, jam, lam, ram, scam, scram, sham, slam, swan, tam, tram, yam, bamboo, camel, cameo, camera, clamor, damsel, enamel, exam, family, famish, gamut, glamor, gamble, hamlet, hammer, ramble, sample

ame*   blame, came, fame, flame, frame, game, lame, name, same, shame, tame, became, mainframe, nickname, overcame, surname

amp   camp, champ, clamp, cramp, damp, lamp, ramp, scamp, stamp, tramp, vamp, decamp, firedamp, revamp, sunlamp

an*   bran, can, fan, man, pan, plan, ran, scan, span, tan, than, van, afghan, airman, bedpan, began, caravan, divan, dustpan, fireman, mailman, rattan, sampan, seaman, sedan, suntan, toucan, wingspan

and   band, bland, brand, gland, grand, hand, land, sand, stand, strand, ampersand, backhand, command, contraband, demand, disband, expand, farmhand, firebrand, handstand, offhand, quicksand, reprimand, understand, withstand

ane	cane, crane, lane, mane, pane, plane, sane, vane, wane, airplane, arcane, germane, humane, hurricane, inane, inhumane, insane, membrane, methane, mundane, octane, profane, propane, seaplane, sugarcane, urbane, urethane, windowpane
ang	bang, clang, fang, gang, hang, pang, rang, sang, slang, sprang, tang, twang, boomerang, mustang, overhang, shebang
ank*	bank, blank, clank, crank, dank, drank, flank, frank, lank, plank, prank, rank, sank, shank, shrank, spank, stank, swank, tank, thank, yank, gangplank, outflank, outrank, riverbank, sandbank
ant	ant, cant, chant, grant, pant, plant, rant, scant, slant, decant, eggplant, enchant, extant, gallivant, houseplant, implant, supplant, sycophant, transplant
ap*	cap, clap, flap, gap, lap, map, nap, scrap, slap, snap, strap, tap, trap, wrap, bootstrap, burlap, catnap, entrap, firetrap, gingersnap, handicap, hubcap, kidnap, mishap, mousetrap, overlap, pinesap, stopgap, thunderclap, wiretap
are	blare, dare, fare, flare, glare, hare, mare, pare, rare, scare, share, snare, spare, square, stare, tare, ware, airfare, aware, beware, compare, declare, ensnare, fanfare, hardware, nightmare, prepare, stemware, threadbare, welfare
arm	arm, charm, farm, harm, alarm, disarm, firearm, forearm, rearm, sidearm, underarm, yardarm
art	art, cart, chart, dart, kart, mart, part, smart, start, tart, apart, counterpart, depart, impart, outsmart, pushcart, rampart, restart, upstart
ash*	bash, cash, dash, gash, hash, lash, mash, rash, sash, abash, brash, clash, crash, flash, gnash, slash, smash, stash, trash, potash, rehash, splash, thrash, cashew, cashier, fashion, dashboard
at*	bat, cat, chat, fat, flat, gnat, hat, mat, pat, rat, sat, scat, slat, spat, that, acrobat, autocrat, bobcat, brickbat, bureaucrat, butterfat, chitchat, combat, copycat, democrat, diplomat, doormat, format, habitat, hemostat, muskrat, nonfat, photostat, rheostat, wildcat
atch	catch, latch, match, patch, scratch, snatch, thatch, crosspatch, dispatch, outmatch, potlatch, rematch, unlatch
ate*	crate, date, fate, gate, late, mate, plate, rate, sate, skate, slate, state, abate, calculate, candidate, create, debate, disintegrate, dissipate, donate, elate, elevate, estimate, excavate, inmate, irate, irritate, locate, migrate, motivate, mutate, negate, notate

aw*	caw, haw, jaw, law, maw, paw, raw, saw, claw, draw, flaw, gnaw, slaw, thaw, bylaw, macaw, squaw, straw, bawdy, brawl, crawl, drawl, shawl, trawl, dawn, fawn, gawk, hawk, lawn, pawn, tawny, yawn, dawdle, lawman, lawyer, tawdry, jawbone, rawhide, sawdust, sawmill
ay*	bay, clay, day, gay, gray, hay, lay, may, pay, play, ray, say, stay, stray, sway, tray, way, allay, anyway, ashtray, away, betray, birthday, castaway, dismay, doorway, foray, freeway, gateway, hearsay, holiday, mainstay, payday, portray, relay, someday, subway
eal	deal, heal, meal, peal, real, seal, squeal, steal, teal, veal, zeal, appeal, conceal, congeal, cornmeal, ideal, piecemeal, oatmeal, ordeal, repeal, reveal, surreal
eam	beam, cream, dream, gleam, ream, seam, scream, steam, team, airstream, daydream, inseam, midstream, moonbeam, sunbeam, upstream
ear	clear, dear, ear, fear, gear, hear, near, rear, sear, shear, smear, spear, tear, year, appear, arrear, disappear, endear
eat*	beat, bleat, cheat, cleat, heat, meat, neat, peat, pleat, seat, treat, wheat, browbeat, buckwheat, defeat, downbeat, drumbeat, entreat, heartbeat, mincemeat, offbeat, overheat, repeat, retreat, upbeat
ed*	bed, bled, bred, fed, fled, led, pled, red, shed, sled, sped, wed, coed, edit, pedal, cheddar, credit
eck	check, deck, fleck, heck, neck, peck, speck, wreck, bedeck, bottleneck, breakneck, crookneck, flyspeck, henpeck, paycheck, redneck, roughneck, shipwreck
ect	aspect, bisect, collect, connect, correct, deflect, deject, detect, dialect, direct, dissect, effect, eject, infect, insect, inspect, intersect, neglect, object, perfect, protect, reflect, respect, select, subject
eed*	bleed, breed, creed, deed, feed, freed, greed, heed, need, reed, speed, steed, tweed, weed, airspeed, aniseed, birdseed, exceed, inbreed, indeed, linseed, misdeed, nosebleed, proceed, ragweed, seaweed, succeed
een	between, green, keen, queen, screen, seen, sheen, spleen, teen, canteen, careen, eighteen, evergreen, foreseen, fourteen, Halloween, overseen, sunscreen, tureen, velveteen, windscreen
eep	beep, cheep, creep, deep, jeep, keep, peep, seep, sheep, sleep, steep, sweep, weep, asleep, oversleep, upkeep
eer	cheer, deer, jeer, leer, peer, queer, sheer, sneer, steer, veer, career, commandeer, domineer, engineer, mountaineer, musketeer, pioneer, reindeer, veneer, volunteer

ell*	bell, cell, dell, dwell, fell, quell, sell, shell, smell, spell, swell, tell, well, yell, barbell, befell, bluebell, bombshell, doorbell, eggshell, farewell, foretell, inkwell, nutshell, oversell, stairwell
end	bend, blend, fend, lend, mend, send, spend, tend, trend, vend, addend, amend, append, ascend, attend, commend, comprehend, condescend, contend, defend, depend, descend, dividend, expend, extend, intend, offend, portend, pretend, subtrahend, suspend, upend
ent	bent, cent, rent, scent, sent, spent, tent, went, cement, consent, event, extent, foment, intent, invent, lament, orient, percent, resent
ept	crept, kept, slept, swept, wept, accept, adept, concept, crept, except, inept, intercept, overslept, percept, precept, transept, upswept, windswept
ert	pert, alert, assert, avert, concert, controvert, covert, culvert, desert, dessert, disconcert, divert, exert, expert, extrovert, inert, insert, introvert, invert, overt, pervert, revert, subvert
est*	best, chest, crest, guest, jest, lest, nest, pest, quest, rest, vest, west, wrest, zest, armrest, arrest, attest, bequest, congest, conquest, contest, detest, digest, divest, infest, ingest, invest, request, suggest
et	bet, get, jet, let, met, net, pet, set, vet, wet, yet, abet, alphabet, bayonet, cadet, dragnet, duet, egret, forget, inlet, parapet
ew*	blew, brew, ched, crew, dew, drew, few, flew, hew, knew, mew, new, pew, screw, shrew, skew, slew, spew, stew, pewter, sewage, cashew, curfew, eschew, mildew, nephew, review
ice*	ice, dice, lice, mice, nice, rice, vice, price, slice, spice, trice, twice, advice, device, entice, splice, thrice
ick*	brick, chick, click, crick, flick, kick, lick, nick, pick, prick, quick, sick, slick, stick, thick, tick, trick, wick, airsick, derrick, gimmick, handpick, homesick, limerick, lipstick, maverick, sidekick, rollick, seasick, yardstick
ict	strict, addict, afflict, conflict, contradict, convict, depict, derelict, district, edict, evict, inflict, interdict, predict, restrict, verdict
id	did, grid, hid, kid, lid, skid, slid, squid, acid, arid, aphid, avid, candid, carotid, cuspid, fervid, flaccid, florid, fluid, frigid, horrid, humid, insipid, intrepid, languid, liquid, livid, rapid, rigid, solid, sordid, splendid, squalid, tepid, timid, torpid, valid, vapid, vivid
ide*	bride, chide, hide, pride, ride, side, slide, stride, tide, wide, abide, aside, astride, bromide, chloride, collide, confide, decide, dioxide, divide, fireside, fluoride, outside, oxide,

	peroxide, preside, provide, reside, roadside, subside, suicide, sulfide
ig	big, brig, dig, fig, jig, pig, rig, sprig, swig, twig, wig, bigwig, shindig
ight*	bright, fight, flight, fright, knight, light, might, night, plight, right, sight, slight, tight, airtight, alright, copyright, daylight, delight, firelight, fortnight, headlight, highlight, hindsight, limelight, midnight, skylight, spotlight, starlight, stoplight, tonight, twilight
ill*	bill, chill, dill, drill, fill, frill, gill, grill, hill, kill, mill, quill, sill, skill, spill, still, swill, thrill, till, twill, anthill, distill, doorsill, downhill, fiberfill, foothill, freewill, fulfill, goodwill, handbill, instill, landfill, playbill, sawmill, treadmill, windchill, windmill
im*	brim, dim, grim, him, prim, rim, shim, skim, slim, swim, trim, vim, cherubim, seraphim
ime	chime, crime, dime, grime, lime, prime, slime, time, anytime, bedtime, daytime, lifetime, lunchtime, maritime, mealtime, meantime, nighttime, noontime, overtime, pantomime, ragtime, sometime, sublime, teatime
in*	chin, grin, pin, skin, spin, thin, tin, twin, win, akin, begin, chagrin, doeskin, kingpin
ind	bind, blind, find, grind, hind, kind, mind, rind, wind, behind, humankind, mankind, mastermind, rebind, remind, rewind, spellbind, unkind, unwind, womankind
ine*	dine, fine, line, mine, nine, pine, sine, tine, vine, wine, aline, brine, shine, spine, swine, thine, twine, whine, alpine, bovine, byline, canine, cosine, define, devine, equine, feline, iodine, refine, reline, shrine, supine, ninety, winery, dinette, nineteen
ing*	bring, cling, ding, fling, king, ring, sing, sling, sting, string, thing, wing, wring, zing, anything, awning, bedspring, bowstring, bullring, downswing, drawstring, earring, hamstring, handspring, latchstring, offspring, plaything, shoestring, upswing, wellspring
ink*	ink, blink, brink, chink, clink, drink, fink, kink, link, mink, pink, rink, shrink, sink, slink, stink, think, wink, hoodwink
int	dint, flint, glint, hint, lint, mint, print, quint, splint, sprint, squint, stint, tint, blueprint, footprint, imprint, newsprint, peppermint, skinflint, spearmint, thumbprint, voiceprint
ip*	chip, clip, dip, drip, flip, grip, hip, lip, nip, quip, rip, ship, sip, skip, slip, snip, strip, tip, trip, whip, zip, airship, catnip, equip, fingertip, flagship, kinship, outstrip

ir*	fir, sir, stir, whir, astir, nadir, tapir, birch, bird, birth, circa, dirge, dirt, dirty, firm, first, girl, girth, mirth, circle, circuit, giraffe, girdle, mirage, piranah, sirloin
ire	dire, fire, hire, mire, shire, sire, squire, tire, wire, acquire, admire, aspire, attire, backfire, bonfire, conspire, desire, empire, entire, esquire, inquire, inspire, perspire, quagmire, require, respire, retire, sapphire, satire, shire, vampire
ish	dish, fish, swish, wish, abolish, accomplish, anguish, astonish, banish, blemish, catfish, cherish, codfish, dervish, establish, famish, fetish, finish, furbish, furnish, garish, garnish, lavish, nourish, perish, publish, punish, radish, ravish, relish, varnish
it	bit, fit, hit, kit, knit, lit, pit, quit, sit, skit, wit, acquit, admit, commit, credit, emit, omit, permit, retrofit, submit, transmit
itch	ditch, flitch, glitch, hitch, itch, pitch, snitch, stitch, switch, twitch, witch, backstitch, bewitch, hemstitch, topstitch, unhitch
ob*	blob, cob, glob, gob, job, knob, lob, mob, rob, slob, snob, sob, throb, corncob, doorknob, hobnob, kabob
ock*	block, clock, crock, dock, flock, frock, knock, lock, rock, shock, smock, sock, stock, bedrock, deadlock, gamecock, hemlock, livestock, o'clock, padlock, peacock, roadblock, shamrock
og	bog, clog, cog, dog, fog, flog, frog, grog, hog, jog, log, slog, smog, analog, backlog, bulldog, bullfrog, catalog, dialogue, eggnog, epilogue, hedgehog, leapfrog, polliwog, underdog, watchdog, waterlog
oil	boil, broil, coil, foil, soil, spoil, toil, airfoil, charbroil, embroil, hydrofoil, parboil, recoil, subsoil, tinfoil, topsoil, trefoil, turmoil
oke*	awoke, broke, choke, coke, joke, poke, smoke, spoke, stoke, stroke, woke, yoke, artichoke, backstroke, bespoke, cowpoke, evoke, heatstroke, invoke, keystroke, provoke, slowpoke, sunstroke
old	bold, cold, fold, gold, hold, mold, scold, sold, told, behold, billfold, blindfold, enfold, foothold, foretold, freehold, household, manifold, marigold, outsold, retold, scaffold, tenfold, threshold, toehold, undersold, unfold, uphold
ond	bond, fond, pond, abscond, beyond, blond, correspond, despond, fishpond, frond, millpond, respond, vagabond
one	bone, clone, crone, lone, prone, shone, stone, throne, tone, zone, acetone, alone, backbone, condone, cortisone, enthrone, flagstone, headphone, hormone, limestone,

	methadone, monotone, ozone, postpone, silicone, telephone, wishbone
ong	bong, gong, long, prong, song, strong, thong, tong, wrong, along, furlong, headlong, headstrong, lifelong, oblong, prolong, sarong, sidelong, singsong, scuppernong, tagalong
op*	chop, crop, drop, flop, hop, mop, pop, prop, shop, stop, top, airdrop, backdrop, bellhop, blacktop, dewdrop, doorstop, gumdrop, hardtop, hilltop, lollipop, outcrop, raindrop, rooftop, tabletop, teardrop, treetop, workshop
ope	cope, dope, grope, hope, lope, mope, rope, scope, slope, antelope, envelope, gyroscope, horoscope, interlope, isotope, microscope, periscope, telescope, tightrope
or*	for, nor, born, cord, cork, corn, ford, fork, form, horn, lord, morn, pork, torn, worn, acorn, adorn, chord, flora, glory, scorn, shorn, short, snort, sport, stork, story, sword, sworn, thorn, decor, abort, aorta
ore*	chore, more, score, shore, snore, spore, store, tore, wore, adore, anymore, before, bookstore, carnivore, commodore, deplore, drugstore, encore, explore, folklore, herbivore, ignore, implore, seashore, semaphore, sophomore, therefore
orm	dorm, form, norm, storm, brainstorm, chloroform, conform, deform, hailstorm, inform, landform, outperform, perform, platform, reform, transform, uniform, windstorm
ort	fort, port, sort, tort, abort, airport, assort, carport, cavort, cohort, comport, consort, contort, davenport, deport, distort, escort, exhort, export, extort, import, passport, purport, report, resort, retort, short, snort, sport, support, transport
ot*	blot, clot, cot, dot, got, hot, knot, lot, not, plot, pot, shot, spot, trot, allot, apricot, ascot, ballot, cannot, despot, earshot, feedlot, forgot, gunshot, inkblot, jackpot, mascot, ocelot, robot, shallot, sunspot, teapot
ought	ought, bought, brought, drought, fought, sought, thought, wrought, besought, bethought
ound	bound, found, ground, hound, mound, pound, round, sound, wound, abound, aground, around, astound, compound, confound, expound, impound, inbound, outbound, profound, propound, rebound, resound, runaround, snowbound, surround, wolfhound
out*	bout, clout, flout, pout, scout, shout, snout, spout, sprout, trout, about, bailout, blackout, blowout, brownout, cookout, cutout, devout, dugout, fallout, flameout, handout, hideout, layout, lockout, lookout, printout, tryout, walkout, without

ow*	(long o) blow, flow, glow, grow, know, low, row, show, slow, snow, throw, aglow, arrow, below, bestow, borrow, bungalow, burrow, elbow, escrow, follow, inflow, marrow, meadow, mellow, minnow, narrow, pillow, rainbow, shadow, shallow
ub	club, cub, grub, hub, nub, pub, rub, scrub, shrub, snub, stub, sub, tub, bathtub, cherub, washtub
uck*	buck, chuck, cluck, duck, luck, pluck, snuck, struck, stuck, suck, tuck, truck, amuck, awestruck, mukluk, potluck, woodchuck
uct	duct, abduct, adduct, aqueduct, conduct, construct, deduct, destruct, induct, instruct, misconduct, obstruct, product, reconstruct, viaduct
ude	crude, dude, prude, rude, allude, attitude, collude, conclude, delude, exclude, extrude, fortitude, gratitude, include, interlude, lassitude, occlude, protrude, longitude, magnitude, multitude, platitude, plentitude, rectitude
uff	bluff, buff, cuff, fluff, gruff, muff, puff, ruff, scruff, scuff, snuff, stuff, dandruff, earmuff, foodstuff, handcuff
ug*	bug, chug, dug, drug, hug, jug, lug, mug, plug, pug, rug, shrug, slug, smug, snug, thug, tug, bedbug, earplug, firebug, fireplug, humbug
ult	cult, adult, catapult, consult, difficult, excult, insult, occult, result, tumult
um*	chum, drum, glum, gum, hum, plum, slum, sum, album, cadmium, calcium, cranium, decorum, eardrum, forum, fulcrum, lithium, maximum, minimum, modicum, optimum, premium, quantum, rostrum, sanctum, serum, stadium, sternum, tantrum, uranium
ump*	bump, chump, clump, dump, frump, grump, hump, jump, lump, plump, slump, stump, thump, trump, mugwump
un	bun, fun, gun, nun, pun, run, shun, spun, stun, sun, begun, handgun, homespun
ung	bung, clung, dung, flung, hung, lung, rung, slung, sprung, strung, stung, sung, swung, wrung, hamstrung
unk*	bunk, chunk, clunk, drunk, dunk, flunk, funk, hunk, junk, plunk, punk, shrunk, skunk, slunk, spunk, stunk, sunk, trunk, debunk, chipmunk
up	cup, pup, backup, blowup, checkup, holdup, linkup, pickup, roundup, setup, teacup, windup
ure	cure, lure, pure, allure, coiffure, demure, endure, epicure, impure, insecure, manicure, mature, obscure, pedicure, procure, secure

ust	bust, crust, dust, gust, just, lust, must, rust, thrust, trust, antitrust, disgust, distrust, encrust, entrust, sawdust
ut	but, cut, glut, gut, hut, jut, nut, rut, shut, strut, abut, catgut, coconut, crosscut, donut, haircut, halibut, peanut, rebut, shortcut, uppercut, walnut, woodcut
y*	by, cry, dry, fly, fry, my, pry, sky, sly, spy, sty, try

Note: Pronunciation of og may vary for children in different regions.
*Rimes with an asterisk are part of many different words, according to Cheek, Flippo, & Lindsay (1997) and/or Fry (1998):

Cheek, E. H., Flippo, R. F., & Lindsey, J. D. (1997). *Reading for success in elementary schools.* Dubuque, IA: Brown & Benchmark.

Fry, E. (1998). The most common phonograms. *The Reading Teacher, 52,* 620–622.

APPENDIX B

Letter-Sound Neighborhoods

Consonant Letter-Sound Neighborhoods

Single Consonant Neighborhood

Letters in a single consonant neighborhood represent the sounds heard in the following words:

B,b	boat	buffalo	P,p	popcorn	pineapple
C,c	cat	city	Q,q	queen	quack
D,d	dish	donkey	R,r	rabbit	raisin
F,f	fish	fox	S,s	salad	daisy
G,g	game	gem	T,t	toad	turtle
H,h	hat	hippopotamus	V,v	valentine	volcano
J,j	jet	jam	W,w	wagon	wave
K,k	kangaroo	kite	X,x	fox	exit
L,l	lamp	lollipop	Y,y	yellow	barnyard
M,m	monkey	mask	Z,z	zoo	zipper
N,n	nut	nest			

W,w and **Y,y** act as consonants when they are onsets, as in **wagon, wafer, yellow,** and **barnyard.**

Though **Y,y** represents the consonant sound heard in **yellow** when it is an onset, **Y,y** also acts as a vowel in many letter-sound neighborhoods.

X,x does not occur in many frequently used words and seldom represents the sound heard in **Xray,** a favorite example in ABC books. Though **X,x** represents several sounds, the **"ks"** in **fox** (particularly at the end of words) and the **"gz"** in **exit** are most common.

Consonants that represent more than one sound, such as **c, g,** and **s,** are explained later.

Qu Neighborhood

When **Q,q** is present in spelling, its next-door neighbor is almost always **U,u,** which acts as a consonant.

Onset "kw" Sound	*Middle "kw" Sound*	*Final "k" Sound*
quack q + u = qu	acquit q + u = qu	antique q + u + e = que
quaff	adequate	baroque
quaint	banquet	bisque
quake	conquest	boutique
quality	eloquent	clique
quantity	exquisite	critique
quarter	frequent	grotesque
queen	inquest	oblique
question	liquid	opaque
quick	request	physique
quiet	require	plaque
quill	sequel	statuesque
quit	sequin	technique
quiz	tranquil	torque
quote	vanquish	unique

Words spelled with **que** are borrowed from French and hence reflect the influence of French on our spelling system. Occasionally the **u** in **qu** is silent. Under this circumstance, **qu** represents the "k" heard in **mosquito, quay, croquette,** and **quiche.** This occurs so seldom in English words that it does not merit specific attention. **Q,q** occurs without **u** in a few words, as in **Iraq,** but this is so rare in English that it does not warrant special consideration either.

Twin Consonant Neighborhood

Formed whenever the same consonants are immediate neighbors (double letter), the sound represented is usually that of a single consonant neighborhood, as in **ra__bb__it** and **co__tt__on.** When there is a twin consonant in a word, the consonant sound most often goes with the preceding vowel to form a neighborhood, as in **rabbit** ("rab") and **mitten** ("mit"). The exception is when words are joined together to make compounds, in which case both sounds may be heard, as in **headdress** and **bookkeeper.** For the purpose of dividing words into syllables, the syllable division is between the double consonants (**rab-bit, mit-ten**), and the first syllable is most often the syllable that is accented.

In some words spelled with a double **c,** the first **c** represents the sound of "k" in **kite** and the second the "s" in **save,** as in **accent, accept,** and **accident.**

When suffixes are added to some words, such as **slam** and **wrap,** consonants are doubled, as in **slamming** and **wrapped.** Whereas it is easy to infer the pronunciation of the twin consonant neighborhood, it is challenging to learn when (and when not) to double consonants in writing suffixes.

Consonant Blend Neighborhood

The sounds represented by letters in a consonant blend neighborhood are joined together during pronunciation. Knowledge of the single consonant neighborhood transfers to the blend neighborhood, so readers need only learn how sounds are blended together during pronunciation.

Two-Letter Blends

***bl** Neighborhood*

black   b + l = bl
blame
blanket
blaze
bleach
blew
blight
blind
blizzard
block
blond
blouse
blossom
blue
blush

***cl** Neighborhood*

clam   c + l = cl
clasp
class
clay
clean
clever
cliff
clip
clock
clod
cloth
cloud
club
clump
cluster

***fl** Neighborhood*

flag   f + l = fl
flake
flame
flare
flat
flea
fleet
flesh
flight
fling
float
flood
flour
flow
fluid

***gl** Neighborhood*

glad   g + l = gl
glance
glare
glass
gleam
glen
glide
glimmer
glimpse
glitter
globe
gloom
glow
glue
glutton

***pl** Neighborhood*

place   p + l = pl
plane
planet
plank
plant
plastic
play
please
pledge
plenty
plod
plot
plow
plum
plus

***sl** Neighborhood*

slab   s + l = sl
slant
slap
sleep
slice
slide
slim
slip
slit
sliver
slobber
slogan
slope
slouch
slow

***br** Neighborhood*

bracelet   b + r = br
brag
brain
brake
branch
brass
brave
bread
breeze
bride
brim
broil

***cr** Neighborhood*

crab   c + r = cr
cradle
craft
crash
crawl
cream
creature
crew
crib
cricket
crop
cross

***dr** Neighborhood*

dragon   d + r = dr
drain
drama
drape
draw
dream
dress
drift
drill
drink
drip
drop

broom
brown
brush

fr Neighborhood

frame   f + r = fr
frank
free
freeze
fresh
fright
fringe
frock
frog
front
frost
frown
frozen
fruit
fry

tr Neighborhood

track   t + r = tr
trade
train
trap
treat
tree
trial
tribe
trick
trim
troll
tropic
trout
truck
trunk

sm Neighborhood

smack   s + m = sm
small
smart
smash
smear
smell
smelter
smile
smirk
smock

crown
crush
crust

gr Neighborhood

grab   g + r = gr
grain
grand
grape
grass
grateful
great
green
grew
grill
grip
groom
ground
grow
grump

sc Neighborhood

scale   s + c = sc
scan
scare
scarf
scoff
scold
scone
scoop
scope
score
scotch
scour
scout
scowl
scuttle

sn Neighborhood

snack   s + n = sn
snail
snake
snap
snarl
sneak
sneeze
snicker
sniff
snob

drown
drug
drum

pr Neighborhood

prefer   p + r = pr
present
press
pretty
pride
prim
print
prize
probe
problem
proof
proud
prove
prude
prune

sk Neighborhood

skate   s + k = sk
skeleton
sketch
skew
ski
skid
skillet
skim
skin
skip
skirt
skit
skull
skunk
sky

sp Neighborhood

space   s + p = sp
spade
spaghetti
spark
speak
speed
spell
spend
spice
spider

smog	snoop	spill
smoke	snout	spoon
smooth	snow	sport
smudge	snub	spout
smug	snuff	spun

st Neighborhood	*sw* Neighborhood	*tw* Neighborhood
stack s + t = st	swallow s + w = sw	tweed t + w = tw
stain	swamp	tweezers
stamp	swan	twelve
station	swarm	twenty
steak	sway	twice
steel	sweep	twig
steeple	sweet	twilight
stiff	swell	twill
still	swift	twin
stir	swim	twine
stock	swing	twinkle
stone	swipe	twirl
stop	swish	twist
store	switch	twit
storm	swoop	twitch

Sk, sm, sp, and **st** occur at the beginning and the end of words, as in **mask, prism, clasp,** and **last.** All the other two-letter blends occur at the beginning of words, not the end.

The letters **wr** do not form a blend neighborhood. When they are next-door neighbors, the **w** is silent, as in **wrap, write,** and **wreck.**

Some letter combinations, such as **nd, mp, ld, nt, lk,** and **nk,** form a blend neighborhood at the end of words, as in **stand, jump, held, sent, talk,** and **sink.** In my experience, the blend neighborhoods at the end of words are most easily learned as rimes (see Appendix A).

Three-Letter Blends

scr Neighborhood	*spl* Neighborhood	*spr* Neighborhood
scram s + c + r = scr	splash s + p + l = spl	sprain s + p + r = spr
scramble	splat	sprang
scrap	splatter	sprawl
scrape	splay	spray
scratch	spleen	spread
scrawny	splendid	spree
scream	splendor	sprig
screech	splice	spring
screen	splint	sprinkle
screw	splinter	sprint
scribe	split	sprite
script	splotch	sprout
scrod	splurge	spruce
scroll	sprung	spry

squ Neighborhood	*str* Neighborhood
squabble s + qu = squ	strap s + t + r = str
squadron	strawberry
squall	streak
squander	stream
square	street
squaw	strength
squawk	stress
squeak	stretch
squeamish	stride
squeeze	strike
squid	string
squint	stroke
squire	stroll
squirrel	strong
squirt	structure

The following letters in a three-letter blend neighborhood represent two sounds.

chr Neighborhood	*sch* Neighborhood	*thr* Neighborhood
christen ch + r = chr	schedule s + ch = sch	thrash th + r = thr
Christmas	schema	thread
chromate	schematic	threat
chromatic	scheme	three
chrome	schizoid	thresh
chromium	schizophrenia	thrift
chromosome	scholar	thrill
chronic	scholastic	thrive
chronicle	school	throat
chronology	schoolbook	throb
chrysalis	schoolhouse	throne
chrysanthemum	schooner	throng

Except for the frequently used words **Christmas, school,** and **schedule, chr** and **sch** are not often present in the words readers and spellers encounter every day. This is not the case for **thr,** which is part of many words authors routinely use. Generally speaking, up through third grade children read more words with two-letter blends than three-letter blends. I suggest you teach the three-letter blends after readers know common two-letter blends.

Consonant Digraph Neighborhood
The letters in a consonant digraph neighborhood represent one sound that is very different from the sounds the letters represent individually.

ch Neighborhood	*ph* Neighborhood	*sh* Neighborhood
chain	phantom	shade
chalk	pharaoh	shadow
challenge	pharmacy	shady
change	phase	shark
channel	pheasant	sheep
check	phenomenon	shell

cheer	phenotype	shelter
cheese	philander	ship
cherish	philanthropic	shirt
chili	philosophy	shock
chimpanzee	phobia	shop
chip	phone	short
choose	phoneme	shot
church	photograp	show
churn	physical	shuffle

Other sounds that the **ch** digraph neighborhood represents are the **"sh"** heard in **chagrin** and the **"k"** heard in **choir.** Even though **ch** represents sounds other than that heard in **chirp,** this is the most frequent sound and so it is a good sound to try first.

The digraph **ph** commonly represents the **"f"** heard in **phone.** Every now and then **ph** represents the sound of **"p,"** and sometimes **ph** is silent.

th Neighborhood	*th* Neighborhood	*wh* Neighborhood
(*Voiceless*)	(*Voiced*)	
thank	than	what
theater	that	wheat
theft	the	wheel
theme	their	when
thermal	them	where
thick	then	whether
thief	there	which
thimble	these	while
thing	they	whine
think	this	whip
thirst	those	whir
thorn	though	whisk
thumb	thus	whisper
thump	thy	whistle
thunder	thyself	why

The examples show that the digraphs **ch, ph, sh,** and **th** occur at the beginning of words. These digraphs also occur in the middle of words, such as **franchise, dolphin, bishop,** and **heathen,** and at the end of words, such as **perch, graph, fish,** and **teeth.**

The letters **th** represent two sounds—the sound heard in **thank** (called voiceless) and that heard in **than** (called voiced). Advise readers to first try the voiceless **"th"** in **thank** and, if that does not form a contextually meaningful word, to try the voiced **"th"** in **than.**

When **wh** precedes **o,** it represents the **"h"** in **who.** The **"hw"** sound in **white** is much more common, so encourage readers to first try the **"hw"** sound and, if that does not form a meaningful word, to next try the **"h"** sound. However, in some American's speech, the **"h"** is not pronounced in a word such as **white;** just the **"w"** is pronounced. This reflects readers' normal pronunciation and hence should not interfere with word identification.

When the letter **e** follows the digraph **th** at the end of a word, such as in **bathe,** the **th** represents the voiced sound heard in **that.** This explains the difference in pronunciation between **cloth** and **clothe,** and **teeth** and **teethe.**

tch *Neighborhood*

catch   tch = tch
crutch
ditch
etch
fetch
glitch
hitch
itch
latch
match
notch
scotch
stitch
stretch
wretch

Whereas readers should have no trouble inferring that the **t** in **tch** is silent, they must remember to include the **t** in spelling. Hence, **tch** may well be more problematic for spellers than for readers. The **ck** neighborhood (which represents the **"k"** at the end of words such as **back**) and the **ng** neighborhood are not included here because they are quicker to learn as part of the rimes **ack, eck, ick, ock,** and **uck,** or the rimes **ang, ing, ong,** and **ung,** as shown in Appendix A.

Gh also forms a digraph neighborhood. As an onset, **gh** represents **"g,"** though few English words begin with **gh.** When **gh** is not an onset, there are two options: the **gh** is silent, as in **thigh,** or it represents **"f"** as in **laugh.** When words include the sequence **ght,** the **gh** is silent, as in **bought** and **night.** Rimes with **gh** are a shortcut to word learning; look in Appendix A for examples.

S,s as a Next-Door Neighbor

As an onset **S,s** represents the **"s"** heard in **sack,** never **"z."** Only two alternatives, **"s"** or **"z,"** are possible when **s** is a middle or ending neighbor in spelling. **S,s** is not troublesome for most readers and spellers. Encourage readers to form a mind-set to attempt pronunciation with the **"s"** first and, if that fails, to try the **"z."**

"s" Onset	*"s" Sound*	*"z" Sound*
sack	arson	amuse
salad	basic	arise
salt	bus	cause
satin	crisis	chisel
seal	dress	closet
seed	essay	cousin
sell	focus	daisy
sick	grass	drowsy
sift	hassle	fuse
sight	house	his
six	person	please
soap	surpass	raise
sock	tassel	resent
soft	toss	those
sun	verse	turquoise

Sure and **sugar** are exceptions; the **s** in the beginning of these words represents the sound of **"sh."** Additionally, if **i** or **u** follows **s** in the middle of words, **s** may represent the sound heard in **mansion** and **erasure,** or the sound heard in **vision** and **pleasure.**

When -**es** is a suffix as in **dishes** or **washes,** the -**es** represents **"z."**

The Letters c and g as the Next-Door Neighbors of a, o, and u
The ca, co, cu Neighborhoods

When **ca, co,** and **cu** are immediate neighbors, the **c** usually represents the **"k"** heard in **kite** (called a hard sound).

ca Neighborhood	*co* Neighborhood	*cu* Neighborhood
cabbage c + a = ca	coach c + o = co	cube c + u = cu
cabin	code	cuddle
cable	coffee	cuff
cactus	cold	culture
call	color	cunning
camel	comb	cupcake
camp	come	cupid
canary	consider	curb
candle	contest	cure
canteen	control	curious
canvas	cook	curl
cape	copy	curtain
capture	corn	curve
cartoon	cost	custard
castle	cover	custom
avocado	alcove	cut
brocade	balcony	locust
educate	deacon	focus
placate	falcon	mercury
volcano	glucose	secure

The ga, go, gu Neighborhoods

In the **ga, go,** or **gu** neighborhoods, the **g** usually represents the sound associated with the **"g"** in **gate** (called a hard sound).

ga Neighborhood	*o* Neighborhood	*gu* Neighborhood
gable g + a = ga	go g + o = go	gulch g + u = gu
gag	goal	gulf
gain	goat	gull
galaxy	goblet	gulp
gaily	goblin	gum
gallery	golf	gumbo
gallon	gone	gun
gallop	good	guppy
game	goose	gurgle
gang	gopher	gush
gap	gossip	gust
garden	got	gutter

garlic	govern	guy
gate	gown	guzzle
began	Angora	August
legal	cargo	begun
organ	category	bogus
slogan	jargon	disgust
vulgar	lagoon	yogurt

The Letters c and g as the Next-Door Neighbors of e, i, and y
The ce, ci, cy Neighborhoods

In the **ce, ci,** and **cy** neighborhoods, the **c** usually represents the sound associated with the **"s"** in **soap** (called a soft sound).

ce Neighborhood	*ci Neighborhood*	*cy Neighborhood*
cedar c + e = ce	cide c + i = ci	cyberspace c + y = cy
celebrate	cigar	cycle
celery	cinch	cyclist
cell	cinder	cyclone
cement	cinema	cyclops
censor	cinnamon	cygnet
center	circa	cylinder
centigrade	circle	cymbal
central	circuit	cynic
century	circumstance	cynical
ceramic	circus	Cynthia
cereal	citizen	cypress
ceremony	citrus	cyst
certain	city	fancy
certificate	civil	literacy
decent	decide	mercy
excel	excite	pharmacy
faucet	lucid	policy
parcel	pencil	privacy
percent	placid	vacancy

As an onset the **c** in **ci** represents **"s,"** but in the middle of words **ci** represents the **"sh"** sound, as in **social.**

The ge, gi, gy Neighborhoods

When **ge, gi,** or **gy** are neighbors, the **g** usually represents the sound associated with the **"j"** in **jelly** (called the soft sound).

ge Neighborhood	*gi Neighborhood*	*gy Neighborhood*
gelatin g + e = ge	giant g + i = gi	gym g + y = gy
gem	gibe	gypsy
gender	gigantic	gyrate
gene	gigolo	gyroscope
general	gin	allergy
generic	ginger	analogy
generous	giraffe	apology

genial	gist	biology
genius	angina	clergy
gentle	digit	dingy
genuine	engine	ecology
geology	fragile	effigy
gerbil	frigid	energy
germ	legion	lethargy
gesture	logic	liturgy
digest	magic	orgy
diligent	margin	prodigy
halogen	origin	strategy
urgent	tragic	synergy
wage	virgin	zoology

The combinations **ge** and **gi** are not as dependable as the others. Support readers as they learn to first try the sound of "**j**" in **jelly** for **ge** and **gi** and, if that fails, try the sound of "**g**" in **gate.**

Vowel Letter-Sound Neighborhoods

VC Short Vowel Neighborhood

When letters reside in a **VC** neighborhood, the vowel generally represents a short sound. Short vowel sounds are often indicated by a breve (˘), which is explained in the glossary (see Appendix F). A consonant neighborhood before the vowel forms a **CVC** (**cat**), **CCVC** (**brat**), or **CCCVC** (**scrap**) sequence; it does not affect the sound the vowel in the **VC** short vowel neighborhood represents. Likewise, more than one consonant neighbor after the vowel forms a **CVCC** (**back**) or **CVCCC** (**batch**) sequence that does not affect the short vowel sound.

Short Vowel Sounds

a	in **apple**
e	in **elephant**
i	in **igloo**
o	in **olive**
u	in **umbrella**

aC Neighborhood	*eC Neighborhood*	*iC Neighborhood*
act a + C = at	bet e + C = ebb	bit i + C = it
bath	depth	him
camp	hem	drip
cast	left	fill
fact	let	lift
gas	men	limp
last	mess	miss
man	neck	mint
match	nest	nip
pass	pen	pig
path	pet	pin
ramp	press	rib
sad	red	risk

tap	set	sick
tramp	shed	tip

oC Neighborhood	*uC Neighborhood*	*yC Neighborhood*
drop o + C = odd	cut u + C = up	analyst y + C = abyss
got	dug	crypt
hot	dust	cyst
job	Dutch	Egypt
lock	fun	gym
mob	gum	hymn
not	luck	lynch
odd	lump	myth
opt	mud	nymph
pop	mulch	onyx
posh	numb	polyps
rock	nut	symbol
spot	shrug	syndrome
top	trunk	synergy

Sometimes the vowel in a **VC** neighborhood represents a long sound, as in **cold** (**old**), **bolt** (**olt**), **find** (**ind**), **night** (**ight**), and **child** (**ild**). Considered within the context of rimes, combinations like these are quite predictable and, hence, best learned as rimes (see Appendix A). The short sound, however, will usually result in a meaningful word. Advise readers to try the short sound first, and, if that does not produce a meaningful word, to try a long sound.

VCe Long Vowel Neighborhood

In the **VCe** neighborhood, the **e** is silent and the preceding vowel usually has a long sound, which is often indicated by a macron (¯) and explained in the glossary (Appendix F). A consonant neighborhood before the vowel forms a **CVCe** (**save**) or a **CCVCE** (**slave**) sequence and does not affect the sound that the vowel in the **VCe** long vowel neighborhood represents.

Long Vowel Sounds

a	in **cave**
e	in **gene**
i	in **bike**
o	in **code**
u	in **cube**
y	in **type**

aCe Neighborhood	*eCe Neighborhood*	*iCe Neighborhood*
bake a + Ce =	cede e + Ce =	bike i + Ce =
cage	delete	chive
chafe	extreme	dime
chase	mete	hide
date	gene	jibe
face	impede	mice
flake	obese	mime
game	plebe	pile
gave	recede	pine
lane	scene	prize

made	scheme	quite
maze	secede	rile
plate	serene	ripe
tale	theme	rise
wage	these	size

o+ Ce Neighborhood	*u+ Ce Neighborhood*	*y+ Ce Neighborhood*
bone o + Ce =	accuse u + Ce =	acolyte y + Ce =
choke	amuse	analyze
code	cube	argyle
dome	cute	enzyme
doze	duke	genotype
drove	dune	lyre
hose	execute	megabyte
mope	fume	neophyte
note	fuse	paralyze
phone	huge	pyre
probe	immune	rhyme
quote	mule	style
robe	mute	thyme
stole	plume	ftyke
those	yule	type

There are some marked exceptions to the **VCe** long vowel neighborhood. For one thing, it is not conventional for English words to end in the letter **v,** so **e** is tacked on to avoid spelling **have** as **hav, love** as **lov,** and **live** as **liv.** Words spelled with **r** conform to the **r-controlled (Vr)** neighborhood, which explains the pronunciation of **care** and **more.** When the last syllable in a word is **ate** or **ite,** and when the syllable is not stressed in pronunciation, the **a** in **ate** and the **i** in **ite** do not represent a long sound, as in **frigate, climate, private, granite, definite,** and **opposite.** Some loan words from French, such as **cafe,** are exceptions and are pronounced accordingly.

VCCe Short Vowel Neighborhood

In the **VCCe** neighborhood, the vowel generally represents a short sound and the **e** is silent. A consonant neighborhood before the vowel forms a **CVCCe** (**dance**) or **CCVCCe** (**chance**) sequence; it does not affect the sound the vowel in the **VCCe** neighborhood represents.

b<u>adge</u>	d<u>ense</u>	inv<u>olve</u>	pr<u>ince</u>
bal<u>ance</u>	f<u>ence</u>	l<u>ance</u>	r<u>inse</u>
br<u>idge</u>	Fr<u>ance</u>	l<u>apse</u>	s<u>alve</u>
br<u>onze</u>	f<u>udge</u>	l<u>odge</u>	s<u>ince</u>
ch<u>ance</u>	h<u>inge</u>	n<u>udge</u>	t<u>ense</u>
d<u>ance</u>	imp<u>ulse</u>	pl<u>unge</u>	w<u>edge</u>

Dge usually represents "**j**" and the final **e** is silent. Never an onset, **dge** is included in the spelling of many different words and hence readers have ample opportunities to learn this neighborhood through reading and writing. If the short vowel sound does not result in a meaningful word with a **VCCe** neighborhood, advise readers to try the long sound.

The **VCCe** short vowel neighborhood is challenging to spellers inasmuch as the **e** is sometimes dropped when suffixes are added to words, as in **lodging** and **dancing.**

Cle Neighborhood

Ble, cle, dle, gle, kle, ple, tle, and **zle** are typically found at the end of words and may represent intact units of pronunciation. They are usually pronounced as separate syllables.

ble Neighborhood

able   b + le = ble
audible
bubble
double
enable
fumble
marble
nibble
noble
pebble
quibble
ramble
stable
viable
warble

cle Neighborhood

article   c + le = cle
barnacle
bicycle
chronicle
circle
cubicle
cycle
icicle
miracle
obstacle
oracle
particle
spectacle
uncle
vehicle

dle Neighborhood

bridle   d + le = dle
bundle
candle
dawdle
fiddle
girdle
handle
hurdle
middle
muddle
needle
noodle
poodle
puddle
riddle

gle Neighborhood

angle   g + le = gle
bangle
beagle
bugle
dangle
eagle
gargle
giggle
haggle
jingle
mingle
single
tangle
toggle
waggle

kle Neighborhood

ankle   k + le = kle
crinkle
periwinkle
rankle
sparkle
sprinkle
tinkle
twinkle
wrinkle

ple Neighborhood

ample   p + le = ple
apple
couple
crumple
dimple
example
people
purple
sample
scruple
staple
supple
temple
topple
triple

tle Neighborhood

beetle   t + le = tle
bottle
cattle
chortle
gentle
hurtle
little
mantle
startle
subtle

zle Neighborhood

bamboozle   z + le = zle
dazzle
drizzle
embezzle
fizzle
frazzle
guzzle
muzzle
nozzle
nuzzle

title   puzzle
turtle   sizzle
whittle

Ble is pronounced as **"bul,"** cle as **"kul,"** dle as **"dul,"** gle as **"gul,"** kle as **"kul,"** ple as **"pul,"** tle as **"tul,"** and **zle** as **"zul."** These neighborhoods pose challenges to spellers inasmuch as the **e** is sometimes dropped when suffixes are added to words, as in **bubbly** and **bubbling.** In words such as **whistle** and **trestle,** the **t** is silent. Exceptions are so few that they do not pose a problem and so do not merit special attention.

In words such as **stable, cycle, cradle, bugle, wrinkle, dimple, title,** and **puzzle,** the first vowel either (1) represents a long sound because it is part of a CV long vowel neighborhood (as the **CV** in **sta-ble**) or (2) a short sound because it is in a separate **VC** short vowel neighborhood (as the **VC** in **puz-zle** in which the twin consonant neighborhood is divided). Refer to Chapter 6 for information on the syllable structure of words and how this affects pronunciation.

VV Long Vowel Neighborhood with an a or e

In the **VV** neighborhoods of **ai, oa, ay, ee, ey,** and **ea,** the first vowel represents a long sound and the second is silent.

ai Neighborhood	*oa Neighborhood*	*ay Neighborhood*
bait	oat	bay
brain	cloak	clay
chain	coast	day
maim	load	may
paint	loaf	pay
quail	loan	play
raid	oak	ray
sail	road	say
snail	roam	slay
trail	soak	stray
trait	soap	tray
waist	toast	way

ee Neighborhood	*ey Neighborhood*	*ea Neighborhood*
beef	abbey	appeal
creek	alley	beach
creep	barley	cheap
deed	cagey	defeat
feel	covey	dream
feet	donkey	heap
flee	galley	leaf
green	hockey	mean
keep	honey	ordeal
meet	jersey	reap
need	key	reveal
queen	kidney	scream
reef	medley	streak
seem	money	squeal
tree	valley	team

Sometimes two adjacent vowels in the **VV** long vowel neighborhood are referred to as a vowel digraph because two letters represent one sound.

Y,y is a vowel when it follows **a** and **e**, thereby creating the **VV** long vowel neighborhood of **ay** and **ey**.

Most of the time **ai** represents long **a**, but occasionally it represents the sound heard in **said** (seldom the sound in **plaid**). Tell readers to first try the long **a** sound and, should that fail to create a meaningful word, to try the sound heard in **said**.

Ey represents the sound of long **e** heard in **key** and the sound of long **a** heard in **they**. Advise readers to first try the sound of long **e** and, if that fails to produce a meaningful word, to try the sound of long **a**.

Ea sometimes represents the short **e** heard in **head**. Infrequently, **ea** represents a long **a** as in **great**. Advise readers to first try long **e** and, if that does not form a contextually meaningful word, to try short **e**.

When two next-door neighbors are in different syllables, then both vowels represent a separate sound, as in **trial** and **create**.

Double oo Neighborhood

The double **oo** neighborhood usually represents the sound heard in **school** or the sound heard in **book**.

oo in school	*oo in book*
broom	brook
cool	cook
food	crook
hoop	foot
moon	good
pooch	hood
proof	hook
roost	look
scoop	nook
smooth	shook
soon	soot
spook	stood
spoon	tool
tooth	wood
zoom	wool

Advise readers to try one sound and, if that does not result in a sensible word, to try the other sound.

Vowel Diphthong Neighborhoods

When **ow, ou, oi,** and **oy** are immediate neighbors, these combinations often represent the following sounds in pronunciation:

ow in **cow**
oi in **oil**
ou in **out**
oy in **boy**

ow Neighborhood

brow
brown
clown
cow
cowl
crowd
down
drown
gown
growl
how
plow
scowl
town
wow

oi Neighborhood

boil
broil
coin
doily
foist
join
moist
noise
point
poise
soil
spoil
toil
voice
void

ou Neighborhood

bound
cloud
county
flour
grouch
ground
hour
loud
mouth
noun
ouch
pouch
pound
scout
shout

oy Neighborhood

boy
cloy
convoy
coy
decoy
deploy
employ
enjoy
envoy
foyer
joy
ploy
royal
soy
toy

Ow also represents the long sound of **"o"** in **crow,** so readers have two sounds from which to choose—the **"ow"** in **cow** and the **"o"** (long **o**) in **crow.** If one sound does not work, the other will.

Oi may be part of the multiletter chunks **oise** (as in **noise**) and **oice** (as in **voice**). Encourage readers to draw these conclusions during the normal course of reading and writing.

Though **ou** frequently represents the sounds heard in **out** and **cloud,** these two letters represent several other sounds in words; for example, **soul, tour, group, shoulder, encourage, could,** and **double. Your, pour,** and **four** are examples of other exceptions to the **ou** neighborhood. However, authors use words like **your, four, should, would,** and **could** so frequently that these words are added to children's fluent vocabulary early. If readers cannot identify a contextually meaningful word by associating the sounds heard in **out** and **cloud** with the letters **ou,** encourage them to think of words that are in their speaking and listening vocabularies that include other letter-sound neighborhoods in the words (as the **gr** blend and single consonant letter **p** in **group,** or the single consonant **d** and the **ble** neighborhood in **double**) and that make sense in the reading context.

Vr or r-Controlled Neighborhood

The letter **r** affects pronunciation so that vowels cannot be classified as short or long.

ar Neighborhood

arm
barn
car
chart
dark
far
farm
hard
jar
mart
park
scar
star
tar
yard

er Neighborhood

alert
adverb
butter
ceramic
clerk
differ
exert
fern
herd
inert
perch
person
stern
term
under

ir Neighborhood

bird
chirp
dirt
fir
firm
flirt
girl
shirt
sir
skirt
smirk
stir
third
twirl
whir

or Neighborhood

born
cord
corn
dorm
for
fork
horn
more
north
porch
scorn
sport
store
storm
torch

ur Neighborhood

blur
burn
burst
church
curl
fur
hurt
lurk
nurse
purl
purr
surf
turf
turn
urn

The letters **ar** after **w** represent the sounds heard in **war, warn,** and **warm,** not the sound heard in **car.** This, however, is not overly difficult for observant readers to discover.

CV Long Vowel Neighborhood

In the **CV** neighborhood, the vowel usually represents a long sound.

Ca Neighborhood

<u>ba</u>sin   C + a =
<u>ca</u>nine
<u>cra</u>zy
<u>fla</u>vor
<u>ha</u>ven

Ce Neighborhood

a<u>dre</u>nal   C + e =
<u>de</u>cal
<u>de</u>cency
<u>fe</u>line
<u>fe</u>male

Ci Neighborhood

<u>bi</u>sect   C + i =
<u>chi</u>na
<u>di</u>gest
<u>gi</u>ant
<u>li</u>on

label	he	microscope
labor	legal	migrant
later	me	minus
major	meter	pilot
nation	senile	primate
paper	sequence	silent
sensation	she	spider
tiger	we	tiger
vapor	zebra	title
volcano	zenith	trifle

Co Neighborhood

Cu Neighborhood

also C + o =	bugle C + u =
banjo	cubic
bifocal	cucumber
locate	fuel
molar	funeral
moment	future
nomad	human
October	humid
poem	menu
polar	museum
program	music
rotate	nucleus
social	puny
total	pupa
vocal	tribunal

It is also possible to have two or three consonants preceding the vowel, which form **CCV** (**she**) and **CCCV** (**strident**) sequences.

There are many exceptions to the long vowel sound in **CV** neighborhood, particularly if the neighborhood occurs in a syllable that is not accented; for example, the first syllable in **develop.**

Readers may use the following guidelines to help them decide if the sequence of letters in a word is a **CV** or a **VC** neighborhood:

1. **CV Long Vowel Neighborhood:** The **CV** neighborhood is an open syllable, as explained in Chapter 6. If there is one consonant letter between two vowels (as the **l** in **silent**), many times the first vowel ends a **CV** neighborhood and generally is long (**silent**).
2. **VC Short Vowel Neighborhood:** The **VC** neighborhood represents a closed syllable, as described in Chapter 6. If there are two consonants between two vowels, as in **crimson,** the first consonant often goes with the preceding vowel to form a **VC** neighborhood (**crim**). The first vowel (in this case **i**) is short.
3. The consonant blend neighborhood generally stays intact, as in **secret** (**se-cret,** where the first **e** is long as part of a **CV** long vowel neighborhood) and **membrane** (**mem-brane,** where the first **e** is short as part of a **VC** short vowel neighborhood).
4. The consonant digraph neighborhood generally stays intact; for example, **bushel** (**bush-el**), **fathom** (**fath-om**), **marshal** (**mar-shal**).
5. When words end in a **Cle** sequence, the **Cle** is usually an intact neighborhood, as in **stable** (**sta-ble,** long **a** in preceding syllable), **cycle** (long **i**), **cradle** (long **a**), **bugle** (long **u**)—the preceding vowel is

part of a **CV** long vowel neighborhood—and in **wrinkle** (short **i**), **dimple** (short **i**), and **puzzle** (short **u**)—where the preceding vowel is part of a **VC** short vowel neighborhood, as described in Chapter 6.

6. Prefixes and suffixes are usually intact units in words, such as the **pre** in **prepaid** (**pre-paid**), and the **ly** in **slowly** (**slow-ly**), as explained in Chapter 6.

The Letter Y,y as the Final Letter

The letter **y** at the end of words acts as a vowel. When **y** forms a separate final syllable, it generally represents the sound associated with long **e**, as in **bunny** and **silly**. **Y,y** at the end of words with **no other vowels** represents the sound associated with long **i**, as in **by** and **try**.

Final Syllable (long e)	*Only Vowel (long i)*
any	by
army	cry
baby	dry
body	fly
bunny	fry
candy	my
city	ply
funny	pry
lady	shy
melody	sky
mercy	spy
silly	spry
study	sty
taffy	try
tiny	why

Tell readers to try the sound of long **i** in very short words; the sound of long **e** in longer words. If one sound (long **i** or long **e**) does not work, the other one has a good chance of being correct. When the **ly** is a suffix as in **deeply** and **cheaply**, it represents long **e**. Advise readers to try long **e** if they think the **ly** is a suffix and long **i** if they think it is part of the root word. If one sound does not work, the other probably will.

The au and aw Neighborhoods

When **a** and **u** are next-door neighbors, the sound they represent is generally that heard in **fault**. When **a** and **w** are adjacent in spelling, they represent the sound heard in **straw**.

au Neighborhood	*aw Neighborhood*
assault	awe
because	brawl
daunt	brawn
exhaust	claw
faun	crawl
flaunt	draw
fraud	gawk
fraught	jaw
haul	lawn
maul	prawn
saucer	shawl

staunch	spawn
taught	squaw
trauma	thaw
vault	trawl

The **au** and **aw** neighborhoods are quite reliable. The combination of **au** does not occur at the end of words. The **aw** neighborhood, on the other hand, is used as an onset (**awe**), in the middle of words (**strawberry**) and at the end of words (**draw**).

The ew and ue Neighborhoods

When **ew** and **ue** are next-door neighbors, these letter combinations usually represent the sound in **blew** and **blue.**

ew Neighborhood	*ue Neighborhood*
blew	argue
brew	avenue
chew	blue
crew	due
crewel	fondue
drew	glue
flew	issue
grew	pursue
jewel	rescue
sewage	revue
shrew	statue
shrewd	tissue
slew	true
strewn	value
threw	virtue

The **ue** neighborhood cannot be counted on to represent the sound heard in **blue** when the **ue** follows a **q** or a **g** in spelling, as in **clique, masque, mosque, guess, guest, league, morgue,** and **plague.** When children have lots of experience reading and writing words spelled with these sequences, they learn the sounds letters represent.

APPENDIX C

Prefixes

Prefix	Meaning	Examples
ab	away, from	abnormal, absent
ad	to, toward	advocate, admission
ambi	both, around	ambidextrous, ambiance
ante	before	antebellum, antechamber
anti*	against	antibody, antibiotic
circu/m	around	circumnavigate, circumference
con, com, co	with, jointly	conform, coauthor
contra	against, opposite	contraindicate, contraband
counter	against, opposite	counterclaim, counteract
de*	from, away	debrief, dehumidify
dis*	apart from, not	disembark, disarm
dys	bad, difficult	dysfunctional, dyslexic
en, em*	in	enclose, embattle
epi	upon, in addition	epilogue, epicenter, epitaph
extra	beyond	extrasensory, extraordinary
fore*	in front of, before	foreground, forerunner
hyper	excessive	hyperactive, hypercritical
hypo	less than normal	hypotonic, hypotension
in, im, ir, il*	not	invisible, improbable, irresponsible, illogical
in, im*	in or into	inward, immigrant

inter*	between, among	interact, intermingle
intra	within, between	intramural, intracellular
mid*	middle	midweek, midnight
mis*	wrong, bad, not	misfit, misplace
non*	not	nonsmoker, nonconformist
over*	too much	overlook, overcook
peri	around, near	peripheral, period, perigee
post	behind, after	postdate, postpone
pre*	in front of, before	predate, prepay
pro	forward, before	prologue, proactive
re*	back, again	realign, retell
retro	backward, behind	retrofit, retroactive
semi*	half, partly	semicircle, semisoft
sub*	under, inferior	submarine, substandard
super*	above, in addition	superman, supernatural
trans*	across, through	transport, transplant
ultra	beyond, extreme	ultrasonic, ultraminiature
un*	not	unhappy, unsure
under*	too little	underdone, underestimate

---

*The asterisk shows the twenty most common prefixes found in material read by children in grades three through nine (White, Sowell, & Yanagihara, 1989). When these prefixes have more than one meaning, the meaning listed is that given by White, Sowell, and Yanagihara.

White, T. G., Sowell, J., & Yanagihara, A. (1989). Teaching elementary students to use word-part clues. *The Reading Teacher, 42,* 302–308.

APPENDIX D

Suffixes

Suffix	Meaning	Examples
acity	inclined to	capacity, tenacity
acy	state of being, quality	democracy, bureaucracy
al, ial*	relating to	personal, rehearsal
ance	state of being	excellence, acceptance
arch	ruler	patriarch, monarch
archy	rule by	monarchy, oligarchy
ary	place for, connected with	library, military
ate	acted, state of	dictate, fortunate
cracy	kind of government	democracy, bureaucracy
ed*	past tense	jumped, painted
en*	relating to	frozen, wooden
er, or*	one who	worker, teacher
er*	comparative	faster, slower
ery	occupation, products	dentistry, jewelry
	quality of	snobbery
est*	most (comparative)	fastest, nicest
ful*	quality of	beautiful, plentiful
graph	writing	polygraph, telegraph
hood	state, condition	boyhood, neighborhood
ible, able*	able to, quality of	divisible, readable
ic*	like, pertaining to	historic, scenic

ician	specialist in	physician, electrician
ics	study of	mathematics, genetics
ing*	ongoing	reading, listening
ion, ation, ition, tion*	act or state of	construction, ruination
ish	like, nature of	feverish, selfish
ism	belief or practice of	feudalism, defeatism
ist	one who acts or believes	motorist, defeatist
ite	connected with, resident of	socialite, Wyomingite
ity, ty*	state or quality of	alacrity, gravity
ive, ative, itive*	tending to, relating to	creative, active
less*	without	ceaseless, fearless
ly*	every, in the manner of	friendly, weekly
mania	extreme enthusiasm for	pyromania, kleptomania
ment*	result or state of	excitement, retirement
meter	measure	diameter, barometer
metry	science of measurement	geometry, optometry
(i)mony	state or quality of	matrimony, acrimony
ness*	quality of	fondness, happiness
nomy	knowledge of a field or	astronomy, economy
oid	having shape or form of	alkaloid, humanoid
ology	science of	biology, zoology
ory	place for	dormitory, mandatory
ous, eous, ious*	full of, state of	studious, joyous
path	one who suffers	psychopath, sociopath
pathy	feeling, disorder	empathy, neuropathy
phobia	abnormal fear of	acrophobia, hydrophobia
s, es*	plural	dogs, houses
scope	means of viewing	telescope, horoscope
tomy	operation on, incision	lobotomy, tonsillectomy
(i) tude	state or quality of	latitude, servitude
ure	act or function of	capture, puncture
y*	quality, full of	ability, muddy

---

*The asterisk shows the twenty most common suffixes found in material read by children in grades three through nine (White, Sowell, & Yanagihara, 1989).

White, T. G., Sowell, J., & Yanagihara, A. (1989). Teaching elementary students to use word-part clues. *The Reading Teacher, 42,* 302–308.

APPENDIX E

Greek and Latin Roots

Roots	Meaning	Examples
aer(o) (Greek)	air, atmosphere	aerial, aerospace
am(o/i) (Latin)	love	amorous, amity
anim (Latin)	mind, feeling	animal, animate
ann (Latin)	year	annual, anniversary
anthr (opo) (Greek)	human	anthropology, philanthropist
archa (Greek)	ancient, primitive	archaeology, archaic
art (Latin)	skill	artist, artifact
aqua (Latin)	water	aquatic, aquarium
ast(er) (Greek)	star	astrology, astronaut
aud (Latin)	hear	audience, auditory
aut(o) (Greek)	self	autobiography, automobile
bell(i) (Latin)	war	belligerent, rebellion
bene (Latin)	well, good	beneficial, benevolent
bi (Latin)	two	bicycle, bifocals
biblio (Greek)	book	bibliography, bibliotherapy
bio (Greek)	life	biology, biodegradable
cap (Latin)	head	cap, capital
cardi (Greek)	heart	cardiology, cardiogram
carn (Latin)	flesh	carnivorous, carnage
ceiv (Latin)	take, seize	receive, conceive
cent (Latin)	hundred	century, centipede

centr (Greek)	center	centric, centrifugal
cess (Latin)	go, yield	recess, process
chrom(at) (Greek)	color	chromatic, chromosome
chron (Greek)	time	chronicle, chronic
clam/claim (Latin)	shout	proclaim, proclamation
cord (Latin)	heart	cordial, accord
corp(or,us) (Latin)	body	corporate, corpuscle
cosm (Greek)	universe, order	cosmos, microcosm
cred(it) (Latin)	believe, trust	credible, creditor
cri (Greek)	judge	critic, crisis
culp (Latin)	blame	culpable, culprit
cycl (Greek)	circle, wheel	cycle, bicycle
deci (Latin)	ten	decimeter, decimal
dem (Greek)	people	democracy, democratic
derm (Greek)	skin	dermatology, epidermis
dic(t) (Latin)	say, speak	dictaphone, dictate
doc(t) (Latin)	teach	indoctrinate, document
dogma (Greek)	opinion, teaching	dogmatic, dogma
duc(t) (Latin)	lead	induce, conduct
dyna (Greek)	power	dynamite, dynamic
ethn (Greek)	race, cultural group	ethnology, ethnic
fac (Latin)	to make, do, see	factory, facsimile
ferv (Latin)	boil, seethe	fervent, fervor
fid (Latin)	faith, trust	fidelity, confidential
fin (Latin)	end, limit	final, finite, finish
firm (Latin)	strong, firm	confirm, affirm
flect(flex) (Latin)	bend	flexible, reflex
flor (Latin)	flower, flourish	florist, floral
flu(x) (Latin)	flow	fluid, confluent
frac(t or g) (Latin)	break	fracture, fragment
gen (Greek)	birth, race, kind	generation, genealogy
ge(o) (Greek)	earth	geography, geology
gno(s) (Greek)	know	diagnosis, prognosis
gon (Greek)	angle	polygon, hexagon
grad (gress) (Latin)	go, step	graduate, progress
grat (Latin)	pleasing, grateful	gratitude, gracious
grav (Latin)	heavy	gravity, aggravate
hol (Greek)	whole	holistic, hologram

hydr (Greek)	water	hydrant, dehydrate
ject (Latin)	throw	interject, trajectory
judic (Latin)	judge	prejudice, adjudicate
junct (Latin)	join	junction, juncture
jur (Latin)	swear	jury, perjury
lat (Latin)	carry	relate, translate
liter (Latin)	letter, literature	literal, literate
loc (Latin)	place, put	locate, allocate
log (Greek)	word	dialogue, prologue
luc (Latin)	light	elucidate, lucid
lud(lus) (Latin)	play, mock	ludicrous, illusive
lumin (Latin)	light	luminescent, illuminate
magn (Latin)	great, large	magnitude, magnificent
mal (Latin)	poor, inadequate	malnourished, maladjusted
manu (Latin)	hand	manual, manicure
matr(ern) (Latin)	mother	maternal, maternity
micr (Greek)	small, one millionth	microphone, microgram
mili (Latin)	soldier	military, militant
mill (Latin)	housand	millimeter, millipede
misc (Latin)	mix, mingle	miscellaneous
mit (Latin)	send, soften	transmit, mitigate
mon(it) (Latin)	warn, advise	monitor, admonish
morph (Greek)	shape or form	endomorph, morphology
mort (Latin)	death	mortician, mortal
multi (Latin)	many, much	multiple, multidimensional
mut (Latin)	change	mutate, mutual
nat (Latin)	born	native, nation
neg (Latin)	deny	negative, renegade
ne(o) (Greek)	new	neonate, neophyte
omni (Latin)	all	omnivorous, omnipotent
onym (Greek)	name	synonym, pseudonym
opt (Greek)	see	option, optician
ord(in) (Latin)	order	order, ordinance
ortho (Greek)	straight	orthodontics, orthodox
pale(o) (Greek)	old	paleolith, paleontology
pater (Latin)	father	paternal, paternity
path (Greek)	suffer or feel, disease	sympathy, psychopath
ped (Latin)	foot	pedal, pedestrian

ped (Greek)	child	pediatrician
pel (Latin)	drive, push	propel, compel
phon (Greek)	sound	phonics, phonograph
phot (Greek)	light	photograph, photo
plen (Latin)	full	plentiful, replenish
pod (Greek)	foot	tripod, podiatrist
polis (Greek)	city, state	policy, metropolis
poly (Greek)	many	polysyllabic, polynomial
port (Latin)	carry	export, portable
press (Latin)	press, force	pressure, repress
prob (Latin)	test	problem, probation
psych (Greek)	mind	psychology, psychosis
put (Latin)	think, reckon	computer, dispute
quest (Latin)	seek, ask	question, quest
rect (Latin)	upright, straight	rectangle, resurrect
rupt (Latin)	break	disrupt, interrupt
sat(is) (Latin)	enough	satisfy, satiate
sci (Latin)	know	science, conscience
scribe (Latin)	write	inscribe, subscribe
sect (Latin)	cut	bisect, section
sed (Latin)	settle, sit	sediment, sedative
sen (Latin)	old	senile, senior
sens or sent (Latin)	feel, think	sensation, sensory
serv (Latin)	serve, save	servant, preserve
simil, simul (Latin)	like	simulate, simultaneous
sol (Latin)	alone	solitary, solitude
solv, solut (Latin)	free or loosen, solve	solution, resolve
son (Latin)	sound	sonic, resonance
soph (Greek)	wise	philosopher, sophisticated
spec (Latin)	look, see	spectator, inspect
spir (Latin)	breath	respiration, perspire
sta(t) (Greek/Latin)	stand, stop	stationary, static
strict (Latin)	draw tight	constrict, restrict
stru(ct) (Latin)	build	structure, construct
tact (Latin)	touch	tactile, contact
tain or ten (Latin)	hold	contain, maintain
tech (Greek)	art, skill, craft	technician, technocrat
tele (Greek)	far away, distant	telescope, telephone

tempor (Latin)	time	temporary, temporal
termin (Latin)	end, boundary	terminal, terminate
therm (Greek)	heat	thermometer
tort, torque (Latin)	twist	torture, distort
tract (Latin)	drag, draw	contract, protract
tri (Latin)	three	triceratops, tricycle
turb (Latin)	disturb, confuse	disturb, turbulence
typ (Greek)	stamp, model	typical, type
un (Latin)	one	unicycle, unicorn
ven (Latin)	come	convene, advent
ver (Latin)	true	verdict, verify
verb (Latin)	word	verbal, verbose
vert (Latin)	turn	subvert, revert
vict or vinc (Latin)	conquer	victory, convince
vid (Latin)	see	video, evident
voc (Latin)	voice	vocal, invoke

APPENDIX F

Generalizations for Adding the Suffixes

-s, -ed, -ing, -ly, and -er to Words

The suffixes **-s, -ed, -ing, -ly,** and **-er** are the top five most frequently used word endings according to White, Sowell, and Yanagihara (1989). The following generalizations are helpful inasmuch as they serve as guides when reading and spelling words with the suffixes of **-s, -ed, -ing, -ly,** and **-er.** When teaching children to recognize these common suffixes while reading and to spell words with these suffixes when writing, advise them that the suffixes themselves are always spelled the same. Sometimes, however, the spelling of the root word changes when a suffix is added. And, of course, there are exceptions to these generaliations. Nevertheless, readers and writers will find them helpful because so many words are spelled with these six suffixes.

VC Short Vowel Neighborhood

VC One-Syllable Words

Add **-s** and **-ly** to **VC** short vowel neighborhood words:

bat	=	bats		spin	=	spins
clap	=	claps		sad	=	sadly

dim	=	dimly		stop	=	stops
dog	=	dogs		tan	=	tans
glad	=	gladly		taps	=	taps
hat	=	hats		win	=	wins

-ed, -ing, -er

Double the last consonant before adding **-ed**, **-ing**, and **-er** to words ending with the **VC** short vowel neighborhood:

big	=	bigger		run	=	runner
clap	=	clapped		sad	=	sadder
dig	=	digging		stop	=	stopping
fat	=	fatter		tan	=	tanned
hop	=	hopped		tap	=	tapping
mad	=	madder		win	=	winner

Doubling the last consonant keeps **VC** short vowel words with the **-ed**, **-ing**, and **-er** suffixes, such as **hop–hopping,** from being read as **VCe** long vowel words, like **hope–hoping.** I find that children need a lot of reading and spelling opportunities to successfully use this generalization when they write.

VCC Short Vowel Words

Simply add **-s, -ed, -ing, -ly,** and **-er** to words ending in a **VCC** short vowel neighborhood:

bank	=	banks		limp	=	limply
damp	=	damper		list	=	lists
dust	=	dusted		rest	=	resting
fast	=	faster		sick	=	sickly
hang	=	hanging		talk	=	talking
jump	=	jumped		walk	=	walked

The reason we do not double the last consonant in the **VCC** short vowel neighborhood is that there is no chance of confusing these short vowel neighborhood words with long vowel **VCe** neighborhood words, as explained previously.

VCe Long Vowel Neighborhood

Drop the final **e** and then add the **-ed**, **-ing**, and **-er** to words ending with the **VCe** long vowel neighborhood:

dive	=	diver		mine	=	miner
face	=	faced		page	=	paged
fine	=	finer		race	=	racing
home	=	homely		safe	=	safer
hide	=	hiding		save	=	saving
joke	=	joking		tape	=	taped
lame	=	lamer		wave	=	waving

Simply add **-s** and **-ly** to **VCe** long vowel words. Examples include dives, faces, homely, jokes, mines, purely and safely.

VV (+ C) Long Vowel Neighborhood

When words end with a **VV** Long Vowel Neighborhood followed by a consonant, add the **-s, -ed, -ing, -ly,** and **-er** without changing the root word:

bleed	=	bleeding		float	=	floating
boat	=	boating		green	=	greener

cheap	=	cheaply		mean	=	meaner
cheat	=	cheated		see	=	seeing
creek	=	creeks		team	=	teams
deep	=	deeply		tree	=	trees

Words Ending in the VV combinations of ay, oy, ey

Simply add **-s, -ed, -ing,** and **-er** to words ending in the **VV** combinations of **ay, oy,** and **ey:**

annoy	=	annoying		play	=	plays
boy	=	boys		prey	=	preyed
employ	=	employer		spray	=	sprayer
enjoy	=	enjoying		stay	=	staying
key	=	keys		toy	=	toying
obey	=	obeying		toy	=	toys

Words Ending in Yy

When a word ends in a **y,** change the **y** to an **i** before adding **-es, -ed,** and **-er:**

angry	=	angrier		easy	=	easier
army	=	armies		fry	=	fries
baby	=	babied		lady	=	ladies
carry	=	carried		marry	=	married
cozy	=	cozier		spry	=	sprier
deny	=	denied		tarry	=	tarries
easy	=	easier		tidy	=	tidier

Adding -es to Words Ending in s, ss, ch, sh, x, and z

Add **-es** to words that end in **s, ss, ch, sh, x,** and **z** as in:

beach	=	beaches		mix	=	mixes
bus	=	buses		pass	=	passes
buzz	=	buzzes		porch	=	porches
class	=	classes		rush	=	rushes
dish	=	dishes		tax	=	taxes
fox	=	foxes		waltz	=	waltzes
gas	=	gases		wish	=	wishes

Index